ABRAHAM JC

AND THE SOURCES OF WONDER

Abraham Joshua Heschel (1907–1972) was one of the twentieth century's most influential Jewish thinkers, a respected theologian and enthusiastic civil rights activist who marched to Selma with Martin Luther King, Jr. His theology emphasized the immediacy of wonder and awe, yet his writing was studded with signs of his vast knowledge of traditional scholarship. No other Jewish thinker of note in the twentieth century used such a wide range of texts so extensively.

Abraham Joshua Heschel and the Sources of Wonder is the first book to demonstrate how Heschel's political, intellectual, and spiritual commitments were embedded in his reading of Jewish tradition. By shedding new light on how Heschel's theological project reconciled the demands of tradition and the modern world, Michael Marmur offers an inspirational lesson in how contemporary Jewish thought can embrace both the texts of the past and the challenges of the present.

(The Kenneth Michael Tanenbaum Series in Jewish Studies)

MICHAEL MARMUR is the Jack, Joseph, and Morton Mandel Provost of the Hebrew Union College–Jewish Institute of Religion.

The Kenneth Michael Tanenbaum Series in Jewish Studies

The Kenneth Michael Tanenbaum Book Series features outstanding research on topics in all areas of Jewish Studies. This interdisciplinary series highlights especially research developed within the framework of the University of Toronto's Centre for Jewish Studies. The Centre is an interdisciplinary research and teaching unit with a large and diverse cohort of affiliated faculty and an impressive roster of annual conferences, symposia, and lectures. Reflecting the Centre's vibrancy, the series highlights the best new research by local and international scholars who contribute to the intellectual life of this interdisciplinary community. The series has been enabled by a generous donation from Kenneth Tanenbaum, whose family has long supported the Centre and helped make it a leader globally in Jewish Studies.

General Editor: Jeffrey Kopstein, Director, Centre for Jewish Studies, Professor of Political Science, University of Toronto

For a list of books in the series, see page 281.

Abraham Joshua Heschel and the Sources of Wonder

MICHAEL MARMUR

UNIVERSITY OF TORONTO PRESS
Toronto Buffalo London

ISBN 978-1-4426-5122-7 (cloth)
ISBN 978-1-4426-5123-4 (paper)

∞ Printed on acid-free, 100% post-consumer recycled paper with
vegetable-based inks.

Library and Archives Canada Cataloguing in Publication

Marmur, Michael, author

Abraham Joshua Heschel and the sources of wonder/Michael Marmur.
(Kenneth Michael Tanenbaum series in Jewish studies)

Includes bibliographical references and index.
ISBN 978-1-4426-5122-7 (bound) – ISBN 978-1-4426-5123-4 (paperback)

1. Heschel, Abraham Joshua, 1907–1972.   2. Judaism – 20th century.
3. Jewish philosophy – 20th century.   I. Title.   II. Series: Kenneth Michael
Tanenbaum series in Jewish studies

BM755.H37M37 2016   296.3   C2015-906987-4

University of Toronto Press acknowledges the financial assistance to its
publishing program of the Canada Council for the Arts and the Ontario Arts
Council, an agency of the Government of Ontario.

**Canada Council   Conseil des Arts
for the Arts   du Canada**

ONTARIO ARTS COUNCIL
CONSEIL DES ARTS DE L'ONTARIO
an Ontario government agency
un organisme du gouvernement de l'Ontario

Funded by the   Financé par le
Government   gouvernement
of Canada   du Canada

To Sarah
A Source of Wonder

Contents

Acknowledgments

One day in 2014, working on the Heschel papers housed at Duke University, I chanced upon a page upon which Abraham Joshua Heschel had written out a teaching from the Bratzlav Hasidic tradition. It has found its way into the first chapter of this book, and its translation reads: when one learns Torah (in this case, the teaching of an ancient sage), one kisses the Sage and is kissed by him.

I started studying the work of Abraham Joshua Heschel in a serious way some twenty years ago, and in the course of that time I have often been struck by the intimacy he felt with the great figures of the Jewish past. His knowledge of Jewish literature was immense, but his sense of involvement with the books he read and the individuals evoked within them was even greater. Engagement outstripped erudition. Textpersons, to use a Heschelian term, were ultimately more important than textbooks.

My own acquaintance with the books which Heschel mastered is rudimentary in comparison to his. Nevertheless, by reading the texts Heschel read and thinking about the way the contemporary is grounded in the timeless, I have been able to sense how – in Heschel's own terminology – "eternity utters a day." From the first time I read Heschel I have had a sense of closeness to this man, who I never had the privilege of meeting in person. That sense has never been weakened or threatened by examining his ideas with recourse to critical tools, by analysing his methods or considering the implications of his thought. Indeed, the more rounded my appreciation of Heschel's life and work has become, the closer I have felt to him. I do not think it necessary to close one's eyes in order to embrace the presence of the departed Sage, or to sense his reciprocated embrace.

Working on this project has also allowed me to enjoy the collegiality and friendship of many men and women. At the Hebrew Union College – Jewish Institute of Religion, my professional and intellectual home for most of my adult life, many colleagues have provided invaluable assistance across our four campuses and various disciplines. Sheldon Zimmerman and the late Arthur Grant were very supportive when the idea was taking shape. To the President of HUC-JIR, Aaron Panken, and to the Dean of our Jerusalem school, Naamah Kelman, special thanks are due. Through Naamah and her family (her father Wolfe Kelman and his special link with Heschel is mentioned in this book) the presence of Heschel has been all the more palpable.

The Director of Libraries David Gilner and the Jerusalem librarian Batya Kaplan deserve gratitude along with the entire library team. Ilan Shalev helped me create a database that serves as a kind of Heschel concordance and that has given me a systematic grounding in Heschel's Bible. In the course of recent years I have also enjoyed making use of the bibliographical and archival resources of the Jewish Theological Seminary, the National Library in Jerusalem, and Duke University. The Heschel Papers at Duke offer an extraordinary opportunity to research aspects of Heschel's life and work beyond his published writings. They are a treasure.

That my work brings me into contact with the administration and faculty of HUC-JIR every day is one of the great blessings of my current position. Faculty colleagues have helped me think through a number of issues, and saved me from countless errors. Among them I want to mention in particular Yehoyada Amir, Jason Kalman, Barry Kogan, David Levine, Dalia Marx, Michael Meyer, Michal Muszkat-Barkan, Richard Sarason, and Rachel Sabath Bet-Halachmi. From within the informal fellowship of Heschel scholars around the world, I want to express particular thanks to Dror Bondi, Alexander Even-Chen, Shai Held, Edward Kaplan, Gordon Tucker, and Yehudah DovBer Zirkind, all of whom have provided help and offered new perspectives.

Susannah Heschel has been very generous with her time and wisdom. She gave permission for all citations from her father's writings, and she also offered many invaluable insights and suggestions. She will notice as she reads the final version that I did not take act upon all her suggestions, but they all stimulated me to think carefully.

Warren Zev Harvey served as my dissertation advisor at the Hebrew University, as I worked on Heschel's *God in Search of Man* (often referred to in this book as *Search*). His support and wisdom helped give this book its shape and focus. David Ellenson has been a great friend and source of encouragement throughout this project. Had he not allowed me to pursue my passion for Heschel, this book would never have come into existence. Writing about Heschel with him (we co-authored an article about a responsum dedicated to the teenage Abraham Heschel of Warsaw) has been one of the highlights of our friendship. Arthur Green has provided advice and inspiration in equal parts. Among other teachers, friends, and colleagues, mention should be made of Arnold Eisen, Marcel Marcus, and Paul Mendes-Flohr, as well as the late Louis Jacobs.

Nikki Littman has been a wonderful editor as this book has undergone its various metamorphoses. It is reasonable to assume that wherever clarity wins out over obscurity in the coming pages, her steady hand can be discerned. Carl Pace prepared the index and provided further assistance, and the team at the University of Toronto Press (from which I will mention Len Husband and Wayne Herrington in particular) has been exemplary in its graciousness and professionalism. An example of this is provided by the photograph they chose for this book's cover. This image, provided by the Jacob Rader Marcus Center of the American Jewish Archives, shows Heschel against the backdrop of the Hebrew Union College in Cincinnati in the early 1940s. Here is the subject of this book in mid-life, a text of some kind balanced on his knee. Europe is in flames and the future uncertain. We see him situated somewhere between the library and the street, between contemplation and action, between wonder and outrage. The connection with the College where I teach and work only makes the picture more appropriate.

A book of this nature is replete with references and allusions and awash with names, many of them unfamiliar to the non-specialist reader. To stop and explain each one of them would have made the work twice as long and half as readable. Occasionally I have included a date or some other clue in order to orient the general reader. If anyone is motivated to find out more about the individuals and the books which populate these pages, I will count this a success. The line separating solid scholarship from stolid pedantry is gossamer thin. If any section of this work seems to veer into the domain of the latter, I have tried to ensure that within a few sentences some accessible conclusion or insight is offered.

This book is about sources and wellsprings, about tradition and immediacy. In a comment to Genesis 32, the medieval Spanish exegete Bachya ben Asher notes that a spring can dry up, but a source is ever renewed. That is why God is referred to as "the source of living water" (Jeremiah 17:13). We are living in times in which the sanctity of humanity is often desecrated in the name of tradition. As the author of Proverbs 25:26 understood, springs can be muddied and sources polluted. In surrounding his thought with sources of Jewish tradition, Abraham Joshua Heschel was suggesting that our own springs are supplied by deep sources, literary and human, ancient and contemporary. It is up to each of us to use our spiritual intuition to determine how to put these sources to good use.

Thanks to Heschel, I have had an opportunity to reflect on the significance of sources, and thanks to him I have learnt that this reflection cannot avoid contemporary application in the political and social spheres. Heschel's readers and heirs are called to resist the abuse of sacred texts to justify inhumanity. I will cite one from a long catalogue of such abuses around the world. Some months before the completion of this work, Jewish terrorists committed an arson attack on a church on the Sea of Galilee and left a quotation from the Jewish liturgy sprayed on the wall. I found myself feeling relief that Heschel had not been alive to witness such a desecration of sources, and of the Source.

While horror and sadness abound, joy and gratitude also pervade. Here in Jerusalem, my family is a source of wonder every day. My father Dow has always been my first reader and primary intellectual interlocutor, as well as fulfilling his even more primary parental role alongside my mother Fredzia. My children Miriam, Nadav, and Gaby constantly provide reasons for hope and celebration. They may be surprised to discover that my concern with Heschel, which has been alive as long as they have, is in fact a concern for the possibility of an engaged and resonant Jewish response to the challenges faced by their generation. I have in fact been writing to or about them all this time.

This book is dedicated to my wife Sarah Bernstein. Her generosity of spirit has allowed me to bring this project to fruition along with my other responsibilities. She has been a source of wonder, encouragement, partnership, laughter, and love for more than thirty years. The advice from Genesis 21:12, "whatever Sarah tells you, listen to her voice," has never let me down. Listening to her voice usually involves thinking, engaging, and growing.

For me, to be a Jew means to be invited to place my personal loves and commitments in a wider context, and to connect with ages long past as well as with eras yet to come. Acknowledging the embrace of my family and friends, I want to express gratitude for the opportunity to sense the kiss of sages long departed. That embrace inspires me as I continue my work of helping to prepare new generations of Jewish leadership. Taken together, this melding of present, past, and future is a profound blessing. I believe the source of this blessing to be inexhaustible.

ABRAHAM JOSHUA HESCHEL
AND THE SOURCES OF WONDER

Chapter One

Abraham Joshua Heschel: Heir and Pioneer

The purpose of this book can be described from three starting points: a person, a question, and a phenomenon.

The person is Abraham Joshua Heschel (1907–1972). His interests were deep and wide, and his legacy is rich and varied. Over forty years after his death, his passions and insights still resonate. While the burgeoning secondary literature on Heschel provides many valuable insights,[1] none of it will provide as much reward as a close and attentive reading of Heschel himself.

Heschel's multifaceted legacy has been the subject of intense interest over the last decades. The challenge recently thrown down concerning Heschel – "What is there left to be said?"[2] – should act as an unnerving caution to anyone proposing to add to the plethora of studies already available. One of the reasons why so many scholars, thinkers, and popular writers return to Heschel is that he straddled domains often regarded as distinct: social activism and spiritual exploration, Europe and America, conservatism and radicalism.

The justification for offering another item to the Heschel bibliography relates to a question at the heart of this volume: what is the relationship between Heschel's repeated emphasis on elemental unmediated human responses to God's call on the one hand and his intensive references to the sources of Jewish tradition on the other? The book aims to demonstrate how Heschel read Jewish tradition and how it served him as a lens through which to perceive contemporary reality.

Heschel is the theologian of awe, wonder, and radical amazement. He privileged faith over creed, response over doctrine. His writing turns to the reader in the present tense, seeking to highlight the immediacy of the current human condition. A number of the titles of his works in

English emphasize this current state: Who is man? he asks. Man is not alone, he proclaims. God is in search of man, he affirms. How, then, are we to understand the fact that most of his works are replete with references to sources of various kinds, most of them taken from Jewish literature? What is the connection between Heschel's emphasis on the immediacy of the moment, the experience of the present event, and the location of his thought in its specific historical and cultural context? Heschel, who described sacred history as "an attempt *to see the past in the present tense*,"[3] grapples with present dilemmas and experiences through the prism of the past. This book aims to describe how and to discuss why he does this.

If this book aims to add to the literature on our first starting point – Heschel – by focusing on our second starting point – the question of his use of traditional sources – it also is intended to make some contribution to a discourse concerning a wider phenomenon, namely, the nature of tradition in a modern context. While Heschel was far from being a typical representative of the contemporary Jewish condition, his intense engagement with both the many layers of Jewish tradition and the actual conditions of the twentieth century provides a highly instructive test case. Can modern-day Jews seeking to grapple with the moral, political, and spiritual challenges of their day do so from within the sources of Judaism? What is the role of tradition in the construction of a contemporary critique and a compelling theology? It is this broader phenomenon of tradition in a non-traditional age which provides a frame in which this book may be read.

The rise of a modern sensibility has been accompanied by intense speculation on the role that tradition ought to play in contemporary culture. T.S. Eliot, a man rarely compared with the subject of this present work,[4] wrote an essay in 1919 entitled "Tradition and the Individual Talent." The subject of his essay is the Western poet, and yet his words may help define the issue at stake in a consideration of the literary, theological, and cultural project of Abraham Joshua Heschel:

> The historical sense compels a man to write not merely with his own generation in his bones, but with a feeling that the whole of the literature of Europe from Homer and within it the whole of the literature of his own country has a simultaneous existence and composes a simultaneous order. This historical sense, which is a sense of the timeless as well as of the temporal and of the timeless and of the temporal together, is what makes a

writer traditional. And it is at the same time what makes a writer most acutely conscious of his place in time, of his contemporaneity.[5]

Replace Homer with the Bible and all that follows in the spiritual output of the Jews over three millennia, and this may be read as a description of Heschel's mission. The temporal and timeless, this moment alongside millennia of Jewish and human endeavour, are melded into a simultaneous existence and a simultaneous order.

Heschel's work and life can be read as an attempt to model a Judaism of resonance out of its own sources. A recurrent theme in his thought is the existence of a deep stratum of meaning, often obscured by layers of convention; depth theology distinct from formal doctrine; a unitary faith at the heart of diverse creeds; an insistent voice speaking out from the generations. For him, the great works of the Jewish canon are not to be understood primarily as reflections of their own time but rather as prisms through which an ancient and always current light is refracted. In this book we hope to explore the way in which a Jew steeped in the sources of his tradition faces contemporaneity and puts this canon to use[6] in his attempt to offer a response to the particular challenges of the twentieth century.

Eliot's ideal modern poet "can neither take the past as a lump, an indiscriminate bolus, nor can he form himself wholly on one or two private admirations, nor can he form himself wholly upon one preferred period."[7] To have a well-modulated and mature approach to the legacy which is "in his bones," we would therefore expect to see evidence of a discerning engagement with tradition ranging across epochs and genres. This book sets out in search of such evidence as it considers the ways in which Heschel harnesses the sources of Judaism in his quest for immediacy and profundity.

There is one more possible way in which extensive reference to classical sources might be understood. While some quote as a sign of their submission to the dictates of tradition, others insist on the primacy of the modern. In the stirring conclusion to his essay on "Quotation and Originality," Ralph Waldo Emerson suggests a clear hierarchy inherent in the relationship between past and present, and in so doing he makes his own modernist affiliation clear:

We cannot overstate our debt to the Past, but the moment has the supreme claim. The Past is for us; but the sole terms on which it can become ours are its subordination to the Present. Only an inventor knows how to borrow, and every man is or should be an inventor ... This vast memory is only raw material. The divine gift is ever the instant life, which receives and uses and creates, and can well bury the old in the omnipotency with which Nature decomposes all her harvest for recomposition.[8]

Would this manifesto be acceptable to Heschel? In grappling with the challenges that the twentieth century presented to Jews and to all people, what role is played by the accumulated wisdom of the preceding thirty centuries? Does the old retain its freshness, or is it recycled in the mulch of the new?

In an attempt to respond to these questions, we will adopt a quasi-archaeological approach. After this introductory chapter, each stratum of Jewish creativity is considered as it comes to expression in Heschel's work. Towards the end of the work these various strands are brought together in a discussion of the creation of Heschel's unique lexicon and his approach to some of the burning issues of his times.

By looking at sources cited in almost fifty years of creativity,[9] I hope to shed light on the theological project of one of the most significant thinkers of the twentieth century and to contribute to an understanding of the complex dynamics between tradition and modernity. The *aspaklaria* of the generations, a Heschelian term that will be explored extensively, can be understood as a complex optical device through which the past is seen through the prism of the present, and the present perceived through the prism of the past.

Heschel and His Sources

Many attempts have been made to capture the essence of the life and thought of Abraham Joshua Heschel. Positioned mainly on the radical edge of the communal mainstream, Heschel forged a unique path. Each decade of his life represented a significant metamorphosis. At the age of ten, he was a Hasidic prodigy in Warsaw; at twenty, a modernist Yiddish poet leaving Vilna. The thirty-year-old Heschel was part of the spiritual resistance movement of Jewish intellectuals in Nazi Germany. Heschel at forty had recently arrived at the Jewish Theological Seminary in New York, after spending most of the war years at the Hebrew Union College in Cincinnati.

Heschel at fifty was the author of a string of theological works – *The Sabbath, Man Is Not Alone, Man's Quest for God*, and *God in Search of Man* – that placed him in the first rank of American Jewish thinkers. At the age of sixty, Heschel was penning a theological response to the events of the Six Day War. At that stage of his life he was one of the leading voices of conscience, interreligious dialogue, and spiritual awakening in American society, having also published two volumes of a monumental study of rabbinic theology, reworked his Berlin dissertation into *The Prophets*, and published a collection of his more popular articles entitled *The Insecurity of Freedom*. Five years later, having recently completed a study of Menahem Mendel of Kotzk, whose spirit had presided over his earliest years, Heschel died.

His literary legacy includes poetry; studies of great figures from the biblical, rabbinic, medieval, and early modern periods; original works on prayer and theology; and a host of articles and lectures on issues both timely and timeless. Along with his books, Heschel bequeathed a legacy of passionate activism rooted in both conscience and tradition. He was an heir and a pioneer.

Abraham Joshua Heschel has been portrayed as a poet, a scholar, a theologian of the deed, a master of prayer, a 1960s icon of social protest, a Hasid, and much besides.[10] A number of his staunchest advocates have insisted that there is a hidden rigour and structure to his thought. Keys capable of unlocking the Heschel enigma have been suggested: phenomenology;[11] pathos;[12] piety;[13] the inversion of normative Western object-subject relations;[14] trenchant resistance to the temptations of the Enlightenment[15]or perhaps a profound embracing of the blessings of modernity;[16] the overcoming of the self;[17] and more.

Although this book will suggest some aspects of Heschel's writings that have been overlooked or underestimated, there is no master key on offer here. In my reading, Heschel's thought is more suggestive than explicit. To use a Heschelian distinction, trawling Heschel's work for the kind of "strict logical arrangement" he associated with the Sephardi tradition would be a futile exercise. His work is better characterized by the "inner wrestling and a kind of baroque emotion" typical of Ashkenazi writers.[18]

Heschel's intensive reliance on quotations and references from various kinds of sources is both remarkable and largely ignored. The sources are quoted and alluded to in both the body of the text and the extensive footnotes and endnotes to almost all of his writings. These notes are often overlooked, since for most of the readers of his theological works his repeated references to obscure sources culled from twenty centuries of Jewish creativity might appear inaccessible and perhaps irrelevant. And yet, even a cursory reading of his works reveals that almost all[19] are widely populated by a diverse range of sources, mainly, although not exclusively, taken from Jewish tradition. No other Jewish thinker of note in the twentieth century, appealing to an audience of modern Jews and non-Jews, used such a panoply of texts, and so extensively.

When, in his 1937 monograph on Abravanel, Heschel described his subject as being at home in all fields of religious literature, in Halakhah, Aggadah, religious philosophy and exegesis, as well as Christian theology and Islamic philosophy,[20] he was describing the range of his own learning and interests.

This grounding in sources was acquired in Heschel's youth. In 1930 the young Heschel, not yet thirty, was asked if his recently published poems had been influenced by Rainer Maria Rilke. Heschel's response was both prickly and informative: "I didn't have to study in Rilke's *cheder* to recognize that there is a God in the world. I had other teachers, other paths, other images."[21]

Almost forty years later, Heschel was asked in an interview if he had been greatly influenced by Martin Buber. His reply was reminiscent of his previous response: "I would not say so. I consider the important insights in Buber to be derived from Hasidic tradition, and these I knew before I met him."[22]

In both cases, when asked explicitly, Heschel stated that the most important influences were exerted upon him at an early stage of his development. He engaged in a lifelong conversation with teachers, images, and insights culled from his earliest years and honed in the decades that followed. In the course of this book, these influences and their significance in Heschel's lifework will be traced. Some influences which came to bear on his later development, including non-Jewish religions and philosophies, will also be discussed.

Heschel's prodigious learning was not unparalleled among Jews of his generation, nor did he outshine Buber, Rosenzweig, Levinas, Soloveitchik, and others in the profundity of his insights. However, in the eyes of Neusner, Peli, and others, his mastery and deployment of such a broad range of sources set him apart. With greater intensity than any of these or of other great modern Jewish thinkers, Heschel deployed the literary sources of Judaism as he grappled with the dilemmas of the present time.

In the epilogue to his study of Heschel's approach to Revelation, Lawrence Perlman commented:

The excitement ... of Heschel's intellectualism is that his achievement is framed in terms of almost every conceivable facet of Judaism. Heschel's thought is replete with references to Kabbalism, Hasidism, Medieval philosophy and Rabbinic thought ... Heschel's use of these sources indicates the immense amount of work to be done in understanding their contribution to his theology and in his contribution towards their significance.[23]

Describing Heschel's work as "a scholarly goldmine," Edward Kaplan also proposed that Heschel's references be elucidated.[24] This book attempts to follow the advice given by Perlman and Kaplan. After considering the ways in which Heschel related to each major period and genre of Jewish literature, a new reading of some central Heschelian motifs will be offered.

Heschel's Audiences

That Heschel had more than one audience is evident from even a perfunctory perusal of his biography. We find Heschel the adolescent writing brief Halakhic commentaries in a Hebrew journal published in Poland and directed at the ultra-Orthodox community, followed by Heschel the young Yiddish poet in Vilna writing in a different genre and for a different audience. Within a few years, he is to be found adopting the vocabulary of scholarly German to gain his doctorate, while simultaneously addressing the wider community by means of articles in the Jewish press.

The move to America denoted not only another linguistic shift but also a profound cultural realignment. Both in Germany and the United States, it would appear that Heschel's primary audience was a Jewish readership well versed in the literature of the West and less conversant with the classics of Judaism. There were, to be sure, other readers who found meaning and significance in his works, but it was to such a moderately affiliated Westernized Jew that Heschel's major theological works were primarily directed, at least on the surface. As he moved from Cincinnati to New York and, in time, from his study room to the front line of American public life, his audience broadened and increased.

Even in America, Heschel continued to write in different languages, clearly with his different audiences in mind. It is instructive to compare two works written during the 1960s. Until its recent translation,[25] Heschel's masterly Hebrew discussion of rabbinic theology, *Torah min*

Hashamayim, was impenetrable to anyone unversed in the conventions and idioms of rabbinic Hebrew. At the other end of the spectrum, the audience at Stanford University, where he delivered the lectures that were later adapted into *Who Is Man?*, was not expected to know Hebrew or to be acquainted with traditional Jewish sources in order to appreciate his brief examination of the human condition. The text contains few quotations of any kind and most of the cultural references are designed to be understood by Western-educated Christians and Jews of the postwar era.

For a further example of Heschel's ability to relate to different audiences simultaneously, an examination of the similarities and disparities between Heschel's two late works on the Kotzker Rebbe – *Kotzk* and *A Passion for Truth* – provides illuminating insights. It is not simply the fact that one is penned in Yiddish, the other in English. The two books are clearly variations on the same theme, and there is much they have in common. But one is not a strict translation of the other,[26] and they further highlight Heschel's heightened sensitivity to his various audiences.

Abraham Joshua Heschel showed considerable skill in "reading" his audience and suiting his writing to the preferences and sensitivities of his readers. His own biography, however, was far removed from the life details of such putative readers, and he lived much of his life with a strong consciousness of his maladjustment to the dominant society.[27] His life and work demonstrate an extraordinary blend of engagement and estrangement, enthusiasm and despair, a thirst for the contemporary with a hunger for the eternal.

Throughout his intense life in the various cities of his residence – marching at Selma, Alabama, and negotiating at the Vatican; in synagogue services and political demonstrations; in libraries and lobbies – Heschel found ways of reaching out to others despite, or perhaps because of, his own sense of alienation.

His quotation and citation of a broad range of sources serve to communicate a double message: that in reading Heschel, readers are encountering an authentic link in the chain of traditional scholarship; and yet, that they are also reading a man who understands the foundations on which their own cultural assumptions are based.[28] Heschel typically wrote with what has been described as a "second hand,"[29] addressing himself to contemporary audiences while placing himself in the context of Jewish literature through the ages.

God in Search of Man among Heschel's Works

This book pays particular attention to *God in Search of Man*, which was published in 1955. Hillel Goldberg offers a striking appraisal of the work's impact:

> It was Heschel who explained, out of the sources of Judaism, the reasoning of Jewish particularity to a culture beginning to question the legitimacy of the melting pot, to tolerate ethnic diversity, to create the conditions for Jewish self-acceptance. The special resonance in Heschel's particularistic emphasis derived from his attempt ... to explain to Jews and gentiles alike how a Judaism with the strength of its specificity could nurture salvation for all.[30]

How does a scion of Hasidic dynasties, born in Warsaw in 1907, speak to postwar American Jews and non-Jews from the sources of Judaism? How is a message of universal meaning sculpted from the bedrock of Jewish tradition? To what extent are Heschel's claims foisted onto that tradition, and to what extent do his claims and insights flow authentically from the sources he quotes? What, indeed, is the purpose of the 1,500 sources quoted and cited in *God in Search of Man*, both in the body of the text and in the extensive endnotes? In attempting to answer these questions, I hope to shed light on the entire Heschelian enterprise.

It has been argued convincingly by Arnold Eisen that *God in Search of Man* is given disproportionate attention among Heschel's books and articles.[31] It is important to consider all of his literary output – spanning as it does languages, decades, and genres – while also taking into consideration his social and political activities. The only privilege given to *Search* in this book is that there has been a rigorous and systematic review of the sources quoted and cited therein. In the course of this book, parallels and contrasts are additionally gleaned from all of Heschel's other major works.

The choice to emphasize *Search* is not arbitrary. Its impact on young American Jews in search of a language to express their Jewish yearnings has been described well by Eisen. The very first lines, decrying religion as "irrelevant, dull, oppressive, insipid," grabbed his attention immediately.[32] There is indeed much to capture the imagination of the Jews of postwar America, including stirring prose, daring theological formulations, and a strident critique of spiritual torpor.

God in Search of Man provides a rehearsal for many, though by no means all, of the major themes of Heschel's life and work. Coming as it did some years before his encounter with Martin Luther King and his entry into the Civil Rights movement, the dimension of social and political activism is much less distinct in this work than it was to become in later years. It is also noticeable that the life of prayer, which had already occupied Heschel in *Man's Quest for God*, published only a year earlier, receives short shrift in *Search*. Nevertheless, it provides an excellent presentation of many of Heschel's major preoccupations.

God in Search of Man is divided into three parts: "God," "Revelation," and "Response." The parts are roughly equal in length, each of them containing a number of chapters, typically divided into sub-chapters, of which there are over 300. *Search* is composed of these short sections, each perhaps five or six paragraphs in length. This style of composition is typical of much of Heschel's writing.

Alongside the linear development of the book's central theses, there are some concepts and terms to which Heschel repeatedly returns throughout *Search*, among them loneliness, freedom, the symbol, intuition, intention, pathos, ego, love, song, responsibility, language, response, integrity, and – overwhelmingly – perception.

God in Search of Man is about divine pathos and the prophetic capacity to sense it. It is about the cultivation of spiritual awareness. It is about the Bible. It is about the way in which we are called to act in the world. It is about the fate of the Jews and the fate of humanity. It is about eternity and history, the past and the present. Throughout the work these motifs are authorized, authenticated, amplified, and augmented by a plethora of classical Jewish sources out of which the religion of pathos emerges. The sources quoted and cited by Heschel are witnesses. They testify to the God who searches for man, and encourage man not to despair of being found.

Heschel and the Art of Jewish Quotation

The term *quotation* hardly does justice to the array of referential techniques to be found in most forms of literature through the ages: direct quotation, allusion, paraphrase, mention, cliché, echo, suggestion, pastiche, plagiarism, and many more. All of these are examples of what Genette has called "literature in the second degree,"[33] and despite attempts to provide comprehensive taxonomies, the lines between the various techniques remain blurred.[34]

Quotation is a central characteristic of Jewish self-expression. The prevalence of quotation in Jewish culture is attested to by the sheer weight of quoted sources to be found in virtually every genre of Jewish literature. Moshe Idel summarizes this well:

> Jewish culture is a cumulative culture par excellence; it assumes that the earlier is very often the better ... The peculiar propensity to preserve as culturally active numerous layers of classical literature creates the possibility of continuous dialogues, and frictions, between those layers.[35]

As I have argued in an article on the phenomenon of quotation in Jewish culture, this observation holds true across periods and genres and has very few exceptions up to recent times.[36] It is against this backdrop that the quotational practices of Abraham Joshua Heschel should be considered. I regard him as a quintessential exemplar of the Jewish art of quotation, and within his work different functions of quotation are discernible. I want to make special mention of six of them, organized in a way that moves from the past and points to the future. Heschel's horizon looks to posterity, but it is rooted in what we might term "anterity," the multifaceted layers of tradition.

1. Intensive quotation of traditional sources is the quintessential form of "thick" Jewish expression, and for Heschel it was an expression of identity and an act of fidelity. To bring a source in the name of its originator is a Jewish virtue.[37] By presenting his work surrounded by the thoughts and writings of generations of his forebears, Heschel positioned himself within a tradition, or a number of traditions. In so doing, he revealed much of his own conception of Jewish civilization.
2. To cite an authority is to bring the dead back to life. This act of revivification, attested to in rabbinic sources,[38] may be termed citation as resuscitation. It serves to place Heschel not only within a canon of sources, but within an intimate conversation spanning continents and centuries. Through quotation Heschel demonstrated his lineage and paid homage to his ancestors. By evoking the legacy of some of the greatest individuals in Jewish history, Heschel furthered his claim to be both an heir and a pioneer.
3. Both the traditional world of Torah scholarship and contemporary Western scholarly practice value the citation of authoritative sources as a badge of erudition, and they establish guidelines for appropriate

citation practices Heschel established his learning and expertise in the act of quotation.

4. Heschel's sources add authority to his claims. Although Heschel barely offered proofs for his assertions, he ascribed authority to his arguments by placing them within a tradition. In the case of some works, most particularly *Torah min Hashamayim*, this attempt to add the weight of precedent to the work's theological implications is at the heart of the project.

5. Quotation serves to stimulate, amplify, and ornament his arguments.[39] Heschel strove to appeal to the hearts and minds of a diverse audience, and the sources he cited are part of his strategy of communication. The sources bear witness.

6. Heschel's quotation of such a rich variety of sources provides an education for his attentive readers. Although there is rarely an overtly didactic feel to his writing, his works provide an implicit curriculum.

In the course of this book, examples of Heschel's employment of these functions will be discussed. For the purposes of this introduction, some general comments about each of them are in order.

Intelligibility, Identity, and Fidelity: On Tradition

In a 1946 essay on "The Eastern European Era," Heschel declared that "if Isaiah were to rise from his grave and were enter to the home of a Jew, the two would easily understand one another."[40] In 1951, we find a prescriptive statement rather than a description: "Our way of life must remain to some degree intelligible to Isaiah and Rabbi Johanan ben Zakkai, to Maimonides and the Ba'al Shem."[41] In an unpublished talk to Hebrew Union College students in Cincinnati in the early 1950s, Heschel expressed his fear of what he called spiritual assimilation and asked if he and his generation would really be understandable to Johanan ben Zakkai.[42] Later, in a speech in 1965, Heschel placed responsibility for the Jewish future on the current generation: "We are either the last Jews or those who will hand over the entire past to generations to come." He defined a Jew as a "witness to the transcendence and presence of God; a person in whose life Abraham would feel at home, a person for whom Rabbi Akiva would feel deep affinity, a person of whom the Jewish martyrs of all ages would not be ashamed."[43]

Something of Heschel's conception of Jewish tradition is revealed in these comments. In its authentic expression, the Judaism of every generation keeps faith with the essence of that which precedes it. This fidelity is expressed using the criterion of intelligibility: Jews are enjoined to ask not if the Judaism of their day is identical in every detail to that of previous years, but rather if its essential thrust would be comprehensible to the giants of the past. Looking to the future, Heschel was concerned lest the encounter with the forces of enlightenment and modernity bring this chain of intelligibility into doubt.

Despite living through a period of great uncertainty concerning the future existence of Judaism and the Jewish people, Heschel once commented that he would have the words *survey* and *survival* removed from our vocabulary.[44] The threats to Jewish survival were not to be confused with the reasons for Jewish existence. He believed that Judaism had something important to say about the human condition and regarded the maintenance of a distinct Jewish voice to be a universal imperative. "Why remain Jews?" he asked on a note found among his papers, answering his own question as follows: "Because we are witnesses to a Truth which will save the whole world."[45]

Abraham Joshua Heschel produced works on the Bible, rabbinic literature, medieval thought, Hasidism, prayer, Israel, and his own theology. He espoused what Moshe Idel has called a "panoramic approach"[46] to Jewish creativity. This is particularly evident in *Torah min Hashamayim*, in which Heschel presented a typological distinction beyond the realm of rabbinic literature. The dominant thesis of *Torah min Hashamayim*, and a recurrent motif elsewhere in his work,[47] is that a dialectic tension runs through Judaism from the Bible to the present day. Heschel had an integrated conception of Judaism according to which an essential core was present throughout the vicissitudes and upheavals of history.

Heschel's footnotes are replete with combinations of sources, either quoted or cited, reflecting Heschel's view of Jewish civilization as well as his conception of the interrelation between Judaism and the Western philosophical tradition. Note 2 of chapter 1 in *God in Search of Man*, for example, provides a catalogue of sources relating to the theme of self-knowledge. The list ranges from Plato and Aristotle to the nineteenth-century German philosopher Jakob Friedrich Fries, and to Max Scheler, who was still alive at the time of Heschel's arrival in Germany in the late 1920s. Heschel then proceeded to address the theme from the perspective of Jewish literature, referring the reader to three great medieval works: Bahya ibn Paquda's *Duties of the Heart*, ibn Saddik's *Haolam Haqaton*, and Maimonides's *Guide for the Perplexed*. The note ends with a reference to Hermann Cohen's views on the subject and a collection of Hebrew sayings on the theme of self-knowledge.

Thus, in this first substantive note of *God in Search of Man*,[48] Heschel implied in the subtext what the text never asserts explicitly: that the great questions troubling the heroes of Western philosophical tradition were also concerns for the leading figures of Jewish thought.

In general, Abraham Joshua Heschel refuted the tendency to homogenize cultures and to contend that all world views were ultimately the same. He also made this position clear in the first chapter of *Search*: "There is not one but many philosophies, and the divergence between Aristotle and Augustine, the Stoics and the thinkers of India is just as real as the divergence between Moses and Buddha."[49]

In his treatment of the relationship between time and space, for example, he employed different cultures as a contrast – Athens is the opposite of Jerusalem: "It was the glory of Greece to have discovered the idea of cosmos, the world of space; it was the achievement of Israel to have experienced history, the world of time."[50]

Elsewhere, however, classical and Jewish sources are juxtaposed in a more complex way. The chapter entitled simply "God in Search of Man" contains one of the longest quotations in the book, taken from the introduction to Maimonides's *Guide for the Perplexed*. This excerpt is supported by both the Zohar and one of Plato's Epistles.[51] This same reference is used in *The Prophets*, where Heschel cited the Platonic Epistle to contrast the poetic with the prophetic mode of inspiration.[52]

In *Search*, however, there is no indication that the passage from Plato's Epistles is being used in contrast with the Jewish sources.[53]

In the main, the range of sources deployed by Heschel in his various arguments comes from within Jewish tradition. Here too, *God in Search of Man* serves as a fine example of this tendency. Both Maimonides and the Zohar are among the sources employed in an extended note in *Search* on the Jewish conception of time.[54] Elsewhere in that work the Zohar is cited alongside the sixteenth-century *Shulhan Arukh*,[55] the Babylonian Talmud,[56] and Moses ibn Ezra's twelfth-century *Shirat Yisrael*.[57]

In *God in Search of Man*, each century of Jewish creativity from the ninth to the twentieth is represented. The diversity of these sources is not only chronological; they span every major genre of medieval Jewish literature, including ethical homilies; *piyyut*; commentaries on the Bible, Talmud, and Midrash; Responsa; Halakhic codes; poetry; and more. What is true of *Search* is true in large measure of the rest of Heschel's works.

A range of authors and works are deployed in support or illustration of Heschel's central arguments. In *Search*, Rashi's commentary on the Song of Songs is invoked in a discussion of "The Unrevealed Torah," contributing also to the development of Heschelian motifs such as mystery, the perpetual voice of the Divine, and divine inspiration.[58] Joseph Albo is cited to emphasize the centrality of faith[59] and the importance of *kavanah*,[60] and the latter is also mentioned in a reference to Bahya,[61] whose *Duties of the Heart* is cited in support of Heschel's emphasis on holy deeds.[62] Remarkably, Judah Halevi's *The Kuzari* is referred to as the source for a universalistic teaching.[63] Here, then, thinkers of the eleventh, twelfth, and fifteenth centuries inform a twentieth-century discourse.

Heschel described Judaism, with a sideswipe presumably aimed at Mordecai Kaplan, as the art of surpassing civilization.[64] Nonetheless, he did have a picture of Jewish civilization – one which differed sharply from that of Kaplan – at the heart of which is the notion of polarity and integration: Halakhah and Aggadah, prophecy and apocalypse, choice and obligation, immanent and transcendent conceptions of the Divine, Ishmael and Akiva, Maimonides and Nachmanides, the Ba'al Shem Tov and the Rebbe of Kotzk.

Heschel created a mosaic of quotations, choosing the order in which to place various traditions.[65] By emphasizing the components of Jewish tradition throughout his work, Heschel placed himself within a canon and a context. By quoting, he engaged with tradition.

Citation as Resuscitation: Heirs and Pioneers

In *A Passion for Truth*, Heschel quoted with approval the dictum of the Talmud of the Land of Israel: "He who quotes a tradition in the name of a sage should at the same time to be able to sense his presence."[66] He suggested that the Ba'al Shem Tov "urged students to seek communion with the sages as well as comprehension of their ideas" and cited the case of another sage, Reb Mendel of Rymanow, whose intense desire to see a medieval commentator, Rabbi Isaac Alfasi, eventually led to Alfasi's reappearance centuries after his demise.[67]

As so often with Heschel, that which he ascribed to the heroes of old was in some sense a reflection of his own self-understanding. Abraham Joshua Heschel (whose own name was an evocation of a forebear) is indeed to be seen within the context of a tendency within Jewish tradition to link citation with resuscitation.[68] Bringing figures of the past to life was not regarded by him as an esoteric procedure. Rather, it was an expression of Heschel's humanism – his sense (learned from the Ba'al Shem Tov) that "one should be capable of learning more from people than from books."[69] Tradition is not to be understood as some impersonal abstraction: it involves intimate acts of transmission.

Arnold Jacob Wolf recalled Heschel telling him "that every word he wrote was originally a quotation from a classic Jewish source."[70] This echoes the observation by Hannah Arendt that Walter Benjamin's "greatest ambition was to produce a work consisting entirely of quotations."[71] Benjamin, Arendt claimed, "knew that the break in tradition and the loss of authority which occurred in his lifetime were irreparable, and he concluded that he had to discover new ways of dealing with the past."[72]

Heschel, too, was conscious of a rupture with Jewish tradition, but unlike Benjamin, he believed that the tools for responding to that rupture were present within Jewish tradition itself. This is not to imply that for Heschel simple adherence to the orthodoxies and norms of Jewish tradition would provide an antidote to the ills of modernity; his conception of Jewish history and of the human condition was far more dynamic and his approach more radical. Rather, it was Heschel's view that in order to be a spiritual heir, it was necessary to be a pioneer, and that in order to be a pioneer, one must be a spiritual heir.[73]

In order to gain a better understanding of Heschel's approach to the voice of tradition in the life of the modern Jew, it is worth dwelling on the two passages where the interrelationship of the heir and the pioneer is mentioned. In *Man Is Not Alone* Heschel wrote,

> To have faith ... does not mean to dwell in the shadow of old ideas conceived by prophets and sages, to live off an inherited estate of doctrines and dogmas. In the realm of the spirit only he who is a pioneer is able to be an heir. The wages of spiritual plagiarism is the loss of integrity; self-aggrandizement is self-betrayal.

To this statement is appended a footnote (of which there are relatively few in *Man Is Not Alone*) designed to illustrate the mandate given by tradition for innovation.[74] Using ancient sources to substantiate a call for innovation is a deliberately paradoxical procedure. Tradition embraces change.

In a 1965 lecture Heschel returned to the theme of heirs and pioneers, but inverted the two terms:

The authentic individual is neither an end nor a beginning but a link between ages, both memory and expectation. Every moment is a new beginning within a continuum of history. It is fallacious to segregate a moment
and not to sense its involvement in both past and future. Humbly the past
defers to the future, but it refuses to be discarded. Only he who is an heir
is qualified to be a pioneer.[75]

By profound engagement with the sources of Jewish tradition in his
writing, Heschel strove to be both an heir and a pioneer. Among critics
and theoreticians of literature, much attention has been paid to the
question of originality. Harold Bloom has written of "the anxiety of influence," suggesting that all strong poets struggle with the fear that
they will not be able to surpass their strong predecessors.[76] It may be
that Heschel's anxiety was of a different kind, closer to what has been
described in a different context as "the anxiety of not being influenced."[77] For heirs of the rabbinic system, it is essential to tie all innovations to former generations, reaching back to Sinai. Heschel speaks the
language of precedent. His declarations carry ancient echoes.

A highly suggestive short chapter at the heart of the second volume
of *Torah min Hashamayim* carries forward the discussion of this rabbinic
notion of Sinai as the source of all apparent innovation. Heschel returned to the distinction between Rabbi Akiva and Rabbi Ishmael,
which is central to the first volume of the work. He suggested that the
tradition according to which no sage can utter any idea that is not in fact
a quotation from his own master is linked to the notion that Moses himself only repeated the words uttered to him by the Almighty. Heschel
noted the existence of another approach by which a sage is entitled to
go beyond that which was spoken at Sinai. He linked it with a position
he attributed to Rabbi Ishmael, maintaining that Moses himself inno-
vated and that God fell into line (as it were) with these innovations.[78]

Rabbi Ishmael came to stand for that part of Heschel's own personality that was in search of innovation. It was the voice of Rabbi Ishmael
that inspired the project of *Torah min Hashamayim*: the search for a mandate for innovation from within Jewish tradition itself. Rabbi Ishmael
represented the human possibility of uttering a new word, while for
Heschel's Rabbi Akiva, each word was a repetition of the primordial
divine utterance. Heschel himself lived in the tension between these
two approaches.

Such an approach typified Heschel's reading of Jewish history
throughout his career. It was peopled with heroic figures – the prophets,

Rabbi Ishmael and Rabbi Akiva, Maimonides, Abravanel, Solomon ibn Gabirol, the Ba'al Shem Tov, Menahem Mendel of Kotzk– and by evoking their presence Heschel placed himself and his readers in their wake. Rather than feeling an affinity with Jewish tradition as an abstraction, it was to these great personalities that he felt a profound attachment. Among his papers, a sentence from the teachings of Rabbi Nachman of Bratslav can be found: "When one learns Torah (the teaching of an ancient sage), one kisses the Sage and is kissed by him."[79] While I do not agree with Moshe Idel's highly speculative claim that Abraham Joshua Heschel saw himself in some sense as the reincarnation or "the spiritual inheritor" of the Ba'al Shem Tov,[80] it is not difficult to see how Idel reached such a conclusion. To use a Heschelian expression from a different context, it is not to "textbooks" which Heschel turns in his exploration of Judaism but rather to "textpeople."[81]

Erudition

Both the traditional sage and the modern scholar are judged by the range, relevance, and accuracy of sources they adduce. By anchoring so many of his works with texts and references, Heschel was not only affirming the resonance and vitality of tradition, and simultaneously educating his readership, but also establishing his bona fides, demonstrating his prodigious command of a diverse range of genres.

In the vast majority of cases in *Search*, as in the rest of his works, Heschel quoted accurately. Occasional slips may be attributed to the fact that Heschel often relied on his own exceptional memory.[82] One of them, the attribution of *Memorabilia* to one ancient Greek philosopher called Xenophanes in *Search* was corrected to another ancient Greek philosopher called Xenophon by the time his 1965 *Who Is Man* was published.[83] Jacob Neusner, who worked for Heschel as an assistant during the composition of *God in Search of Man*, has confirmed Heschel's reliance on his memory in the construction of the text, adding that in the main his recollection of the sources was precise.[84] It is reasonable to deduce that on the rare occasion when the wrong tractate or book was cited, the source of the error was Heschel himself.[85]

It is worth inquiring whether Heschel did justice to the original contexts of the sources he quoted, or whether he was prepared to tear those sources from their original context. There are certainly cases in which he employed a verse or teaching far removed from its original setting. In one such example he offered the words of Korah as a watchword for normative biblical values, despite the fact that in the Bible itself these words are not quoted with approval: "In other religions, gods, heroes, priests are holy; to the Bible not only God but 'the whole community is holy' (Numbers 16:3)."[86] From the perspective of rabbinic Judaism, there is nothing remarkable in this willingness to remove sources from their original context. In terms of Heschel's oeuvre, however, this is a rare phenomenon. When writing in Hebrew, he would enjoy the possibilities inherent in the dislocation of a phrase from its original context, but this was invariably achieved with a high level of playfulness, and involved creating a pact of erudition between author and reader.

One example of this playful misprision[87] can be found in the posthumously published third volume of *Torah min Hashamayim*. While developing an elaborate optical metaphor, according to which one "sees" with two eyes – the eye of reason and a spiritual faculty – Heschel invoked the Halakhic principle that he who is blind in one eye is exempt from the commandment of seeing. Only a reader versed in the literature of the Rabbis can appreciate the comment on its various levels.[88]

In the great majority of cases, Heschel offered readings of classical sources that stayed close to the spirit and "plain meaning" of the text. He regarded this as the Jewish way: "The symbolists claim that the literal meaning of Scripture is not the important matter, only the spiritual truths hidden beneath it; while Jewish tradition insists that the biblical verse must never be divested of *peshat*, of its naked meaning."[89]

Significantly, however, Heschel warned against the elevation of *peshat* to an exclusive prism through which reality should be approached. In a Hebrew lecture delivered in 1958, he spoke against interpreting Jewish history simply in terms of facts and raw data, and then pointed out that the word *peshat* contains the same letters as the word *tipesh*, "stupid."[90]

This ambivalence with regards to the plain meaning is discussed at length in *Torah min Hashamayim*, and the two positions are epitomized by Rabbi Ishmael and Rabbi Akiva, "man of *peshat*" and "man of mystery," respectively.[91] Heschel strove for an integration of the two: a deep respect for the text in its context, coupled with a profound sense that there was more in heaven and earth than *peshat* could explain.[92]

While few doubted his learning, a good deal of controversy surrounded the profile of Heschel as a scholar of Judaism. In the original Hebrew edition of *The Sages*, E. E. Urbach cited Heschel's *Torah min Hashamayim* as an example of the neglect of rudimentary scholarly techniques. Urbach stated that the book was nothing more than a translation of Heschel's own theological views as encountered in *God in Search of Man*, with the addition of a garment comprised of quotations woven across the generations in neo-Hasidic style.[93] The suspicion that Heschel's scholarship served his own theological agenda and was inaccurate or too broad-ranging – and consequently superficial – seems to have been shared by such giants of modern Jewish scholarship as Saul Lieberman and Gershom Scholem.[94] Others held a very different view. Seymour Siegel described the very work disparaged by Urbach as "an achievement of great significance in the history of Jewish thought."[95] Gerson Cohen concluded that "Heschel was what he purported not to be, a textual scholar,"[96] and Neusner concurred, acknowledging the enormity of his scholarly achievement, while criticizing what he regarded as deficiencies of method.[97]

To what extent is Heschel taken seriously as a scholar today? His works still appear frequently on course bibliographies in Jewish Studies courses in a variety of fields, but usually as theology, not scholarship. Steven Katz applauded "his uncovering of hitherto unknown original sources" in the area of Hasidism, and scholars of the Hasidic movement still cite Heschel, although not with universal approval.[98]

Heschel's achievements in the field of scholarship have been defended against the accusation of dilettantism, but none would suggest that Heschel functioned primarily as a conventional textual scholar. The interrelationship between his scholarship and theology was summarized thus by Fritz Rothschild: "Heschel, the research scholar, explored the documents of the past in order to make certain that Heschel, the creative thinker, could make his message true and authentic."[99]

Heschel's works bear witness to the tension between the research scholar and the creative thinker. While he rarely engaged in overt polemics, his approach to tradition and learning can be understood as an implicit critique of dessicated scholarship and the jousting and pettifoggery often typical of academic life. His writing and teaching demonstrated a wish for credibility with a variety of audiences, earned by dint of his mastery of a range of genres. Once obtained, this credibility was to serve Heschel's higher purpose – a compelling and passionate portrayal of Jewish tradition in encounter with the burning questions of the day.

Authority

Abraham Joshua Heschel experienced in his own life a profound transition into modernity but was never cut off from the wellsprings of creativity he found to be at the heart of Judaism. He disagreed emphatically with those who maintained that Jewish life could continue to thrive at one remove from the rhythms and insights of Jewish tradition. To an ideological conference in Jerusalem in 1958 he declared,

> We have no power to issue decrees. But it is our duty to teach and pro-claim: "Guard the legacy of ages! Without the study of the Torah, without the Sabbath, without festivals, prayer, and attachment to God – there is no Jewish existence."[100]

For Heschel, the "power to issue decrees," the authority of religious leaders or religious texts to legislate conformity was a thing of the past.[101] The authority invoked by constant reference to the texts of Jewish tra-dition inhered in the authenticity of the prophetic experience and in the piety and sincerity of the post-biblical sages who were cited.

It is worth reflecting on the Heschelian conception of truth. In a dis-cussion of Saadia Gaon's view on this topic, Heschel planted a signifi-cant comment in a footnote: "Saadia does not mention the definition of truth as that which one cannot help believing."[102]

It was this definition, as much as or more than what he called "the standard definition of truth as the agreement of ideas with reality,"[103] which guided Heschel's own understanding of the nature of truth. The categories of reason are inadequate to contain this overwhelming, un-deniable truth.

In his English work on the prophets, Heschel returned to this distinc-tion between differing conceptions of truth and his belief in the inade-quacy of the strict rationalist definition:

> Defining truth as the conformity of assertion to facts, we may censure the prophets for being inaccurate, incongruous, even absurd; defining truth as reality reflected in a mind, we see prophetic truth as reality reflected in God's mind, the world *sub specie dei*.[104]

To Heschel, the conception of truth as simple correspondence seemed both inadequate and unworkable from a Jewish perspective. On the other hand, he was not prepared to abandon the canons of rational discourse. His search for an approach combining both a commitment to the rational method and a willingness to step beyond it is described in the essay on Saadia and appears as a description of Saadia's own system.

In this description, reason aids revelation in the interpretation of "questionable passages in Scriptures." Since there is only one truth:

whatever is found in Scripture that seems to contradict speculation, or experience, or to disagree with another biblical passage or an oral tradition, should not be taken literally but explained metaphorically ...

This "hermeneutical rule" is based on two assumptions: that "some Scriptural texts ought to be interpreted metaphorically and not literally," and that "biblical teachings are in accordance with human reason."[105] Heschel went on to stress that Saadia rejected the complete allegorization of the Bible, but he "does not clearly determine when the method of metaphorical interpretation must be applied and when it must be dispensed with."[106]

While Heschel took issue with Saadia on a number of counts, it appears that in this regard Heschel was in fact describing his own approach. Adducing a verse or some other sacred text cannot lend unassailable authority to a particular viewpoint. It is incumbent upon each individual to see whether the truth claim in question can be squared with reason and conscience. For this reason, Heschel's sources are rarely brought as evidence of the veracity of a claim. Rather, they may inspire, encourage, enlighten, provoke, or in some other way move the reader. Since we have no power to issue decrees, the impact of the sources is emotive, not statutory.

Stimulation, Amplification, and Ornament

Heschel had reservations about the importance attached to sermons. "The sermon, unlike prayer, has never been considered as one of the supreme things in this world."[107] Nonetheless, reference to the homiletic tradition may prove helpful in understanding Heschel's rhetorical strategies.

In an important work on Jewish preaching, Marc Saperstein quoted a "Polish moralist" on the appropriate way to cite classical texts in sermons:

> What does the truly wise rabbi do? He bases his rebuke on the simple meaning of biblical verses. It is as if the verses themselves were uttering the rebuke. Then, as the simple meaning enters the ears of the listeners and pleases them, the rebuke emerging from the sermon automatically enters their ears as well.[108]

The technique of allowing the verses (and later, sources) to speak for themselves is to be found throughout Heschel's work. There are only very rare instances of a close reading or interpretation of sources. Usually, those sources are invited to move the heart and stir the soul. Then the veracity and validity of Heschel's argument may penetrate the mind.

Two of Heschel's books began as lectures: *The Earth is the Lord's* and *Who Is Man?* It is interesting to note the lack of any significant structural difference between these works and the rest of his books (although these two works are very light on quotations). Throughout his oeuvre he displayed a preference for short subsections, pungent epigrams often based in wordplay, and a tendency to close sections and chapters with resonant quotations from the Bible and post-biblical sources. All of his works, not only those which began as lectures, bear the traces of sermonic and performative influence.

Occasionally, for example, Heschel repeated a biblical verse for rhetorical effect. In chapter 8 of *Search*, for example, Isaiah's phrase "the whole earth is full of his glory" is employed as a refrain, recurring five times either as a quotation or slightly paraphrased.[109] In chapter 9, another verse from Isaiah plays a similar role.[110]

Heschel's preference for the concluding quotation illustrates his belief in the power of Jewish tradition to move the contemporary individual. The arguments in *Search* are not always constructed with philosophical rigour, nor do they depend on close literary analysis.[111] Instead, they are designed to provoke a response in the reader closer to that of a participant in an event than that of a reflective reader considering the literary qualities or logical precision of a written work.

Footnotes tend to detract from a book's immediacy. They often provide a more reflective and discursive dimension to the text.[112] It is all the more remarkable that Heschel even made use of some of these rhetorical techniques within the notes. We do not find only dry references and marginal comments in his notes – there too, he was often engaged in a passionate argument.

An early case of such a deployment of sources involving biblical material can be found in the chapter on wonder in *Search*. The section entitled "Stand Still and Consider" ends with a quotation from Psalms 139 to which a footnote has been appended.[113] The curious reader will find in that note not some reflection on the meaning of the verse from Psalms but rather three verses from Job, quoted in full and without comment.[114] This is hardly the traditional use of the scholarly note. Similar cases of what may be termed "resonating footnotes" can be found elsewhere in the work,[115] and they contribute to one of the most prominent rhetorical characteristics of the book: the use of Jewish sources not typically to embellish or to bolster the authority of a claim made by the author, but rather to move and persuade, much like the testimony of a witness.[116]

Shaul Magid has written that "the tzaddik does not teach us something embedded beneath the text's surface – he uses the text to teach us something outside the text. By embodying the text, his *torah* becomes Torah; his teaching becomes God's will."[117]

This description does indeed hold true for Heschel. The text points to something outside itself, an insight yielded only to the person willing to engage fully. More than the quoted sources justify, more even than they exemplify – Heschel's sources testify.

They also beautify. Heschel's penchant for the concluding quotation has been previously noted. He often used traditional sources "in apposition" to each other or to his own argument. By this grammatical term, I mean that Heschel often merely quoted a text and then left it to his listener or reader to construct meaning and draw conclusions. In his 1967 work on Israel, where a clear polemical intention to move and inspire is at work, this method is taken a stage further, and an entire section of the book comprises fourteen verses of Ezekiel, quoted without commentary.[118]

Heschel employed ancient texts to illustrate and elucidate. In demonstrating the contrast between the Ba'al Shem Tov and the Kotzker Rebbe in his final work, for example, verses from Kings and Ecclesiastes are used to evoke the latter, while the Song of Songs and a rabbinic tradition about the harp of David are employed to portray the former.[119] The voices of Heschel's protagonists are given ancient resonances. Indeed, the echoes are intertextual, since use of the Song of Songs links the Ba'al Shem Tov with his rabbinic predecessor, Rabbi Akiva.

Education

Despite some attempts to glean a systematic educational philosophy from Heschel's writings, he was hardly a theoretician of education.[120] It should also be mentioned that while he was not always a great success as a pedagogue in the classroom, Heschel was nonetheless regarded by many as their teacher. He taught by example, in conversations, and also in his writings. The attentive reader is invited to explore a wide array of sources and to engage with many different aspects of Jewish and world literature. One function, then, of the prevalence of quoted and cited sources in his works is as an educational prompt. These notes are not primarily intended to dazzle his readers or to go over their heads, but rather to go into their hearts and their heads, and to invite them to become further engaged.

At the end of his 1972 interview with journalist Carl Stern,[121] Heschel implored young people to study the great sources of wisdom rather than the best-sellers. In a sense, his own works offer a curriculum to anyone interested in following it. Heschel's message of wonder is accompanied by sources of wisdom.

Starting with the observation that the past and present commingle in Heschel's work, I have tried to set out a range of aspects and functions which may also help to introduce this remarkable figure. Abraham Joshua Heschel was a rhapsodist,[122] in the spirit of the origin of this word, singing and sewing fragments together. He was a weaver of exalted song, binding the fidelity of the heir to the courage of the pioneer: "This is the meaning of existence: to reconcile liberty with service, the passing with the lasting, to weave threads of temporality into the fabric of eternity."[123]

Chapter Two

Heschel's Bible and the Hermeneutic of Surprise

Thinking Biblically

To hear the voice of the Bible is to undergo an experience capable of inducing real change. Heschel's is a hermeneutic of surprise, being taken in or overwhelmed by the immediacy of the Bible, across centuries and contexts.

In June 1937 a review of a recently-published Bible concordance appeared in a German Jewish journal. The reviewer was the thirty-year-old Abraham Joshua Heschel, who argued that unlike a dictionary or encyclopedia, a concordance seeks the meaning of words purely within the context of the Bible itself. He added a comment that epitomized a view he held throughout his life: "The Bible is the only appropriate commentary on itself."[1]

This claim for the unique standing of the Bible informed his doctoral dissertation on prophecy, written in the thirties, and it is to be found in *God in Search of Man*, where we learn that "the Bible is its own witness. The evidence for its unique origin is that of *self-evidence*."[2] "It is through the Bible that we discover what is in the Bible ... we must accept the Bible in order to know the Bible."[3]

Heschel afforded unique status to the Bible as a book, but even more fundamentally as an attitude. In pleading for "the intellectual relevance of the Bible," he argued that in order to read and understand the Bible it was necessary for modern theology "to recover the uniqueness of biblical thinking, of categories with which to face ultimate problems."[4] Heschel repeatedly spoke of a biblical way of thinking at the heart of Jewish consciousness: in order to understand what the Bible says, one has to understand life as seen by the Bible.[5]

This notion of biblical thinking would not be immediately familiar to the critical scholar, to whom the Bible is the repository of perhaps one thousand years of creativity, containing many voices and a range of approaches. Nor would such a concept be immediately familiar to a traditionalist, for whom fidelity to the Halakhic system would typically be presented as the apogee of "Torah-true" behaviour. Heschel certainly meant by this term neither adherence to the documentary hypothesis nor compliance with a normative work of the Jewish legal tradition such as the *Shulkhan Arukh* (although he incorporated both into his own world view).

Heschel frequently contrasted the biblical way of thinking with other philosophies and cultures. Plato's definition of man as "that creature who is constantly in search of himself" is contrasted with the "biblical mind" according to which "man is not only a creature who is constantly in search of himself but also a *creature God is constantly in search of.*"[6] "Against the conception of the world as something just here, the Bible insists that the world is creation."[7] "To the Greek mind, man is above all a rational being ... To the biblical mind, man is above all a commanded being ..."[8]

Heschel urgently wished to present the biblical world view as an alternative to the zeitgeist. Modern man lacks "consciousness of the problem to which the Bible refers."[9] Nevertheless, the modern malaise presents an opportunity for the reintroduction of biblical thinking: "There is a genuine hunger for religious teaching and religious understanding ... When we witness the collapse of so much of self reliance and so many certainties then the Biblical message has tremendous power."[10]

Heschel bemoaned "the elimination of the Hebrew Bible from the greater part of the world,"[11] and the twentieth century's "growing alienation from the Bible."[12] In an interview which was broadcast shortly after Heschel's death, he decried the "complete decline of the Bible in American education."[13]

Heschel was keen to stress that the Bible "is a book about man. It is not theology from the point of view of man but rather anthropology from the point of view of God."[14] This reading of the Bible allowed him to put the reading of the Bible at the forefront of his social and political concerns.[15] The idea that the Bible was a book about humanity was not only understood in terms of social reform and political agitation. It was also understood to mean that within the pages of the Bible a person might find an echo of his or her own yearnings and failings. This intimate dimension notwithstanding, the Bible represented for Heschel the ultimate antidote to a rampant narcissism.

In a 1953 paper Heschel bemoaned the fate of the Book of Psalms in the Jewish community of his day:

> The attitudes recorded in some of the Psalms are no less important, we might assume, than the events recorded in the Book of Judges. Yet how few Psalms are taught in our schools while the Books of Judges and Samuel are always taught. "Christianity is a wonderful religion," a Jewish woman active in a Temple, remarked. "Why does not Judaism have a Book of Psalms?" We say that we have given the Bible to the world. Have we not given it away?[16]

Two years later *God in Search of Man* appeared, and it may be regarded as Heschel's attempt to redress the balance and to reclaim the Psalms, which are quoted twenty times more than the Books of Judges and Samuel together.

It is possible that Heschel hinted at his social and religious purpose in placing such emphasis on the Bible in the second volume of *Torah min Hashamayim*,[17] where he paraphrased a story from the Babylonian Talmud (*Avodah Zarah* 4a). After they observed that a Babylonian Amora was no great expert on the Bible, some sectarians in Caesarea asked Rabbi Abahu how he came to be so knowledgeable in Scriptures. He answered, "We [in the Land of Israel] who have many sectarians at hand busy ourselves with Scripture, but the Babylonian scholars who do not have sectarians at hand do not busy themselves with Scripture."[18]

His reading of the story in the context of a discussion on the status of the Book of Deuteronomy is forced to the point of incongruity. So why is the story told? It might be permissible to read this tale as a kind of autobiographical aside to his Hebrew-reading audience. He was explaining, perhaps, that just as in the case of Rabbi Abahu in Caesarea, the particular circumstances of his environment had caused him to relate intensively to the Bible.

Writing in America of the 1950s, Heschel found in his repeated evocation of "biblical man" and the "biblical world view" what Daniel Breslauer has described as "a symbol of Judaism that would cut across the boundaries set by variations in observance."[19] An appeal to the normative rabbinic literature which characterizes *Torah min Hashamayim* would not have succeeded in reaching a rapidly assimilating North American Jewish community, let alone the increasingly large Christian following he was attracting.[20] Evoking the imagery of the Old Testament throughout his career helped Heschel reach Protestants, Catholics, and Jews alike.

For the last thirty years of his life Heschel warned of the crisis facing a world increasingly deaf to the Bible:

> The Bible may be found in the hotels, but it is not to be found in the homes or in the minds. Few of our contemporaries have ever absorbed the challenge of the prophets or the grandeur of the Book of Genesis ...[21]

Something of his self-understanding comes to light in this critique. He set himself the goal of broadening the contemporary audience of the Bible. He was a witness for the reality of God and the centrality of the Bible and set himself the task of bringing it into the homes and minds of his audience.

The second part of *God in Search of Man* includes a lengthy defence of or paean to the Bible, stressing repeatedly its uniqueness. The Sinai moment, the Bible, and even the very idea of revelation are described as incomparable and wholly unprecedented.

Heschel declared the primacy and uniqueness of the Bible as testimony, not as reasoned argument. Heschel's claims for the Bible have been examined in an essay by Jon D. Levenson, in which he gave special prominence to the arguments put forward in the second part of *God in Search of Man*. Levenson exposed some of the methodological omissions and deficiencies that are to be noted in any serious discussion of Heschel on Scripture.[22] Levenson noted that Heschel made claims about the Bible rather than justifying hypotheses. He quoted approvingly the judgment of Arthur Cohen that Heschel was "bored with argument"[23] and committed instead to a stirring rhetorical representation of faith.

The claims for the Bible's status in the second part of *Search* are indeed often unsubstantiated and unconvincing – it is described, for example, as a work "free of any tinge of vested interests, of class or nation; free of any regard for persons ... unconstrained by any false deference to any institution."[24] These rhetorical flights and declarations of faith ring less true than much else in the book.

Heschel was genuinely distressed by the arrogance of those who believed that some literary or archaeological key could unlock the mysteries of the Bible. He complained that "we itemize the Bible and tear it to pieces instead of immersing ourselves in ... [its] thoughts."[25] He may also have been concerned that his own critique of unthinking fundamentalism might be interpreted as irreverence. Most of all, he was distressed at the thought that many Jews had become estranged from the text and the spirit of the Bible. He wanted to persuade his readers that the Bible was sublime and sui generis. Often this case is not so much argued as pleaded.

Heschel's Biblical Hermeneutics

In a 1944 article entitled "Reason and Revelation in Saadia's Philosophy," Heschel engaged in an extended discussion of the biblical hermeneutics of one of the greatest figures in Jewish thought, Saadia Gaon. He argued that for his subject "reason and revelation are not antagonistic to each other but supplementary so as to act in concert for a common goal. There is only one truth, but two ways to lead to it."[26] Saadia's approach attested to "the superiority of revelation rather than the inferiority of reason" and placed Scripture as "the greatest gift to man, except that of life itself."[27]

In the article Heschel related to a hermeneutical rule in Saadia's thought according to which any part of Scripture which seems to contradict reason should be understood metaphorically. However, he noted that Saadia "strongly rejects the complete rationalization of the Bible," which turns everything into an allegory.[28]

Despite his reservations about Saadia's rationalism, Heschel's description of Saadia's hermeneutical method paralleled his own approach. In *God in Search of Man*, Heschel related to the theme of "questionable" passages, now categorizing them as either "commonplace" or "harsh." These verses, either mundane or brutal, "lead one to feel that God is not present in them." In the first case, Heschel seemed to adopt Saadia's approach, reminding his readers that "the Bible has more than one level of meaning."[29]

Heschel's approach was quite different with regards to scriptural passages presenting moral difficulties. This "extremely difficult problem" evoked a radical response. Heschel stated that "not every utterance in the Bible is to be regarded as a norm or a standard of behavior."[30] He proceeded to discuss the special status of the prophet, who questions God's judgment and pleads for divine mercy,[31] and closed the section with a rabbinic text designed to illustrate "the independence of human understanding and its power to challenge a prophet's claim."[32]

Adopting a more apologetic tone, Heschel also argued that the eternal truths of the Bible cannot be considered solely from the perspective of one generation or one moral sensibility. The most extreme expression of this defensive posture is found in the rhetorical question "Shall we presume to sit in judgment in the name of morality over those who taught the world what justice means?"[33]

A range of strategies, then, were employed in Heschel's attempt to grapple with the challenge presented by certain passages of Scripture.[34] He was surely describing his own project when he wrote that a

> philosophy of religion has to carry on a battle on two fronts, trying to win-
> now false notions of the fundamentalist, and to dampen the over-confidence
> of the rationalists. The ultimate task is to lead us to a higher place of knowl-
> edge and experience, to attachment through understanding.[35]

Time and again, we find Heschel in search of a position that steers a course between these two poles. He treated with disdain a slavish adherence to the "plain" meaning of the text, yet also derided a wholly metaphorical reading.[36]

There is hardly any biblical exegesis in Heschel's works. Rarely do we see extended or close readings of a passage or chapter. This phenomenon is strikingly apparent in the two works Heschel wrote on the prophets of the Bible. Both the German and English versions of this work are replete with quotations from the Bible, but they show very little sustained commentary on the texts. The quoted sources speak to the readers; they are rarely interpreted explicitly by the author.[37]

Rather than expound or analyse the sources, Heschel encountered them in the context of what he called in *Search* "responsive interpretation":[38] when trying to understand a biblical expression such as "God spoke," it must be accepted that

> it refers to an idea that is not at home in the mind, and the only way to
> understand its meaning is by *responding* to it. We must adapt our minds to
> a meaning unheard of before. The word is but a clue; the real burden of
> understanding is upon the mind and soul of the reader.[39]

Here the hermeneutic of surprise is at work. In an important insight, Alexander Even-Chen and Ephraim Meir have drawn a parallel between Buber's understanding of the Bible and Heschel's approach to prayer. Referring to his 1939 article on prayer, they note that for Heschel it is in prayer that the power of words can transform those who pray and carry them beyond where they would otherwise be able to go.[40]

Indeed, Heschel's discussion of the power of words to transform, expressed in German in the 1930s and thereafter in *Man's Quest for God*, offers a significant parallel with Heschel's own reading of the Bible, which "has the words that startle the guilty and the promise that upholds the forlorn. And he who seeks a language in which to utter his deepest concern, to pray, will find it in the Bible."[41]

Heschel sought a contemporary reading of the Bible, but he was by no means uncritically modern. One aspect of the modern enterprise which he found repugnant was the tyranny of suspicion. He complained that the phrase "Love thy neighbour as thyself" had now been replaced with "Suspect thy neighbour as thyself."[42] *Suspicion* here denotes the opposite of surprise, a kind of knowing world-weariness which negates the possibility of an encounter with the sacred.

From his days in Berlin, Abraham Joshua Heschel maintained an ambivalent view of scientific biblical criticism. While acknowledging that "it was modern critical scholarship that paved the way for the understanding of the literal and historical dimensions of the Bible that we now consider indispensable for theological understanding,"[43] he argued against turning the Bible into a specimen for dissection or a piece of literature to be reviewed along with the latest novel. In an essay on Protestantism, Heschel penned a critique of biblical criticism summarizing his views on the matter:

> Into his studies of the Bible the modern scholar brings his total personality, his increased knowledge of the ancient Near East, his power of analysis, his historic sense, his honest commitment to truth – as well as inherent skepticism of biblical claims and tradition. In consequence, we have so much to say *about the Bible* that we are not prepared to hear what the Bible has to say about us ... The sense of the mystery and *transcendence* of what is at stake in the Bible is lost in the process of analysis. As a result, we have brought about the desanctification of the Bible.[44]

In *Search* Heschel disparaged a banal dichotomy between a naive fundamentalism on the one hand and a patronizing, reductive rationalism on the other hand. "It is incorrect to maintain that all words in the Bible originated in the spirit of God."[45] The words of Scripture are "the only lasting record of what was conveyed to the prophets," yet they are "neither identical with, nor the eternally adequate rendering of, the divine wisdom."[46]

In a move both conservative and radical, Heschel maintained that a
non-fundamentalist approach to Scripture was sanctioned by tradition
itself. This is in fact one of the central themes of *Torah min Hashamayim*.[47]
His statement in *Search* that "the prophetic words were given to us to be
understood"[48] was a personal restatement of the position identified in
his later Hebrew work with Rabbi Ishmael.

For Abraham Joshua Heschel, the claims of modern scholarship were
a necessary but insufficient part of a contemporary religious sensibility.
Often he presented the approach of biblical criticism as accurate but
beside the point:

> The essence of our faith in the sanctity of the Bible is that its words contain
> that which God wants us to know and to fulfill. How these words were
> written down is not the fundamental problem. That is why the theme of
> Biblical criticism is not the theme of faith …[49]

Heschel argued that while the historical claim of Mosaic authorship may be an issue for theology, depth theology should engage far
more with the mystery of Moses's prophecy.[50] He criticized both the
attempt on the part of experts to make sweeping claims about the
Bible as a whole and the tendency to atomize and dissect the biblical
text.[51] Modern biblical criticism had for Heschel forsaken that humility which should accompany any attempt to read and understand the
sacred text.[52]

One familiar strategy by which liberals have grappled with the dilemma of considering Sinai in the light of historical perspective and modern
text criticism has been the notion of continuing revelation. Heschel rejected the view expressed, for example, in the 1937 Columbus Platform of
the North American Reform Rabbinate, that "revelation is a continuous
process, confined to no one group and no one age"[53] and argued against
it with passion. Though he did not take issue with the concept of historical development, he believed that any attempt to flatten out all moments
of revelation as being of equal significance was an affront to the deepest
insights of Judaism. He expressed the view that "the term 'continuous
revelation' [was] as logical as the term 'a round square.'"[54] He preferred
instead the notion of continuous understanding. "The word was given
once; the effort to understand it must go on for ever."[55]

Heschel's biblical approach is presented in contrast to concepts of
relentless unfolding processes – in this sense, attempts to link Heschel

with process theology seem inappropriate.[56] In contrast to any view, religious or scientific, that emphasizes the inexorable playing out of an undifferentiated process, Heschel's theology of prayer and of the Bible privileges the unsettling creative moment, the possibility of turning, the potential for change. He read the Bible with this possibility constantly in mind.

Rather than explicate the words of the Bible, Heschel preferred the hermeneutic of surprise. He tended to quote verses, often at length, in the hope that the ancient text would penetrate the barriers of hyper-scepticism and hyperrationalism and simply be heard, as if for the first time. I believe that the lack of biblical exegesis in his oeuvre is one of its most remarkable features and speaks to the heart of Heschel's approach. Patently, it did not indicate any incapacity on his part to dwell on the meaning of texts.[57] Rather, I would suggest that this exegetical silence is in itself a commentary and a statement. Throughout his career Heschel strove to have the Bible speak for itself.

Perhaps the only example of Bible commentary offered by Heschel in *Search* is found in a section entitled "The Paradox of Sinai."[58] The fact that the bush described in the third chapter of Exodus burned yet was not consumed is understood to be an expression of the paradox of revelation and concealment.

Divine wisdom, Heschel argued, can be imparted when divine power is hidden. This is a fascinating insight in and of itself, but here it is noteworthy for being perhaps the only example in the entire work of what I would term biblical exegesis.

Rather than explicate, Heschel's approach was to allow the Bible to speak for itself, and to create opportunities for the reader or listener to be struck by the power of the biblical words. He eschewed the possibility of "knowing" too much about the text, consistent in his view that the Bible itself is its only appropriate commentary.

How the Bible Is Deployed

Looking at the published work of Abraham Joshua Heschel over the decades, some quantitative data about his use of particular biblical sources emerges.

The following books were cited most intensively in his writings, in descending order: Isaiah, Exodus, Psalms, Jeremiah, and Deuteronomy. At the other end of the spectrum, Micah, Jonah, Ruth and the Song of Songs were among the books he quoted least.

These sources were not equally spread across his oeuvre: some were deployed in a disproportionate way in certain works. So, for example, over half of the references to the Song of Songs in Heschel are to be found in *Torah min Hashamayim*, with only a handful of such references in the rest of his writing. The same is true of the Book of Joshua, which is almost invisible in the rest of his work.

It is instructive to consider in more detail *God in Search of Man*, by far the most replete with biblical material of his overtly theological works. There are no fewer than 650 biblical quotations and references in the book; only his Hebrew work on the rabbinic concept of revelation and the English version of his book on prophecy contain more biblical references. *Man Is Not Alone*, published some four years earlier, contains fewer than one hundred.

The biblical book most commonly cited in *Search* is Psalms. Nowhere ✓ else in his writings does it occupy such a prominent place, although as noted above, it is one of Heschel's favourite sources. *God in Search of Man* accounts for one quarter of all Job citations in Heschel's work.[59] A section in one of the chapters is entitled "The Test of Job" and relates to that biblical work. Other biblical books that feature more prominently in *God in Search of Man* than they do in other writings by Heschel are Daniel, Proverbs, and Ecclesiastes. In short, there is a preponderance of Wisdom literature material used in *Search*.[60] Not only are they intensively cited, they tend to play an important role in the book's arguments – between them, the Books of Job and Psalms account for one half of the extended biblical quotations in *Search*.

Abraham Joshua Heschel's Bible was at the same time both the pre-eminent source of his religious insight and a strategic common denominator. In *God in Search of Man* the canon is oriented towards the individual: the Psalms and the Book of Job speak to the searching individual. There is relatively little mention of law or of community.

The Bible is extensively positioned in the foreground of *God in Search of Man*. By foreground I mean the body of the text, in contradistinction to the endnotes found at the end of each chapter, where the Bible plays a minor and sporadic role.[61] Perhaps the most eloquent proof of this "foregrounding" is to be found in the almost total lack of biblical allusion in the book. There are few allusions, indirect references, or biblical asides. Almost every biblical reference is clearly marked and noted.[62] Unlike texts of other genres, Heschel's Bible is part of his explicit language.

The Bible is quoted and cited in a variety of ways and with a number of different purposes in *Search*. One phenomenon, which can be termed *quotation clusters*, occurs when a number of biblical phrases are marshaled in a parade of quotations. Occasionally this is for the purpose of illustrating a point by listing examples:

> With amazing consistency the Bible records that the theophanies witnessed by Moses occurred in a cloud. Again and again we hear that the Lord "called to Moses out of the midst of the cloud" (Exodus 24:16); that the Lord appeared and spoke to him "in the pillar of a cloud" (Numbers 12:4; Deuteronomy 12:5; Psalms 99:7); the "Lord descended in the cloud" (Exodus 34:5; Numbers 11:25); "the glory of the Lord appeared in the cloud" (Exodus 16:10); "I will appear in the cloud" (Leviticus 16:2).[63]

Elsewhere, clusters are employed for the advancement of an argument based on the Bible.[64]

Search contains almost one hundred examples with entire verses and extended biblical quotations. They are used for a variety of purposes and in a number of ways, particularly in the early parts of the book. For example, "For all the appreciation of reason and our thankfulness for it, man's intelligence was never regarded in Jewish tradition as being self-sufficient. 'Trust in the Lord with all thy heart, and do not rely on thine own understanding' (Proverbs 3:5)."[65]

Often, the form exemplified here is followed. Heschel makes a statement and then uses the verse to prove, demonstrate, epitomize, or emphasize his point.[66]

There are also over fifty cases of verse "chunks," segments ranging from two to six verses. Often, although not always, these verse are set apart on the page so that their impact is enhanced. For example, a section called "The Contingency of Nature" contains the following:

> What are the foundations of the earth? There are no natural foundations. The foundations of the world are not of this world. The earth continues to exist because of Him
>> That sits above the circle of the earth
>> And the inhabitants thereof are as grasshoppers ...
>> That brings princes to nothing.
>> He makes the judges of the earth as a thing of naught.
>> Scarce are they planted
>> Scarce are they sown
>> Scarce has their stock taken root in the earth;
>> When He blows upon them, they wither,
>> And the whirlwind takes them away as stubble. Isaiah 40:22–4[67]

Heschel wanted his readers to hear the voice of the Bible and hoped his books would provide the conduit to such an encounter. The reader is invited to be a listener and to hear the voice of Scripture. One means to this end is the deployment of biblical verses and passages, particularly noticeable at the ends of sections and chapters. Heschel employed here a technique of juxtaposition or apposition, whereby the biblical quotation acts as an explanation, illustration, amplification, or fulfilment of a point made previously in his own words.[68]

This technique of apposition informs all of Heschel's theological works. In *Man Is Not Alone*, for example, there is only one case of a section of the book starting with a biblical verse in the manner of classical midrashic discussions, while there are several cases of sections ending this way.[69] In this same book, there is also an example of the most extreme case of this technique of apposition, when an entire psalm is simply appended to the chapter.[70] For Heschel, writing in 1951 on the hiding God, no commentary could add to the words of the psalmist.[71]

Heschel's Bible was deployed in a variety of ways: by emphasizing certain works; by placing the biblical material in the "foreground" of most of his texts; by using clusters of verses and extended quotations; and by constructing his argument in such a way that the Bible's voice can be heard without explanation.

Further Modes of Deployment

On occasion Heschel offered decontextualized readings of the Bible that came directly from rabbinic literature. On two occasions in *Search*, for example, he cited verses from the Book of Job and claimed that they referred to the Torah, in line with rabbinic readings of these verses.[72]

Sometimes Heschel's translations were tailored to suit his theological agenda. The expression from Job 28:23, "God understands the way to it, He knows its place," is unclear: to what does God know the way? Various suggestions have been offered in both traditional readings and modern critical treatments: God understands the way to Torah, or the needs and frailties of the people of Israel, or even aspects of God's own divinity.[73] Heschel joined this tradition of appropriating the text in light of its ambiguity and informed his readers that at stake in the verse is the "search for meaning."[74] Another verse whose meaning is unclear, Psalms 51:8, is similarly fitted into the Heschelian vocabulary, and is rendered "'Thou desirest truth in the inwardness' of man."[75] These instances of what can be termed misprision or creative misreading are most remarkable for their paucity. The biblical sources quoted in *Search* and throughout his work are accurately quoted. They are manipulated to suit the author's needs and predilections, as, by definition, sources always are. But this manipulation falls firmly within the normative hermeneutical field one would expect an heir to Jewish tradition and modern scholarly methods to inhabit.

Certain keywords and passages were used by Heschel throughout his career. It will suffice to consider the case of one verse, Psalms 119:19, one of forty verses which appear ten times or more in the Heschel literature. Although this verse is remarkable in the versatility of its usage, it is by no means unique. By following its path we are also witness to the way in which ideas and sources are used and reused in the furtherance of Heschel's theological project.

This verse is translated by Heschel in different ways, as if to emphasize the indeterminacy of its meaning and the fluidity of its translation. It reads, variously, I am a stranger (neophyte, sojourner) on the earth; do not hide Thy commandment from me.

There are four distinct ways in which this verse is deployed by Heschel in books and articles from 1949 to 1972. It is worth noting that this verse, a watchword for displacement and alienation, entered Heschel's theological vocabulary only after his move to the United States and the destruction of Eastern European Jewry.

In its earliest appearance, the verse is found among a cluster of quotations relating to the nature of the Jewish religion: "It has often been said that Judaism is an earthly religion, yet the psalmist states, 'I am a sojourner in the earth.'"[76]

Three years later, the same passage – and indeed the two paragraphs that surround it – was repackaged for use in *Man Is Not Alone*. In the paragraph preceding the verse from Psalms the word *mystic* was replaced by the word *spiritual* with some additional stylistic changes,[77] but it is the same argument, virtually word for word. Both in the essay on Jewish mysticism and in the popular work on religion in general and Judaism in particular, this verse was used to counteract the commonly held notion that Judaism is primarily concerned with the here and now. It was meant to indicate an alternative reality, one in which our stay in this world is but transient and fleeting.

If the verse in question was thus used to express the essence of Judaism, it was also used most extensively to say something about the human condition in general and perhaps about the modern scourge of alienation in particular. This usage first came to light in a 1953 essay on prayer, in direct polemical contrast to an opinion quoted from E.S. Ames's popular work on religion:

> If "prayer is the expression of the sense of being at home in the universe," then the Psalmist who exclaimed, "I am a stranger on earth, hide not thy commandments from me" (119:19), was a person who grievously misunderstood the nature of prayer. Throughout many centuries of Jewish history the true motivation for prayer was not "the sense of being at home in the universe" but the sense of *not* being at home in the universe ... *The Shekhinah is in exile*, the world is corrupt, *the universe itself is not at home* ...[78]

In a 1956 essay on Reinhold Niebuhr, the notion of man's essential alienation was widened still further:

> We do not feel "at home" in the world. With the psalmist we pray, "I am a stranger on earth, hide not Thy commandments from me" (119:19) ... in a world where His will is defied, where His kingship is denied, who can fail to see the discrepancy between the world and the will of God?[79]

Here, too, Heschel expressed man's essential alienation in terms of divine exile, maintaining some of the turns of phrase from earlier incarnations of this paragraph. But the overtly liturgical context is now downplayed and the verse comes to be a motto for contemporary alienation in general.

The idea of linking the verse from Psalms with the concept of alienation stayed with Heschel until his last days. In the chapter on this topic in *A Passion for Truth* he stated that "alienation was a condition affecting the lives of the ancient Prophets of Israel, and it may have found an expression in the Psalmist's outcry 'I am a sojourner on earth' (Psalms 119:19)."[80]

In *God in Search of Man*, the strand of interpretation in which human and divine alienation are linked was refined and emphasized. Ames's comment about the worshipper being at home in the universe was no longer the context for the invocation of the verse, but the original reference to prayer has not been lost. Here we see an activist reading of the verse, and indeed of the very notion of faith:

> The words, "I am a stranger on earth" (Psalms 119:19), were interpreted to refer to God. God is a stranger in the world. The *Shekhinah*, the presence of God, is in exile. Our task is to bring God back into the world, into our lives.

To worship is to expand the presence of God in the world. To have faith in God is to reveal what is concealed.[81]

Considering Heschel's tendency to cite all his sources, this statement contains a mystery of its own. Who are the anonymous interpreters of this verse? And does their interpretation extend to the idea that God is to be brought into the world? The idea that the verse refers to God can be found in the Hasidic work *Degel Mahaneh Efraim*, a book from which Heschel quoted elsewhere in *Search*:[82] "And it is known that the Holy One Blessed be He is like a wanderer in this world, and He has nobody on whom he can bestow the *Shekhinah* ..."[83]

In Heschel's reading, the identification of God as a fellow wanderer was developed into a call for God's rehabilitation in this world, an idea which is not to be found in *Degel Mahaneh Efraim* or any other work I have been able to find. Prayer, far from being an expression of domestic satisfaction, is now seen as an acknowledgment of alienation both human and divine, and a commitment to the expansion of God's presence in the world.

Another interpretation of this verse is to be found in the *Midrash on Psalms*,[84] where the matter under discussion is the human capacity to understand Torah. Heschel also employed this reading of the verse in *Search* at an important point in the discussion of the Bible in Part II. He was intent on pointing to an alternative way of approaching the Bible, one that avoided the obvious pitfalls of fundamentalism and rationalism alike. In touching on the thorny question of sections of the Bible that offend our sensibilities, Heschel pleaded for a combination of honesty, perspective, and humility: not all of the Bible's meanings are immediately apparent to us. In promoting this view, he marshalled a number of sources with no commentary between them. He paraphrased a teaching of the Kotzker Rebbe, quoted the last words of Job (42:3–6) in full, and then brought two teachings from *Midrash on Psalms*, the second of which relates to our verse:

"I am a neophyte in the earth, hide not Thy commandments from me" (Psalms 110:19). Was David a neophyte? But this is what it meant: just as a neophyte comprehends nothing of the Torah, so does man, though his eyes are open, comprehend nothing at all of the Torah. If David, the composer of all the songs and psalms, said I am a neophyte and know nothing, how much more does it apply to us ... For we are neophytes before Thee and sojourners, as all our fathers were (I Chronicles 29:16).[85]

Heschel returned to this midrashic reading of the verse in the first chapter of *Torah min Hashamayim*, once again in the context of a discussion about difficult biblical passages. As part of his description of two overarching approaches to the world and indeed to the Bible, Heschel advanced the view that rationality is insufficient when we attempt to understand Scripture. This Midrash serves as an example of such a view, according to which "the essence of Torah learning is not human understanding and reason, but rather the sanctity of the Torah."[86] In the posthumously published third volume of *Torah min Hashamayim*, Heschel returned to this teaching, yet again in the context of the Torah's unrevealed mysteries, and he astutely linked this to the immediately preceding verse and its treatment in *Midrash on Psalms*,[87] emphasizing the distinction between our present blindness and the promise of future revelation.

In one verse Heschel found a springboard for two ideas that were central to his theology: the alienation of the prophet, of humanity, and indeed of God; and the limits of human reasoning when confronting the mysteries of the Torah. He used the verse in a number of books and articles, applying it in accordance with the dictates of his argument. Interestingly, it has been noted by Avi Sagi that J.B. Soloveitchik tended to quote this same verse when discussing the tension between universalism and particularism.[88] The manner in which certain verses of the Bible have played a significant role in the course of modern Jewish thought is worthy of further research and consideration.

A Hermeneutic of Surprise

To cite the Bible is to choose what to bring to a reader's attention, and what to leave out. Notwithstanding, Abraham Joshua Heschel strove to present the Bible to his readers in a relatively unmediated form and suggested they read it as neophytes, open to the possibility of new understanding.

For Heschel, as for Jewish culture in general, the Bible is the fons et origo, the source of sources from which he drew in the course of his life. More than anything, it served not as a prooftext but as an invitation to encounter, a conduit of meaning. This encounter was born not in reflection but in surprise. The Bible is the most sublime literary distillation of the surprise, wonder, amazement, and awe that are the primal human responses to the mystery of existence. The Bible is also the quintessential expression of the outrage, embarrassment, dissatisfaction, and foreboding that accompany any encounter with great injustice. Heschel's Bible is the crystallized representation of existence, sublime and incomparable.

In his last interview, Heschel reflected on the uniqueness of the Bible. He averred that he did not believe in a monopoly of truth or of divine love. After this clarification of his universalistic commitments, he added, "What has the Hebrew Bible given us in particular that is not to be found anywhere else? I would say the particular appreciation of the greatness of man, of man's tremendous potentiality as a partner of God."[89]

In encountering the Bible, the individual is invited not only to perceive God's call but also to become aware of the human potential to respond to it. This may be the greatest surprise of all.

The text of the Bible held only penultimate significance for Heschel. At the conclusion of the second part of *Search*, he stated that "the meaning of the Torah has never been contained by books,"[90] and earlier in that work he emphasized the status of the Bible as an echo of an event in an epigram pregnant with meaning: "As a report about revelation the Bible itself is a *midrash*."[91]

Over a decade later, moved by the events of the Six Day War, Heschel continued this theme of the dynamic nature of the Bible, molten and never fixed. The Bible is "not a document sealed and finished. It is a book alive, a book that goes on and extends into the present – always being written, always disclosing and unfolding."[92]

How is this notion of the unfolding Torah to be reconciled with what we have noted as his opposition to the idea of an inexorable unfolding process of life? The perpetual writing of human history is, like the written Bible, not the chronicle of some predetermined enactment but rather the record of human encounters, on the intimate and the grand historical scale. In this sense, the Bible is not only revealed in surprise. It is written in surprise.

The hermeneutic of surprise was designed to prod his readers to get beyond the verse, beyond the textual excerpt, and to relate to the divine call and the human response of awe and wonder that are the core of Torah. "There is in the Bible God's word to man, but there is also man's word to God."[93] In moments of true encounter with Scripture, both voices may be heard.

Susannah Heschel has pointed out that her father witnessed at first hand attempts to eradicate the Old Testament and de-Judaize Jesus.[94] This consciousness stayed with him after the Nazi years, causing him to declare in 1965 that "the fate of the Jewish people and the fate of the Hebrew Bible are intertwined"[95] and to observe that "Nazism has suffered a defeat, but the process of eliminating the Bible from the consciousness of the Western world goes on."[96] His approach to the Bible, and his deliberate foregrounding of Biblical verses and concepts in his own original way, were in part a response to the events he himself had seen. Heschel taught that the Bible is its own witness. In his life and work, he sought to express that testimony in terror, love, and surprise.

Chapter Three

A Living Response:
Heschel and the Literature of the Sages

"Where the People Israel Lived"

According to an unconfirmed story, Abraham Joshua Heschel once bought an edition of the Talmud as a birthday present for Martin Buber, and the recipient of the gift thanked the donor, adding, "I have always wanted one of these."[1] The extent to which Martin Buber was in fact steeped in the literature of the Rabbis is not our concern here: it is rather the fact that Heschel differentiated between his own background and that of his erstwhile mentor which is significant. In a 1967 interview Heschel commented, "One of the weaknesses in Buber, who was an exceedingly learned man, was that he was not at home in rabbinic literature."[2]

The irony inherent in this comment would not have been lost on Heschel, knowing that in his formative years Buber had in fact lived in the home of his grandfather, an eminent scholar of rabbinic literature. Nonetheless, Heschel regarded Buber, and indeed most of the leading figures of modern Judaism, as being at one remove from rabbinic culture and literature. A.J. Heschel and J.B. Soloveitchik are rare among the first rank of modern Jewish thinkers in that both were immersed in the world of rabbinic Judaism from birth. Of the two, it was Heschel who made more extensive use of rabbinic literature in his own writings.

Some data from *God in Search of Man* may serve to illustrate the range of rabbinic sources Heschel used in his work. While excerpts from rabbinic literature are fewer (less than half) and less prominently displayed than their biblical counterparts, nonetheless there are over three hundred such sources.

Heschel deployed biblical and rabbinic material in sharply distinct ways in *Search*. In the case of the biblical references, there is a great preponderance in the first part of the book, less than half this amount in the second part, and even fewer in the third. The Bible is a key source for grounding a conception of God, central but less predominant in the matter of revelation, and further consigned to the background in the discussion of response.

Heschel's use of rabbinic sources in *Search* follows a different pattern. The smallest number of examples can be found in the "Revelation" section at the heart of the book and by far the greatest number in the "Response" section. Moreover, in the third section the number of rabbinic sources cited actually exceeds that of the biblical references. The Bible may provide a lexicon for wonder, but it is the Rabbis who help furnish a vocabulary for response. The Bible speaks universal truths. The Rabbis clothe these truths in specificity. The Bible evokes wonder. The Rabbis mandate action.

The most copious citation of rabbinic sources in Heschel's work is to be found in *Torah min Hashamayim*. This book contains more than three times the number of individual rabbinic sources than are to be found in any of three works on a similar topic all of which are replete with rabbinic quotations: Solomon Schechter's *Some Aspects of Rabbinic Theology* (1909), C.G. Montefiore and H.M.J. Loewe's *A Rabbinic Anthology* (1938), or Ephraim E. Urbach's *The Sages* (1969). So intense is Heschel's use of quotation in *Torah min Hashamayim* that Jacob Neusner called it an unreadable work.[3] In my view, however, the book manages to maintain clear focus and fluency while weaving together such a rich thread of citation.

It is beyond doubt, then, that Heschel made intensive use of rabbinic literature, but what role did he ascribe to it? A short 1956 essay, "Teaching Religion to American Jews," may provide a significant clue. In that essay, an anomaly in his description of the desired curriculum for adult Jewish education revealed a certain ambivalence. In Heschel's first statement of curricular intent, the Rabbis are notable by their absence:

> In our quest for forgotten questions, what should we study in our adult education programs? First, the Bible must become the central core of all our studies. Second, we need to devote ourselves to an intense, word-by-word study of the prayerbook. And third, we should attempt to recapture an appreciation of the religious spirit of East European Jewry.[4]

Subsequently, a brief reference is made to each of these three genres, but immediately following the paean to the Bible, Heschel inserted a paragraph entitled "Rabbinic Literature":

> Second in importance is the study of rabbinic sources. These sources contain more than aphorisms, laws, or stories. They are the living response of our people to God's claim on man and examples of our people's effort to live in a way which is compatible with man's dignity as a being created in the image of God. Rabbinic literature is where the people Israel lived for ages, and to its pages all must turn who want to meet that people.[5]

This is the most explicit reflection on the significance of rabbinic literature in all of Heschel's writings, and it is couched ambivalently. Rabbinic sources are both included and omitted from his essential curriculum, and they are then described both as a living response and a past glory.

During his years at the Jewish Theological Seminary, Abraham Joshua Heschel was in close physical proximity to a number of scholars whose work on the rabbis of the period of the Second Temple and the Talmud achieved popularity. The greatest of them, Louis Ginzberg, had a close relationship with Heschel and was involved in bringing Heschel to the seminary. Following Ginzberg's death in 1953, it was men such as Max Kadushin[6] and Louis Finkelstein who were at the forefront of Rabbinics at the seminary. While the distance between his and their offices may have been short, Heschel's approach to the literature and culture of the Rabbis was far removed from theirs. As with the case of Bible scholarship, Heschel walked a different path than many of his contemporaries. While not engaging in any overt polemics with their historical and sociological methods, Heschel offered a different reading of the Rabbis and their continued relevance.

Aggadic Man

For Heschel, the world created by the Rabbis had vital significance so long as it was understood in terms of both of its key poles, Halakhah and Aggadah. He believed that too much attention had been paid to the Halakhic dimension of existence removed from its Aggadic corollary, thus creating a distorted picture. In the introduction to *Torah min Hashamayim*, Heschel contested that "whoever sees in Aggadah mind games or intellectual ornamentation does violence to its essence and squanders its riches."[7] Halakhic literature continued to grow and develop in subsequent generations, but the ideas and insights of Aggadah were largely ignored:

> The teaching of Aggadah eluded the great masters of Jewish religious thought. Thus the study of the most sublime matters languished in Israel. The modern Jew, who thirsts for matters of the intellects, finds in the House of Study only a salty crust and meager rations, and thus rejects the meal.[8]

Rather than the creative tension between Aggadah and Halakhah being maintained, the latter had become inordinately prominent at the expense of the former. Heschel claimed that Judaism was misunderstood as a result. He attributed the abandonment by many modern Jews of their Judaism to this imbalance. In Rebecca Schorsch's formulation, "his polemical intent is to redress the wrong due to Aggadic material – to demonstrate that it is as diverse and as integral a part of Judaism as is Halakhah."[9] More than defending the honour of Aggadah, Heschel regarded its rehabilitation as a crucial step for the future of Judaism.

There are lines of connection between Abraham Joshua Heschel and some other major twentieth-century figures who were engaged in the reinstatement of Aggadah. The first section of *Torah min Hashamayim* undoubtedly owes much to Bialik's seminal essay "Halakhah and Aggadah."[10] Heschel had little use for the latter part of Bialik's argument, which related to tensions inherent within the Jewish national renaissance. However, the opening part of the essay, in which the essential characteristics of the two approaches are described, seems to have informed Heschel's thinking. A close comparison between these two explications of the interrelationship between Halakhah and Aggadah has yet to be undertaken.[11]

Another central figure in Heschel's work is Louis Ginzberg,[12] whose extraordinary contribution to redressing the balance of scholarly interest and encouraging a focus on the Midrash served as a model and an inspiration.

Alan Brill has described Heschel as "Aggadic Man," concluding that *Torah min Hashamayim* "belongs on the shelf with the other great romantic readings of rabbinic Judaism," especially the works of Bialik, Ginzberg, and Agnon. He suggested that "Heschel's unique and most important contribution to the study of *aggadah* was to reintroduce the rabbinic texts in their full strangeness, otherness, and wondrousness."[13]

Brill's reading of Heschel is highly illuminating and by no means uncritical. At one point he compares Heschel's treatment of the Sinaitic revelation to that of S.Y. Agnon, concluding that in contrast to Agnon, Heschel imposed an anachronistic sensibility on the Rabbis. Such a claim is by no means unique. As I noted in chapter 1, a famous assault on Heschel on this count is to be found in the introduction to the original Hebrew edition of Urbach's monumental opus, *The Sages*. Urbach claimed that Heschel's Hebrew work was simply a version of Heschel's own theology, augmented by quotations gleaned from all the ages and varnished with a neo-Hasidic gloss.[14]

The debate concerning Heschel's credibility with regards to the literature of the Sages is reproduced in discussions of his reading of the Bible, medieval literature, Hasidism, and modern philosophy. There is little to be gained from attempting to rank Abraham Joshua Heschel among scholars of rabbinic culture. He was convinced that he had gone a step further than those scholars, following on from David Zvi Hoffman, who had noted a significant distinction between the schools of Rabbi Ishmael and Rabbi Akiva in the domain of Halakhah. By extending this distinction into the realm of Aggadah, Heschel elevated these men to the status of eternal archetypes. He carried the strong conviction that these distinct world views were indeed to be found in the period of the Rabbis (and, being elemental human responses, in all other periods as well). Rather than spending much time on proving this thesis using the tools of *Wissenschaft*, he preferred to let the words and deeds of the Rabbis speak for themselves.

Rabbinic Literature and the Heschelian Lexicon

To judge from his monumental work, the *Theology of Ancient Judaism*, as Heschel termed *Torah min Hashamayim* in English, Heschel did not see the literature of the Rabbis simply as a museum of forgotten treasures.[15] It is, however, no coincidence that hardly any of Heschel's writings on the Rabbis were published in English. It appears that the Sages did not play a central part in his strategy for the revivification of Judaism in postwar America.

Nonetheless, their examples are adduced to illustrate contemporary dilemmas. In *Search*, Heschel quoted a tale from Tractate Shabbat about a sage who falls prey to the temptations of drink and misreads the Torah as a result, the implication being that the transient vanities of the world can obscure the eternal truths of Torah learning and righteous living.[16] Based largely on Rashi's explanations, Heschel provided a phrase-by-phrase exposition of the tale. The story's denouement, in which the sage in question is returned to his previous level of expertise, thanks to the intercession of his colleagues, was not relevant to Heschel's purpose and is therefore excised from his version. Rather, it was the figure of the ancient scholar seduced by the temptations of the day which caught his attention.

Elsewhere in *God in Search of Man*, two extended rabbinic quotations appear in one note as part of Heschel's discussion of "The Problem of Evil." A note on that chapter is situated precisely at the juncture between the general discussion of human evil in the world and the particular invocation of the horrors of the Holocaust.[17] It is the literature of the Rabbis which Heschel employed to provide a kind of theological backdrop. In order to illustrate "what the Rabbis thought about the situation of man," he first referred to a Talmudic discussion of the verse in Habakkuk likening human beings to the fish of the sea[18] and then added a profound teaching from Tractate Sukkah, according to which, in the time to come, the evil inclination will appear to the righteous as a mountain and to the evil as nothing more than a strand of hair.[19] Rabbinic sources were marshalled to illustrate Heschel's belief that good and evil are inextricably intertwined: we find these and several other rabbinic traditions in Heschel's 1956 essay on this theme, offering a Jewish reading of the theology of Reinhold Niebuhr.[20] Rabbinic sources play an important role in what may be termed the Heschelian vocabulary. Not only did Heschel tend to cite particular rabbinic sources as typical of "the Rabbis,"[21] "the ancient men of old," or simply "legend"; he also related to such sources as indicative of "the Jewish mind," "the Jewish way of living," "Jewish observance," "Jewish experience," and "the world of Jewish piety."[22] The most prevalent attribution of this kind is to "Jewish tradition."[23] In other rabbinic citations Heschel adopted certain turns of phrase and included them in his own theological vocabulary.[24] The implication here is that the ancient sages embodied the essential Jewish spirit.

Heschel's use of the literature of the Sages in *Search* is well illustrated by this cluster of rabbinic quotations:

In Hebrew we speak of the mitzvah as if it were endowed with sensible properties, as if it were a concrete entity, a thing. We say, for example, "to appropriate mitzvot," "to acquire mitzvot," "to pursue mitzvot," "to be well-laden with mitzvot";[n3] "even the ignorant men are replete with mitzvot as a pomegranate (is replete with grains)";[n4] "Adorn thyself with mitzvot before Him."[n5] Every mitzvah brings "a good angel into being." Mitzvot are "man's friends,"[n6] his true "offspring," his defenders in the world to come,[n7] his garments, his form. Without mitzvot one is naked.[n8][25]

Most of this section is in fact taken from Heschel's highly important 1949 Hebrew essay *Pikuach Neshama*. He translated, edited, and added to the paragraph, then inserted it into the text of his English work. Having commented in the Hebrew original that the expression involving the pomegranate could not be translated into any other language, within a few short years he had translated the expression and prepared it for consumption by an Anglophone audience.[26]

The Talmudic metaphor of mitzvot from this world reappearing and testifying on behalf of Israel in the world to come was cited as the source of the image of mitzvot as defenders,[27] but the subsequent reference from Genesis Rabbah referred to mitzvot as clothing (and hence a barrier to nakedness). It is a commentary to Genesis Rabbah appearing in the classical edition which developed the image of mitzvah as both garment and as shield, thus implying another meaning of "defenders."[28] Having trawled the rabbinic sources for metaphors of mitzvah, Heschel transformed them into his own rhetoric.

In *Torah min Hashamayim* key aspects of Heschelian thought are presented in rabbinic garb. Divine pathos, for example, is seen in terms of the exile of the Shekhinah[29] and of the mutuality of the relationship between the Jewish people and God.[30] The notion of God's search for man is linked to the rabbinic expression that speaks of "God's appetite" – God desires to see Israel, just as Israel yearns to see God.[31]

I have already noted that Heschel often cited classical texts at the end of sections and chapter. Chapters 5 and 6 of *Search,* for example, both conclude with rabbinic quotations; the former a paraphrase of the discussion in Ecclesiastes Rabbah of the whereabouts of Moses's grave, and the latter a long quotation of the famous Menahot tradition concerning Moses and Rabbi Akiva. Similarly, the section on "The Evil Drive" in chapter 35 ends with a series of five quotations, four of which are Talmudic. Eternal truths are uttered out of the mouth of tradition.[32]

The *Tannaim* in Nazi Berlin

In 1936 Heschel published a series of eight articles entitled "Personalities in Jewish History" in the Berlin *Jüdisches Gemeindeblatt*,[33] the Jewish publication with the largest circulation in Germany at that time.[34] Each article constituted a portrait of a sage of the first and second centuries, from Rabbi Johanan ben Zakkai to Rabbi Hiyya.[35] The pieces were written at a time of unparalleled concern in the Jewish community. The Nuremberg laws had been passed only a few months earlier. The eight articles appeared over six months, starting 23 February 1936, some two weeks before the German reoccupation of the Rhineland, and ending 16 August 1936, the precise date of the closing ceremony of the Berlin Olympic Games.

The title given to this series of articles, "Personalities in Jewish History," deserves attention. From the 1930s until the end of his life, Heschel presented his ideas through the prism of particular individuals. A list of the individuals who populated Heschel's pantheon would include the early biblical prophets, Rabbi Akiva and Rabbi Ishmael, Saadia Gaon, Abravanel, Solomon ibn Gabirol, Maimonides, and later figures such as the Ba'al Shem Tov and Menahem Mendel of Kotzk. This emphasis expressed more than an interest in the philosophies of these individuals. Heschel's understanding of their personalities played a central role in his approach.

In his presentation of rabbinic exemplars to a Jewish community in crisis, a variety of attitudes and strategies is described. Rather than one archetype of heroic resistance, a range of approaches is explicated. The message is not that the radicals or the pacifists or the intellectuals or the Zionists or any one faction in the panoply of Jewish responses can find a mandate in tradition. They all can claim such a mandate, including those on the verge of resignation.

If diversity is one message of these portraits, another is the power of the individual to effect change. Throughout his life Heschel remained convinced of this, in opposition to intellectual trends which emphasized impersonal processes, economic factors, and other structural explanations. In contrast, he emphasized the primacy of the individual and highlighted particular men through whom broad conceptions were explored and developed.

Some twenty years after the appearance of these articles Heschel declared his emphasis on the individual and his resistance to the zeitgeist:

Much has been spoken and written in our midst about nation and society, about the community and its institutions. But the individual has been lost sight of ... The time has arrived to pay heed to the forgotten individual. Judaism is a personal problem.[36]

His choice of individual subjects is worthy of note. Rabbi Ishmael, who was to feature so prominently in Heschel's later work, was not one of the eight sages portrayed in these early pieces. Each of the eight was designed to illustrate a particular sensibility. As one reads these short articles, it is difficult to avoid the sense that the period of Roman rule serves as a cipher for the dramatic and ominous prospects facing the Jews of Nazi Germany. In a number of the pieces, a paragraph describing the desperate conditions of the day was included. Rabbi Johanan ben Zakkai "recognized the hopelessness of the fight against the Romans." Rabbi Gamaliel was an iron patriarch who realized that "only centralization and the creation of a legislative institution, the standing and worth of which would be generally recognized, could save the teaching and the nation from disintegration." Rabbi Akiva's "enthusiastic life took a tragic turn when he joined the Bar Kokhba revolt "with messianic enthusiasm." Rabbi Simeon ben Gamaliel offered a practical, life-affirming approach to a period when "an avalanche of resignation" gave rise to a "fury of despair."

That Heschel saw fit to devote an essay to the tragic and controversial figure of Elisha ben Avuya is itself significant. He saw him as part of a tradition of the "shattering of faith" reaching back to Job. The failure of any apparent reward for piety "gave rise to agonizing doubt about the veracity of faith." The other sages profiled were Rabbi Meir, Rabbi Judah the Prince, and lastly Rabbi Hiyya, who is portrayed as a humble émigré scholar. In each of the articles Heschel showed both a willingness to be critical and a deep empathy with his subjects.

In these long-forgotten pieces the woes and stark choices of contemporary times were woven into Heschel's description of days long past. Pacifism, resistance, emigration, communal self-discipline – all these and other potential responses to the current plight were rehearsed through the lives of these traditional exemplars.

Each one of the articles contains some passages with clear parallels to the actual life situation of its readers. "Mystical speculations, apocalyptic visions and messianic exaltations dominated the spirit of the age" in Rabbi Johanan ben Zakkai's days. The Judaism of Rabbi Akiva's era "found itself at a cultural turning point." Rabbi Simeon ben Gamaliel's era was characterized not by "a collapse of faith but by an avalanche of resignation."[37] This same term, "resignation," appears in the discussion of Elisha ben Avuya, in which Heschel commented that "the shattering of faith is not new in Judaism" and is a theme harking back to Job. Faith in an individual deity leads to trust that there will be an appropriate reward for piety. When this reward fails to come, "resignation" may follow.

The eighth article ("Rabbi Chija") opens with a paragraph whose resonances could hardly have been lost on his readers:

> The Jews in Palestine, the people and the scholars, lived in fear that the Torah might be lost to them. The land was slipping away from them. The leaders had been killed and safety of existence denied. They were, to a large extent, refugees, emigrants and martyrs. Their children could not be taught and the places of instruction for judges could hardly be maintained. Disaster hung over them ...

These early rabbinic sketches contained more than hints of their readers' own predicament. By perusing these short articles, it becomes evident that from early on in his career, Heschel saw the great archetypes of the Mishnah as embodying a debate running the length of Jewish history. Indeed, a reading of Heschel's earliest published writing suggests that the basis of this Akiva-Ishmael distinction occurred to him at a very early stage of his development.

We have noted that Rabbi Ishmael did not merit an article of his own among the eight portraits. Nonetheless, one can find *in nuce* the dichotomy later to be found at the heart of *Torah min Hashamayim*. In these early essays it is Rabbi Simeon ben Gamaliel who expressed an Ishmaelian sensibility. Following Rabbi Ishmael, Rabbi Simeon ben Gamaliel "found himself in a deep spiritual conflict with Rabbi Akiva": the latter stands for study, the former for action. Akiva "saw in every idiom of the Torah a subject for interpretation," while Rabbis Ishmael and Simeon ben Gamaliel held that hyperbole need not be understood hyperliterally. The Akivan approach favoured astuteness and mental acrobatics; the Ishmael-Simeon axis privileged knowledge and a pragmatic approach.

"Fathers of the Universe"

In *Torah min Hashamayim*, two *tannaim* are presented as the fulcrum of Jewish history. The Ishmael-Akiva dichotomy is presented as an echo of earlier tensions and a precursor of tensions yet to come. Rabbi Akiva's views are linked with apocalyptic literature and Rabbi Ishmael's with the classical prophetic tradition.[38] Akiva's perspective is heavenly while Ishmael's is this-worldly. Akiva is an ideologue of martyrdom; Ishmael prefers to live to serve God another day. Akiva finds meaning in the crowns on the letters; Ishmael believes the text was written in the language of human beings. In the wake of these great archetypes, the subsequent great debates of Judaism take shape. Heschel summarized his approach in the posthumously published third volume, in which he asserted that the "changes and disagreements of subsequent generations have their roots in the systems of these two 'Fathers of the Universe.'"[39]

The Rabbis in general and these Sages in particular were regarded by Heschel as the spring from which many of the key debates about life's great questions derived. He posited a profound disagreement between the Ishmaelian and Akivan schools concerning the vision seen by Moses at the moment of revelation. Heschel suggests that Akiva's view, namely that Moses did indeed see the figure of the Divine, is perpetuated in the Amoraic period, while the school of Rabbi Ishmael opposes this view. The debate continues on into the Middle Ages and beyond.[40]

Heschel's earliest publications foreshadowed his later fascination with the distinction between Rabbi Akiva and Rabbi Ishmael. Aged fifteen and sixteen he published brief paragraphs in a Polish journal in Hebrew, noting problems and offering solutions to Talmudic questions.[41] In the first of these pieces he related to an extended discussion in the Babylonian Talmud concerning twofold compensation for articles stolen from the house of someone entrusted with safekeeping (as described in Exodus 22:6–8), and fourfold and fivefold compensation for animals slaughtered or sold by a thief (Exodus 21:37). The young Heschel noted the fact that in setting out his ruling on this particular issue, Maimonides makes use of a hermeneutical principle which differs from the normative voice used in the original Talmudic discussion.[42]

Forty years after writing this short article, a more mature Heschel was addressing the distinction between the hermeneutical approaches[43] discussed here in the first volume of *Torah min Hashamayim*. This work presents a bold thesis, namely an application of the distinction between the schools of Rabbi Ishmael and Rabbi Akiva. Heschel claimed that these two schools of opinion represent two ways of understanding the world and what lies beyond it.

Towards the beginning of this first volume, Heschel suggested that the difference between the Akivan and Ishmaelian approaches was related to their respective applications of the hermeneutical principles he discussed in the earlier 1922 article. In volume 1 Heschel ascribed the difference in approach[44] between Rabbi Akiva and Rabbi Ishmael to their teachers, Nahum of Gimzo and Nehunyah ben ha-Kanah, respectively.[45] Rabbi Ishmael learned from Nehunyah that "since the Torah spoke in human language, we must interpret its languages by using concepts susceptible to human understanding."[46] In contrast,

> Nachum of Gamzo and Rabbi Akiva believed that a gulf separates the language of the Torah and the language of humans ... Now the principle of generalization and specification is appropriate for understanding words spoken by human beings, but it is not always sufficient to appreciate the intention of words spoken on high. We cannot grasp the mysteries of Torah with rational tools, using the pincers of logic alone.[47]

In the second volume of his Hebrew masterwork[48] Heschel cited a later section of this Talmudic discussion in his presentation of the fundamental difference between the two rabbis in their understanding of the concept of Torah from Heaven. For Rabbi Ishmael, the entire Torah was not revealed at Sinai. Rather, the general rules were revealed there and the details were made known in the Tent of Meeting. In Rabbi Akiva's view, the Torah was revealed in its entirety on Sinai and repeated thereafter.

Decades earlier, in the 1922 note, the teenage Heschel had noticed that Maimonides adopted an Ishmaelian position rather than the Akivan approach apparently favoured in the conclusion of this particular Talmudic discussion. There is, of course, no indication that he would have formulated the question in this way at that stage of his development. It cannot be proven that Heschel carried the more radical religious ideas of his later years with him from his early youth. It is, however, noteworthy that at fifteen he was asking a question that was to appear at the core of his work forty years later.

With which of these two Fathers of the Universe did Heschel identify during the course of his life? Some have attempted to provide a definitive answer to this question. A recent article claims that there is no doubt about the matter: Rabbi Akiva is the hero of the work. While Heschel identified with Rabbi Ishmael on the legal plane, in matters of theology and Aggadah, it is Rabbi Akiva who prevailed.[49]

This observation is borne out by neither my reading of *Torah min Hashamayim* nor a comparison between this work and the rest of the

Heschelian canon. It is certainly the case that Rabbi Akiva is identified with the single most prevalent and influential theological notion
in Heschel's thought: divine pathos.[50] But there is repeated evidence
that the Ishmaelian viewpoint is defended and, on occasion, clearly
preferred.[51]

Heschel's Rabbi Ishmael comes to represent a historically minded,
this-worldly approach that is both radical in its theological implications
and moderate in its practical applications. Even before writing *Torah
min Hashamayim* Heschel was marshalling rabbinic sources in furtherance of a moderate theology. An excellent example of this tendency can
to be found in *Search*, where he asserted that the claim that every iota of
the law was revealed to Moses is "a theological exaggeration." He then
proceeded to offer a critique of hyperlegalism:

> In their zeal to carry out the ancient injunction, "make a hedge about the
> Torah," many Rabbis failed to heed the warning, "Do not consider the
> hedge more important than the vineyard." Excessive regard for the hedge
> may spell ruin for the vineyard.[52]

Heschel found a traditional echo of his critique in a saying from
Genesis Rabbah attributed to Rabbi Hiyya.[53] He had already deployed
this text in *The Sabbath*, as support for his contention that the "ancient
rabbis knew that excessive piety may endanger the fulfillment of the
essence of the law,"[54] and he returned to it on two occasions in *Torah min
Hashamayim*. In volume 2, Rabbi Hiyya's dictum is brought among other teachings that represent an Ishmaelian sense of moderation against
Akivan extremism.[55] The fullest exposition of these ideas comes in the
third volume, where an entire chapter is devoted to the concept of *kol
hamosif gore'a*, namely that "more is less."[56]

Rabbi Hiyya's teaching became a slogan of moderation, and it is the
moderate, rational, Ishmaelian Heschel who presented it in *Search*. This
attempt to find an authentic Jewish lexicon of moderation is one of
Heschel's boldest theological ambitions.

Gedalia Haber, a young Israeli scholar, has argued that it is possible
to discern a consistent Heschelian dogmatic approach according to
which the Akivan position is to be preferred in some matters and the
Ishmaelian in others. His assumption that there is such a clearly consistent world view waiting to be discovered does not tally with my own
reading of Heschel's work. Haber is right, in my view, to redress the
balance and note that both Fathers of the Universe play a key role in

Heschel's work, but he is misguided in his attempt to uncover the road-map which will explicate each preference and judgment.[57]

Reuven Kimelman noted two essential differences between Heschel's book on the Sages and foundational works by Schechter, Moore, and Urbach. In his view, "Heschel's work on rabbinic thought continues his work on biblical thought."[58] The second distinction relates to what Kimelman terms "the modality of presentation." The dichotomy between Rabbis Akiva and Ishmael is often typological rather than historical, and it exemplifies what Kimelman calls "a collaborative pluralism." "With non-finality as his watchword, Heschel invited the reader to engage in the ongoing rabbinic quest for the meaning of revelation and of God's involvement with humanity."[59]

Kimelman is correct in both assertions. Abraham Joshua Heschel's conception of Jewish culture and of human nature spanned the generations. However, it is the two *tannaim*, Rabbi Ishmael and Rabbi Akiva, who are presented as the personification of this typology. The fact that they were of the generation of destruction is of significance: the survivors of one destruction look back to survivors and martyrs from a previous cataclysm in Jewish history for inspiration.

In his preface to *Heavenly Torah*, Gordon Tucker pointed out that the Hebrew term *Avot Ha'Olam* bears more than one translation. Rabbi Akiva and Rabbi Ishmael are not only Fathers of the Universe, they are also eternal paradigms, historical figures who come to embody ideas and orientations which are ever present in history.[60] Students recall that when challenged by them to say with whom he himself identified, Heschel indicated that he saw himself as the heir of both. In Heschel's reading, we all bear both Akivan and Ishmaelian traces.

On the Sources of *Kavanah*

Both his Hasidic roots and his understanding of contemporary realities convinced Heschel that something other than Halakhic precision or prodigious study was now called for.[61] Already in the 1950s he declared, "As a Jew committed to Halakhah, I say to you that Halakhah is not the central issue of this generation. This generation does not know how to study or what to study."[62]

This statement implied that the Jews of postwar America were ill equipped to engage in Halakhic discourse. However, Heschel's critique was not limited to the ignorance of his contemporaries. It also extended to the tendency of the Halakhic system itself to irrelevance, when transformed into what he witheringly termed "pan-Halakhism." In his view Halakhah should not be considered in isolation, and such a lack of perspective misconstrues the essence of Judaism.[63]

After his earliest publications, Heschel never published in the Halakhic genre.[64] It would be wrong, however, to conclude that he eschewed Halakhah as a realm necessary for the full understanding of Judaism, capable of yielding great meaning, even to disenfranchised moderns. I want to conclude this chapter by referring to the longest footnote in *God in Search of Man*, which appears at the end of chapter 31, "Kavanah," and is over a page in length. It constitutes a description of some of the key claims in "an ancient controversy among scholars of Jewish law whether the presence of *kavanah* – of the right intention in carrying out one's duty – is absolutely required for the performance of all religious acts."[65]

This discussion was unlikely to have been immediately understandable to the majority of Heschel's contemporary readers. It draws upon the Mishnah, the Talmud, and a little-known late Halakhic work, *Athvan Deoraitha*. Why did Heschel choose to expatiate in this way on the Halakhic category of *kavanah*? In an article published recently,[66] David Ellenson and I proposed that this note be read in the context of a question, purportedly asked by the adolescent Heschel, which found its way into a *responsum* published in 1924. We argue that thirty years later, in a world almost unrecognizable from the one he previously inhabited, Heschel was motivated by the same core concerns.

The extended note and other references to the question of *kavanah* can be further understood by looking at other work produced by Heschel in the period leading up to the publication of *God in Search of Man*. Speaking on the subject of Jewish prayer to the Conservative Rabbinical Assembly in 1953, Heschel took issue with an approach that he believed to be prevalent in the Conservative Movement of the time. He attacked the equation of pedantry with piety, an attitude he believed promoted a conception he called religious behaviourism: namely, the unwitting reduction of Judaism to a sort of sacred physics, with no sense for the imponderable, the introspective, or the metaphysical.[67] Heschel attributed the popularity of this doctrine to the desire to respect and conform to traditional norms which is the major motive for fulfilment of religious ritual.

In the course of this lecture, Heschel made clear that the question of prayer "is a problem of universal significance,"[68] and in discussing it, he considered the interrelationship of Halakhah and Aggadah in general. In his specific treatment of prayer, Heschel cited and rejected a number of popular views on the subject. Prayer should not be judged in terms of synagogue attendance, or seen as a tool for the promotion of Jewish unity. It should be seen as neither simply an ancestral institution nor a means of satisfying an emotional need.

At the heart of this analysis of the contemporary crisis of prayer is the tension between *keva* and *kavanah*, regularity and spontaneous intention. During this same lecture Heschel pointed to a distinction between the de jure and de facto primacy of *kavanah* over *keva* in prayer:

> In regards to most aspects of observance, Jewish tradition has for pedagogic reasons given primacy to the principle of *keva*; there are many rituals concerning which the law maintains that if a person has performed them without proper *kavanah*, he is to be regarded *ex post facto* as having fulfilled his duty. In prayer, however, Halakhah insists upon the supremacy of *kavanah* over the external performance, at least, theoretically.
>
> ... In reality, however, the element of *keva*, of regularity, has often gained the upper hand over the element of *kavanah*.

Subsequently, Heschel attempted to describe the elusive concept under discussion: "*Kavanah* ... is more than paying attention to the literal meaning of a text. It is *attentiveness to God, an act of appreciation of being able to stand in the presence of God.*"[69]

In *Search* Heschel was to contest religious behaviourism, and more specifically the claim that faith is not afforded any intrinsic merit by Judaism. In a section entitled "A Religion without Faith,"[70] a number of traditional sources are marshalled against this position. Of the seven footnotes, six relate to rabbinic sources and one is a quotation from Schechter's *Studies in Judaism*, authoritatively summarizing the normative beliefs of the Sages. In other words, it is the sages of the Talmud – not the philosophers, the Hasidim, or even the prophets – who are used to defeat the claims of the religious behaviourists.[71]

In the same year as Heschel criticized the Conservative rabbinate on the issue of "religious behaviourism," he also addressed the Central Conference of American Rabbis. In the presence of the religious leadership of the Reform Movement, Heschel's emphasis was quite different. Most of the lecture was given over to a defence of *keva*, a vigorous argument in favour of regularity and consistency. He declared, for example,

"A Jew is asked to take a *leap of action* rather than a *leap of thought*: to surpass his needs, to do more than he needs in order to understand more than he does."[72]

At the end of his presentation, Heschel quoted disapprovingly a survey of Reform Jewish lay practice in which Morton M. Berman issued a call to increased ritual observance "to meet a fundamental need of every human being for *symbolism* and *ceremonialism*."[73]

One might expect that Heschel would have approved of any approach encouraging greater observance, but instead he responded with outrage. If Jewish life, he claimed, is reduced to an assortment of customs and ceremonies, the attempt to explicate and preserve it instead trivializes and kills it. Here again the concept of *kavanah* is introduced into the discourse: "A religious act is something in which the soul must be able to participate; out of which inner devotion, *kavanah*, must evolve. But what *kavanah* should I entertain if entering the *sukkah* is a mere ceremony?"[74]

Both of these 1953 lectures were integrated into Heschel's 1954 work, *Man's Quest for God*, in which he developed more ideas relating to the concept of *kavanah*, where it is understood as a form of self-disclosure. It is not an act of cogitation or concentration but an attempt "to deepen the mutual allegiance of man and God."[75] Perhaps the most revealing references to *kavanah* are to be found towards the end of *Quest*:

> There is a difference between symbolic understanding and what tradition means by *kavanah* ... *Kavanah* is awareness of the will of God rather than awareness of the reason for a *mitzvah*. Awareness of symbolic meaning is awareness of a specific idea; *kavanah* is awareness of an ineffable situation. It does not try to appropriate what is part of the divine mystery. It is *kavanah* rather than symbolic understanding that evokes in us ultimate joy at the moment of doing a *mitzvah*.[76]

By examining these references to *kavanah* in the period leading up to the composition of *Search*, the lengthy footnote on the subject may be better understood. Heschel was walking a theological tightrope: on the one hand, he argued that the Jewish response to God necessitated the performance of deeds. On the other hand, he argued that "it is a distortion to say that Judaism consists exclusively of performing ritual or moral deeds, and to forget that the goal of all performing is in *transforming* the soul."[77]

Heschel sought a combination of formal adherence and enthusiastic intention. He asserted that "the individual's insight alone is unable to cope with all the problems of living. It is the guidance of tradition on which we must reply, and whose norms we must learn to interpret and to apply."[78] However, he was vigorously opposed to any attempt at transvaluation or reinterpretation in the name of social utility or psychological well-being.

In view of the delicacy of his mission, it is not surprising that the issue of *kavanah* is handled in a somewhat complex manner. In the course of *Search*, Heschel taught that "the absence of the right intention does not necessarily vilify the goodness of a deed of charity,"[79] but also that "the chief aim and purpose of the mitzvot performed with our body is to arouse our attention to the mitzvot that are fulfilled with the mind and the heart, for these are the pillars on which the service of God rests."[80]

The extended educational footnote on *kavanah* brings all these various strands together and plots a course between the extremes. Why this somewhat convoluted treatment of the subject? There is a polemical explanation which cannot be ruled out, and it relates to Heschel's long-standing theological disagreement with one of his colleagues at the Jewish Theological Seminary, Mordecai Kaplan. I believe that the existence of rationalist, functionalist, and most particularly Kaplanian attempts to explain the fulfilment of the commandments in terms of social utility and psychological health pushed Heschel to state that performance without any explicit *kavanah* was preferable to quasi-anthropological explanations, which rob the mitzvot of their grandeur. The long discussion of what he terms "an ancient controversy" did in fact reflect a contemporary controversy, one in which he himself was a protagonist.

The literature of the Rabbis, Halakhah, and Aggadah together were understood and deployed by Heschel as the home of Jewish particularity, the place where Judaism lived. He believed that in order for rabbinic tradition to live and be relevant, the twin poles of rabbinic consciousness, Halakhah and Aggadah, must each find their voice. If the Bible is the key source for insights on how to perceive the world around us, the Sages teach us how to respond to that world. If the Bible is where the human condition achieves sublime expression, the distinctive voice of Judaism emerges in the literature of the Rabbis.

Chapter Four

From Contemplation to Practice:
Heschel's Two Maimonides

Heschel in Medieval Context

In 2010 and 2012 Micha Goodman published two best-selling works in Israel, on Maimonides and Judah Halevi, respectively. Few modern thinkers are mentioned in either of the works; Abraham Joshua Heschel appears in both. Heschel's double appearance is a testament not only to the regard in which Goodman holds Heschel. It is also a reflection of the extent to which Heschel's thought bears traces of the great Jewish thinkers of the Middle Ages.

Most of this chapter will relate to Maimonides, who exercised a profound and complex influence on Heschel. Halevi is less central in Heschel's work, although he does play a significant role, particularly in *Search*.[1] In that work Heschel first introduces the concept of God in search of man, quoting a phrase from the Book of Job: "Thou dost hunt me like a lion (10:16)."[2] Other sources from the liturgy and the midrashic literature are also quoted, but no textual support for the bold theological declaration that gives the book its name is as substantial as that of Judah Halevi. Claims from *The Kuzari* concerning divine initiative in human affairs are extensively quoted in a footnote,[3] while the chapter itself quotes from a sacred poem by Halevi, italicizing the stanza to which Heschel ascribed the greatest importance:

> I have sought Thy nearness;
>   With all my heart have I called Thee,
>   *And going out to meet Thee*
>   *I found Thee coming toward me.*[4]

Many of the key themes of Heschel's book, and indeed of his entire body of written work, are evoked in this liturgical poem: concealment and mystery, glory and wonder, awe and search. This reading supports Goodman's insight that Heschel's conception of faith was a modern iteration of Judah Halevi's piety.[5]

Bahya ibn Paquda,[6] Rashi,[7] and Joseph Albo[8] also feature prominently in *Search* and, in the case of Rashi, elsewhere in Heschel's oeuvre.[9] Other medieval works are marshalled in particular contexts, such as Al-Nakawa's *Menorat ha-Ma'or* in *The Sabbath* and Lonzano's *Derekh Hayyim* in *Man's Quest for God*.[10] But none of these figures receive the attention, both positive and negative, which Heschel afforded to Moses ben Maimon.

Maimonides's Role in Heschel's Thought

In his earlier work, Goodman claimed that Heschel's was the most compelling expression of the religiosity of Maimonides in the *Mishneh Torah* and the *Guide*.[11] The rest of this chapter will describe and analyse the ways in which Maimonides features in Heschel's work, in order to shed light on Heschel's understanding of his own enterprise and to provide a view of Heschel's Maimonides in the context of other modern Jewish readings of "the Great Eagle."[12]

Addressing the Central Conference of American Rabbis in 1954, Samuel Atlas reflected on the contemporary relevance of Maimonides. Atlas expressed his opinion that "in the struggle of ideas, the voice of Maimonides should be heard loudly on the battleground of ideas in favor of reason over unreason." He then went on to bemoan the flourishing of various kinds of mysticism and the "overemphasis on the idea of God as the 'wholly other,' the transcendent, and the ineffable."[13] Maimonides was to be seen as a corrective to this dangerous vogue. In the course of the lecture, Atlas made clear that his reference to the "wholly other" related to Emil Brunner and Karl Barth,[14] but the provenance of the ineffable was left unstated. To Atlas's audience of Reform rabbis, less than three years after the publication of *Man Is Not Alone*, there would have been little doubt that the reference to the ineffable alluded to the Jewish thinker who had brought the term into contemporary Jewish theological parlance – Abraham Joshua Heschel.[15]

In contrast to this perception that the legacy of Maimonides stood against Heschel in the great intellectual and religious debates of the twentieth century, it is particularly noteworthy that no figure was more central to Heschel's own work than Maimonides.

Maimonides's role in Heschel's work was central yet ambivalent. Although he is absent from or peripheral to *Die Prophetie, The Sabbath, Man Is Not Alone, Man's Quest for God*, and other works, no other single post-rabbinic source or author is quoted as frequently as Maimonides in *God in Search of Man*, and Heschel dedicated both a German biography and a Hebrew article to him.[16]

Heschel's Maimonides is multifaceted and at times contradictory. In some cases, his name is invoked as a watchword for greatness and normative Jewish respectability. For example, Maimonides is described in *Search* as the author of a "classical expression" concerning awe and a "great code" of Jewish law, and termed one of "the leading exponents of Jewish thought" and "one of the greatest scholars of the law of all times."[17] However, as discussed below, Maimonides is attacked in that same work and elsewhere for veering away from the true spirit of Judaism.

A simple dichotomy in which Heschel stands for neo-mysticism and Maimonides for archrationalism will not hold. A more nuanced picture of Heschel's understanding and judgment of Maimonides is called for.

Heschel against Dogma

The very first reference to Maimonides in *God in Search of Man* is remarkable.

An entire paragraph is devoted to a summary of the Thirteen Principles. After asserting that all but four of the principles relate to "the realm of ideas," Heschel continued,

> The Maimonidean creed is based upon the premise that it is in ideas that ultimate reality comes to expression. To the Biblical man, however, it is in events, not only in ideas that ultimate reality comes to expression. The substance of Judaism is given both in history and in thought. We accept ideas and recall events. The Jew says, "I believe," and is told, "Remember!" His creed contains a summary of basic ideas as well as a summary of outstanding events.[18]

It appears as though the creed of Maimonides is being contrasted with the living faith of "the Jew." The impression that Maimonides's legacy is being criticized is strengthened in the sentence which follows:

To the Jewish mind, the understanding of God is not achieved by referring in a Greek way to timeless qualities of a Supreme Being, to ideas of goodness or perfection, but rather by sensing the living acts of His concern, to His dynamic attentiveness to man.[19]

While Maimonides espouses (so it is implied) a disembodied and dispassionate Greek philosophy, "authentic Judaism" is based upon concrete events and individuals, and informed by a vision of divine pathos. In this same section, Heschel rejected the notion that the great problem is "how to reconcile the Bible with Aristotle's view of the universe and of man," and presented his own position as an alternative to the implied Maimonidean view.[20]

There is evidence to substantiate such a reading of Heschel's Maimonides, even within his 1935 biography, *Maimonides*. It is the nub of his critique of the *Mishneh Torah*:

> Here lies the inherent defect of his codification: instead of the process, the concept; instead of the case, the law; instead of the people, the matter; instead of history, theory; instead of the living atmosphere, the anonymous authority; instead of the situation, the abstraction.[21]

Earlier in the same work, this tendency to prefer the clean lines of theoretical abstraction over the less symmetrical contours of human history is understood in terms of the distinction between Sephardi and Ashkenazi tradition. Maimonides is presented as the archetypal representative of a Sephardi sensibility. In contrast to the "arches, artful figures, flourishes, and adornments" of the Tosafists in Northern Europe, "the man erecting his colossal structure in Fostat worked without flourishes and without arabesques" and "created a self-contained whole with the simplicity and precise order of straight lines ... "[22]

Heschel objected to the adoption of the Sephardi aesthetic by enlightened German Jewish intellectuals, which had led to the exclusion of the more emotive Eastern European tradition. In a 1953 essay he decried the rise of a neo-Sephardi sensibility and suggested that to judge the cultural life of Eastern European Jews by Sephardi standards "would be equivalent to weighing the beauties of Gothic architecture on the scales of classical Greek."[23]

Judaism, in Heschel's conception, was not to be described by an excessively symmetrical and precise theology. In a 1969 talk he took issue with the notion of divine omnipotence, claiming that Islam was responsible for the introduction of this concept into the theological lexicon of the Jews. Maimonides tried to deal with this challenge "in a very beautiful way," arguing,

> God himself is bound by his own creations and by the reason that permeates these creations. So, in a sense he fought the exaggerated conceptions of omnipotence. But he did not go far enough. I tell you that the idea of Divine omnipotence, meaning, holding God responsible for everything, expecting him to do the impossible, to defy human freedom, is a non-Jewish idea.[24]

The Maimonidean architectonic is splendid and impressive, but its arches and buttresses are made of imported materials. Heschel's objection to the dogma of Maimonides is not that it is antithetical to reason, but rather that it is antithetical to the true spirit of Judaism.

To demonstrate the depth of Heschel's reservations towards what he understood to be a Sephardi hegemony, it can be noted that occasionally Heschel hinted at a link between Maimonides, "that foremost Sephardic master," and Spinoza. Heschel acknowledged that Spinoza rejected the key aspirations of medieval Sephardi philosophy, and yet in his view Spinoza "pushed certain tendencies inherent in that tradition."[25] This statement does far more than establish a link between Maimonides and Spinoza, itself an uncontroversial assertion. Given the great opprobrium reserved by Heschel for Spinoza, it is hard to understand it as anything other than an attack on the cultural milieu in which a conception of the world *in more geometrico* was somehow allowed to develop.

In the English version of his book on the prophets, Heschel once again established a link between Maimonides and Spinoza – and not to the credit of the former. What Heschel saw as Maimonides's opposition to all forms of passion led to a God devoid of emotion. Spinoza continued in this vein and went on to rob divinity of even the capacity for love.[26]

Maimonides seems to fulfil a symbolic role here, representing one pole of a perennial debate. He stands for rationalism, detachment, Greek thinking, and also dogma, as exemplified by the Thirteen Principles. In a speech to Jewish educators in 1969, Heschel made his views in this matter quite explicit: "Let me perhaps tell you bluntly that, while I have great respect for the system of dogmas developed by Maimonides, I have many serious reservations about them."[27]

It is not unreasonable to see Maimonides as the father of Jewish dog-ma.[28] The fact that towards the end of his life Heschel gave vent to these reservations suggests that his mention of the Principles in *Search* was indeed intended to provide a counterpoint to the more authentically "Jewish" view not contained by dogma. A note affixed to the pub-lished version of this talk suggests that *Torah min Hashamayim* offered a kind of extended proof of the assertion, and as such it can be read as an anti-Maimonidean tract.[29] Susannah Heschel has suggested that Maimonides's emphasis on the distance between God and the emo-tions reflects but one aspect of Judaism in its totality and that her fa-ther's theology was an outgrowth of "another tradition in Judaism."[30]

Maimonides between Rabbi Akiva and Rabbi Ishmael

These assertions that Heschel's Hebrew magnum opus set out an alter-native to Maimonides's theological detachment deserve scrutiny. They imply both that Maimonides was the spiritual heir of Rabbi Ishmael and that Heschel expressed a clear preference for the Akivan position – we discussed this latter thesis in the previous chapter.

A case can be made for Maimonides's Ishmaelian lineage.[31] Rabbi Ishmael is described as the apotheosis of "delicacy, intellectual reserve, clear thinking, and sobriety," who sought the middle way and was characterized by "emotional equilibrium." He "expended his energy on clarity and precision, on that which was given to understanding and cognition."[32] This is not precisely a description of Heschel's Maimonides: in the biography, for example, Maimonides deviates at some points from the Aristotelian conception of the mean.[33] Nevertheless, many of these essential characteristics have clear echoes in the popular presen-tation of Maimonides.[34]

In a number of cases the direct link between Rabbi Ishmael and Maimonides is made explicit,[35] nowhere more clearly than at the very end of the highly important introductory chapter to the first volume of *Torah min Hashamayim*:

> The teachings of Rabbi Ishmael, an original creation without parallel in our ancient literature, did not penetrate into the consciousness of the gen-erations. Only indirectly and unconsciously were many Sages influenced by his mode of thought. Hints of this are found in the work of champions of plain-meaning exegesis in the Middle Ages, and in the rationalist ap-proach of some medieval thinkers ... Yet his principle, "the Torah speaks

in human language," became a cornerstone of scriptural understanding, and his views concerning the sacrifices appear again in Maimonides' *Guide of the Perplexed* ...[36]

In *Torah min Hashamayim* Maimonides served as a foil to highlight certain aspects of the rabbinic world view. For example, his opinions of the sensual and corporeal aspects of life as stated in chapters 8 and 9 of Book III of the *Guide* and in the introduction to the *Commentary on the Mishnah* are contrasted with the rabbinic sensibility, to the clear advantage of the Rabbis.[37]

This, then, is the first of Heschel's two Maimonides. He is the epitome of Sephardi symmetry and hyperrationalism, and claims for the normative status of his dogma are regarded by Heschel as overblown. There are indeed specific cases where a position espoused by Maimonides is mentioned and opposed,[38] and in essence the argument of *Torah min Hashamayim* opposes the very notion of authoritative theological dogma. Heschel was keen to undermine any attempt to bring theological debate to a definitive close.[39]

The Second Maimonides

There is, however, another Maimonides who emerges from Heschel's various accounts and treatments. This Maimonides is a passionate defender of the Torah and a dedicated defender of Jewish interests. This is a Rambam of the heart to set against the Maimonides of the mind.

That Maimonides did not fit neatly into a stereotype expressed itself also with regard to the Akiva-Ishmael distinction. Despite the general sense that in *Torah min Hashamayim* Maimonides is aligned with Rabbi Ishmael in the rationalist camp against the Akivan approach, Heschel pointed out a number of instances in which Maimonides seemed to adopt the Akivan stance. In one chapter, for example, Maimonides concurred with Rabbi Akiva that the infringement of Leviticus 19:18 is a matter of will and intention and not simply a question of externally measurable behaviour.[40]

The Akivan aspect of Maimonides is most emphatic in relation to the extensive interpretation of the concept *Torah min Hashamayim*.[41] Heschel noted Maimonides's assertion that it is heresy to suggest that even one letter of the Torah was uttered by Moses of his own accord and not as a result of divine inspiration. He regarded this as an extension and application of the Akivan tendency to apply the notion of the Torah's divinity as widely as possible.[42]

However, even regarding this crucial issue of Revelation, Heschel's Maimonides robustly defended aspects of the Ishmaelian position. In one of the pivotal chapters of *Torah min Hashamayim*, Maimonides is marshalled as the chief supporter of Rabbi Ishmael's view regarding the role of the hermeneutical principles in the process of revelation. At stake in this chapter is the divine sanction for interpretation. Rabbi Ishmael is presented as advancing the view that most of the specific laws and regulations were not given explicitly by God to Moses, but rather that the tools for the subsequent revelation of these divine laws were a major part of the revelation itself.[43]

In a 1965 Hebrew essay on the Hasidic Rabbi Nachman of Kosov, the question of Maimonides's theological lineage was referred to explicitly, albeit in a comment en passant. Heschel offered a brief reprise of his central thesis about the two world views epitomized by Rabbi Akiva and Rabbi Ishmael, and emphasized the two ways of appreciating the value of our this-worldly existence. Whereas Rabbi Akiva placed the emphasis on the world to come, in Rabbi Ishmael's view life was to be lived in this world. Heschel commented,

> Many went in the way of Rabbi Akiba. Even Maimonides could write: "Desolation of the soul is found in the perfection of the body; perfection of the soul is found in the desolation of the body." Later, however, he rejected this view and affirmed that of R. Ishmael.[44]

The Maimonides presented by Heschel has an inherent ambivalence, and this extends beyond the question of his alignment along the Rabbi Akiva–Rabbi Ishmael axis. If the first Maimonides is the archetype of dispassionate rationalism accused of settling for the relatively facile attempt "to reconcile the Bible with Aristotle's view of the universe and of man,"[45] the second Maimonides is a person imbued with radical prophetic passion.

Heschel's second Maimonides is not a carbon copy of one of his *tannaitic* precursors but rather a complex man and multifaceted thinker. If Heschel disapproved of the archetypal hyperrationalist, he showed great empathy with the pioneer leader, motivated perhaps by prophetic inspiration and "ruled by Messianic moods."[46] In a chapter on Halakhic innovation near the end of *Torah min Hashamayim*, Maimonides is presented as a legal decisor, prepared to make reforms when circumstances demanded it. His views are presented next to those of the Ba'al Shem Tov and the Kotzker Rebbe.[47] In the final analysis Heschel's Maimonides is bigger than Heschel's typology. As we saw in our discussion of

Heschel's reading of the Akiva-Ishmael dichotomy, his own commitments and passions also confounded any neat binary structure.

Biography and Autobiography: Maimonides and Heschel

From 1934, when he was offered a commission to write a biography to mark the eight-hundredth anniversary of Maimonides's birth,[48] until the last year of his life almost forty years later, Abraham Joshua Heschel had a strong and complex affinity with the Sage of Fostat.[49] In the biography, Heschel made conscious use of biographical material and folklore of questionable historicity in pursuit of an accessible and sympathetic subject. The result is a Maimonides full of emotion: a young boy in Cordoba pouring out his heart to God in the women's section of the synagogue,[50] an adolescent struggling to control his sarcastic bent [51] and perhaps even his physical urges,[52] a harrowed traveller narrowly escaping a tempest on his way to the Land of Israel,[53] a communal leader defending Jewish interests,[54] even a visionary in a nocturnal audience with Moses after the completion of the *Mishneh Torah*,[55] and so on.

The biographical tendency in the work of Abraham Joshua Heschel came to rich expression in Maimonides. His life (or a somewhat apocryphal version thereof) and times were pressed into service, and they were seen as a foreshadowing of contemporary Jewish experience. Describing the conditions of Jewish life under the Almohades, Heschel wrote these words in Berlin in 1935, when their contemporary resonance would have been unmistakable:

> They suffered through an existence that could not be endured for long. They had to give up their community life in order to survive as individuals. Their houses of prayer and study lay in ruins. The communities shrank visibly because their members kept emigrating ... Their Jewish existence was now an ordeal of courage in a life of peril ... A shadow lay across the lives of the Jews. From the gloom of frightened minds rose a distrust of Providence and an intimation of disaster.[56]

Heschel's Maimonides underwent profound change in the course of his life. In a chapter entitled "The Transformation," we are told that Maimonides is shaped by the traumatic experience of his brother's death. There is a heroic tone[57] to the description of this "spiritual transformation" in the immediate aftermath of which "all that reaches us is a mere echo of the internal bliss that filled his soul."[58]

Heschel not only admired Maimonides, he identified with him, and thus there is a strong autobiographical dimension to the biography. Rémi Brague's comment that "the Straussian Maimonides might be, at least in part, a construction and the projection into the past of a personal project"[59] can certainly be applied to Abraham Joshua Heschel.

Heschel explained the change of emphasis in his own life from study to activism as a direct result of his reworking of the book on prophecy for an English-speaking audience.[60] However, in the last chapter of *The Insecurity of Freedom*, a work setting out Heschel's activist manifesto, it is the example of Maimonides which is given. He translated a section from his 1935 biography that describes Maimonides's "last metamorphosis":

> From metaphysics to medicine, from contemplation to practice, from speculation to the imitation of God. God is not only the object of knowledge; He is the example one is to follow. Human beings whom He seeks to guide in this providence take the place of abstract concepts which constitute the means of the intellectual perception of God.[61]

The decision to place the figure of Maimonides at the very peak of Heschel's social agenda, the finale of *The Insecurity of Freedom*, is no coincidence. He clearly found this example of the progression from the seclusion of study and reflection to engagement with people in society a potent source of personal inspiration. It is interesting to note that in his reading of the *Guide*, contemplation wins out over ritual and ethics.[62] The fact that Maimonides eschewed systematic writing after the *Guide* is adduced as evidence of his change of emphasis.[63] The life of Maimonides is presented as a kind of prooftext for Heschel's interpretation of his thought; the textperson[64] illuminates the text.

Heschel's Scholarly Method

Maimonides occupies a unique position in Heschel's work, presented as both the archdogmatist, against whose passionless divinity Heschel posits the "Most Moved Mover,"[65] and a complex man capable of personal transformation and radical innovation. Maimonides the First is admired for his scholarship and rigour, but opposed, often in sharp tones. Maimonides the Second is a model for Heschel's self-understanding.[66]

Does this bifurcated perspective make Heschel's Maimonides recognizable to contemporary scholarship? Heschel's tendency to make use of legends in the construction of his Maimonidean myth has been criti-cized,[67] and the question may be posed whether it is Maimonides being described or rather Heschel himself. Take for example the following remarkable statement in *Maimonides*:

> The view that natural occurrences are an uninterrupted emanation from God, that the cosmic movements are determined by an incessant striving toward the higher, a yearning to become like the higher, corresponded to Maimonides's own character. It is a *pathos* in the Greek sense: a great pas-sion – that rules the world. And the *pathetic* idea of the universe found its likeness and echo in Maimonides's *pathetic* character.[68]

Barry Kogan has stated that "it is quite mistaken, if not bizarre, to sug-gest that the universe that found its likeness and echo in Maimonides's own character was in *any* sense pathetic."[69] Pathos is a more significant term in the Heschelian, rather than the Maimonidean, lexicon.

The relationship between Heschel's Maimonides and the Mai-monides of contemporary scholarship may be illustrated with refer-ence to a suggestion in the 1945 essay that valuable information regard-ing Maimonides's self-understanding as a prophet can be learned from the *Chapters Concerning Felicity*, "which in the opinion of most scholars was authored by Maimonides."[70] Heschel noted his intention to add support to the opinion of Moritz Steinschneider and Wilhelm Bacher, scholars of a bygone era, regarding the authenticity of this work, while ignoring the fact that the very edition from which he cited the text was preceded by an introduction casting severe doubts on its Maimonidean authorship. Indeed, already by 1935 Gershom Scholem had asserted that Maimonides was not the author, but Heschel sidestepped the claims of contemporary scholarship and preferred to use the text as bal-last for his portrayal of Maimonides the self-styled prophet.[71]

Heschel, Strauss, and Guttmann

A distinction is commonly made between two great streams of Maimonides scholarship in the twentieth century: the naturalistic school associated with Leo Strauss and his followers, and the harmon-istic interpretation of Julius Guttmann, Harry A. Wolfson, and others.[72] George Kohler has persuasively presented this debate between two great twentieth-century experts in medieval Jewish thought against the backdrop of the preceding century. He notes that Guttmann represented a certain liberal world view according to which the postulates of reason and revelation could in theory be harmonized, while for Strauss such a resolution was illusory, and the profound political implications of Maimonides's remarkable perspective could be approached only through an appropriate regard for the role of esoteric writing and concealment in the *Guide*.[73] Where is Heschel in the context of this debate? And how are we to understand his two Maimonides in this light?

Heschel was certainly acquainted with the work of Strauss and Wolfson – in the 1945 essay he referred his readers to both of them in one footnote.[74] On the level of personal contact and influence, there is no doubt that Julius Guttmann had a profound impact on Heschel, who studied under him at the *Hochschule* and addressed words of thanks to him in the introduction to his dissertation.[75] In the first chapter of *Search* he conducted a discussion of religious philosophy and the philosophy of religion that showed signs of Guttmann's influence.[76] Later in the work his presentation of the relationship between Spinoza and Mendelssohn was explicitly based on Guttmann's article on this theme.[77]

It might appear that Heschel's ambivalent view of Maimonides would be congenial to a Straussian position, but this link is more apparent than real. However, in one regard at least, Strauss' approach to Maimonides is mirrored in Heschel – namely, the concern with hints, secrets, and apparent contradictions. The esoteric aspect of the Maimonidean enterprise is stressed more in the 1945 Hebrew article than in the 1935 biography, where it was mentioned only in passing. In the earlier work, for example, Maimonides's declaration in the introduction to the *Guide* that he had not benefited from divine prophecy is quoted without commentary. In the later essay, this statement is treated to a much closer reading, and Heschel asserted that the very denial implies the possibility of that which is denied.[78]

In Heschel's own writings there are a number of hints about hinting. In his essay on Maimonides and prophecy, he asserted that "sages are not in the habit of making public their innermost thoughts,"[79] and in *Torah min Hashamayim*, he advised his readers that the only way to understand the Talmudic conception of prophecy is to pay attention to that which is only hinted at.[80] Heschel saw himself as part of this tradition. His quotation of the Talmudic aphorism that a "man who does not understand what he is being shown by gesture is not worthy to converse in signs before the king"[81] is perhaps indicative of his own approach.

Heschel showed sensitivity to contradictions within Maimonides's writing. Twice in *Search* he pointed his readers to different interpretations offered by Maimonides, highlighting contrasting opinions.[82] While in much of his work two figures from Jewish history are employed in order to denote contrasting views, in Maimonides one man embodies both sides of a dichotomy.

To judge by his prioritizing of *praxis* over *theoria*[83] and his belief in the essential continuity of Jewish philosophy, Heschel is closer in spirit to Guttmann and the harmonizers than to Strauss and the naturalists.

Prophecy and *Imitatio Dei*

David Novak has argued that Heschel's reading of Maimonides played an important role in the development of Heschel's own understanding of the role of the prophet. He argues convincingly that Heschel's approach to divine pathos and the empathy of the prophet owed much to Maimonides's notion of a wordless revelation as expressed in the *Guide* I.65. Indeed, this chapter is itself quoted in both *Search* and *Torah min Hashamayim*.[84] In the final section of this chapter some consideration will be given to the way in which Maimonides is employed to demonstrate how the prophet, the excellent person, and to some extent every person, can be engaged in what Novak calls *"bespeaking* revelation"[85] and what might further be described as enacting God's will.

If Maimonides is largely absent from *Die Prophetie*, he fulfilled an ambivalent role in *The Prophets*. On the one hand, we encounter the archetypal archrationalist, preceded by Philo and the Stoics and succeeded by Spinoza.[86] In this guise Maimonides is the major obstacle to be overcome in the promotion of the concept of divine Pathos. The principle of divine impassibility must be confronted if the Heschelian idea of a responsive and passionate God can be defended in normative Jewish terms.

A footnote in *The Prophets* sheds light on the thinking behind an important passage in *God in Search of Man*. In a section entitled "Inspiration an Event," Heschel quoted a paragraph from chapter 22 of *Search*, and then added,

> An example of conceiving prophecy as a process is Maimonides' theory, according to which prophecy (with the exception of Moses) is a continuous emanation from the divine Being, and is transmitted to all those who are endowed with certain qualities ... through the medium of the Active

Intellect ... Accordingly, prophetic illumination occurs in conformity with natural law or with the order or emanation, while the failure to be inspired is regarded as a miracle.[87]

This approach of seeing prophecy as a process is clearly not one with which Heschel – opponent of the homogenizing process and proponent of the galvanizing event – concurred. On the other hand, it is in *The Prophets* that Heschel presented his definition of prophecy in terms taken, it seems, from his reading of Maimonides:

> The prophet's eye is directed to the contemporary scene; the society and its conduct are the main theme of his speeches. Yet his ear is inclined to God. He is a person struck by the glory and presence of God, overpowered by the hand of God. Yet his true greatness is his ability to hold God and man in a single thought.[88]

Heschel's description of the essence of prophecy is rooted in a particular reading of the last chapters of Maimonides's life, combined with a reading of the last chapters of the *Guide*. Significantly, the 1966 version of the chapter expanded upon the core idea already present in the work written thirty years previously, as the later Heschel refined and deepened his understanding of this higher rung of human endeavour. In the original Heschel wrote,

> The imitation of God now meant service for individuals. Maimonides renounced the postulate of withdrawal ... He could now "speak to other people and at the same time think incessantly about God and stand incessantly before God in his heart even though he was with people physically, just as it is written in the Song of Songs: 'I sleep, but my heart is awake.'"[89]

The source of Heschel's metaphor of prophetic bifurcation would appear to be, then, the *Guide* III.51.[90] However, earlier in the Maimonides's biography, in the chapter on the *Guide*, Heschel stated unequivocally that at that stage of his life Maimonides "put contemplation higher than action."[91] So in a sense the prooftext for Heschel's epitome of prophecy was not only Maimonides's life but also his works.

In the 1945 essay Heschel offered a clear interpretation of the closing chapters of the *Guide*. "The conclusion of the work is a proof for the entire goal of the book."[92] The goal in question is the instruction of the select few in the method required to be elevated to the status of a prophet. The parable of the ruler in his palace, the call for solitude – all of these are interpreted in light of the prophetic dimension.

In these two passages relating to Maimonides's prophetology, Heschel's two versions of Maimonides appear side by side. The same man is presented both as the epitome of dispassionate rationalism and as the model for bifocal engagement with the world and with God. How can these contradictions be reconciled?

Heschel's scholarly method in the 1945 essay and elsewhere may have been regarded in some quarters as dubious, but the key contention – namely, that Maimonides saw himself and his disciples as candidates for prophecy – continues to be discussed among contemporary scholars.[93] Heschel's reading of III.51 and III.54 as providing instructions in prophecy is cited at the end of an important essay by Steven Harvey as a possible way of squaring Maimonides's championing of the solitary life with the often-reported accounts of his communal and social involvement. Harvey cannot accept Heschel's notion that Maimonides was promoting a state of total immersion in thought about God as an achievable possibility for himself and his disciples, since this "is a state Maimonides reserves for Moses and perhaps the patriarchs, and I see no evidence that he suggested or even believed that he himself achieved such a state."[94]

Heschel's Maimonides is a man who undergoes change. His transition from scholarly detachment to social involvement and from abstraction to concrete action is a heroic tale, and it is what ultimately qualifies Maimonides in Heschel's eyes for his status as one of Judaism's greatest figures. We noted above that in the Heschelian typology the Sephardi tradition is seen as symmetrical and generic, while the Ashkenazi tradition is specific and therefore less geometric. It is then of particular importance that in the last chapter of the biography Heschel cited the *Guide* II.20 as evidence of his contention that Maimonides "had arduously labored to attain the knowledge that God, for all the sublimity of His essence, has immediate knowledge of individual things, and not just of the species. The imitation of God now meant service for individuals."[95]

It seems plausible that the reference here is in fact to the *Guide* III.20 and 21,[96] in which the topic of divine knowledge is discussed. If Heschel's reading of Maimonides has anything of great significance to add to the debate about Maimonides, it is perhaps this: he sees Maimonides overcoming Aristotle and therefore reaching out beyond the confines of Greek/Sephardi thought to the very heart of the divine pathos. Ultimately, Heschel's Maimonides is not an Aristotelian;[97] he cannot be if he is to meet Heschel's criteria for being a great Jew. Heschel's philosopher-prophet keeps both ideas of God in mind at the same time: the impassable Deity and the caring God of pathos. Heschel's Maimonides experienced "the inadequacy of all our categories,"[98] and this pushed him beyond the merely intellectual dimension: "After wrestling with the problems and riddles which stood 'at the apex of the world' and concluding that their solution lay beyond the bounds of the human intellect, he thereupon sought to cross the boundary line."[99]

Prophecy begins where the human intellect alone cannot prevail. In chapter 24 of *God in Search of Man*, Heschel quoted extensively from the letter to Rabbi Hasdai, the theme of which is the superiority of prophecy over reason and philosophy.[100] The translation of the letter is highly instructive: "Reason and proof cannot aspire to the level of insight at which prophecy exists – how can they ever prove it or disprove it?"[101]

Elsewhere, though not in all cases, Heschel made use of published translations. But here the material demanded his own rendering, since no English translation was to hand, and Heschel provided a highly contentious reading. His translation here is based on a shift of vocalization of the word *re'aya* from "testimony" or "proof" to "insight," a favourite term in the Heschel lexicon.

This same realization of the inadequacy of categories and reason is also at the heart of a trend towards action. It is as though Heschel concurred with Shlomo Pines's conclusion:

> The only positive knowledge of God of which man is capable is knowledge of the attributes of action, and this leads and ought to lead to a sort of political activity which is the highest perfection of man. The practical way of life, the *bios praktikos*, is superior to the theoretical.[102]

Heschel's formulation of this idea is one of his most famous: "A Jew is asked to take a *leap of action* rather than a *leap of thought*. He is asked to surpass his needs, to do more than he understands in order to understand more than he does."[103]

Throughout his life, Heschel called upon these two figures, Maimonides and the Rambam,[104] symbol of dry rationalism and hero of prophetic passion, in order to fulfil a multitude of functions. By employing the Rabbi Ishmael–Rabbi Akiva typology in his description of the Rabbis, Heschel had two individuals epitomize two central thrusts that characterized Judaism, and indeed the whole human condition. In the figure of Maimonides, these tendencies found a single embodiment.

It is for this reason that Heschel both condemned and condoned Maimonides, and it is for this reason that he identified with him so deeply. This is why Atlas, in his 1954 address, could hint that Heschel was in some sense Maimonides's antithesis, and Goodman could suggest that Heschel was in some way Maimonides's heir. Heschel's Maimonides was an embodiment of rationalist and antirationalist tendencies, a reflection of the Jewish condition, and a foreshadowing of Heschel's own life and enterprise.

Chapter Five

On the Verge of God: Heschel and Kabbalah

Setim ve-Galya: The Presence and Absence of Kabbalah

Was Heschel a mystic? This question has been posed over the years by critics and devotees alike. In a question-and-answer session at Dartmouth College in 1961, Heschel came close to answering the question directly. Responding to the question, "What do you consider a mystic to be?" he said, "A mystic is a person who is about the opposite of myself."[1] However, as he expanded on the theme, it was unclear if Heschel was distancing himself from the terminology of mysticism or from its essence. He noted that he tried not to use the term because it was so heavily loaded with connotations. Attempts to answer the complex question of his relationship to the mystical realm have typically focused on his biography and his theology. In this chapter I want to add a third source of insight: his library.

When one reflects on Heschel's entire body of work, it appears that the kabbalistic paradox *setim ve-galya*,[2] the revealed and the concealed, has particular resonance. It speaks to his understanding of the divine as it is expressed in nature, in Torah, and in deeds. It also characterizes Heschel's relationship with the sources of Kabbalah themselves. This chapter will consider some of the ways in which these sources come to expression.

Analysis of the terms and works to which he referred in his writings may shed light on the question of Heschel's relation to mysticism. Arthur Green suggested that in his English works, "Heschel made almost no reference to the mystical traditions he knew and loved so well, but learned to couch their insights almost entirely in terms of the West's shared Biblical and prophetic legacy."[3] Green observed that *Die*

Prophetie is devoid of reference to Zoharic or other kabbalistic works[4] and noted that Heschel almost never used the word *mysticism* in his theological writings.[5]

To these important insights we can add that in *Man Is Not Alone*, the words *mysticism* and *mystic* do not appear at any point. Keywords which do allude to "mystical" dimensions are *ineffable*, *mystery*, and *enigma*;[6] these may indeed have been more palatable to Heschel's American audience in the early 1950s.

The role of this tradition in the work and thought of Abraham Joshua Heschel is itself *setim ve-galya*, revealed and concealed. While there is little to be found in some of his works, it is prominent in others. In *Man's Quest for God*, for example, the Zohar is quoted twice and mentioned once more, and it does not form a major part of the Heschelian description of prayer, let alone his critique of symbolism. The only explicit reference to the mystical domain in that work is pejorative. "Decisive is not the mystic experience of our being close to Him" but rather "our *certainty* of His being close to us."[7] In *The Sabbath*, on the other hand, the Zohar constitutes one of the most frequently cited sources. Heschel trawled the Zohar for relevant and compelling aphorisms about the Sabbath[8] and showed no reticence in deploying them.

Having noted that explicit references to the mystical domain are rare in *Man Is Not Alone*, it should be added that even there this literature does make a showing. Early in the work, Heschel asserted that "what is intelligible to our mind is but a thin surface of the profoundly undisclosed."[9] To the statement that "unity is beyond, not within reality," a reference to the second introduction to the *Tikkunei Zohar* is appended.[10]

Throughout Heschel's work, scant attention is paid to the sefirotic system. In his essay on the mystical element in Judaism he seemed more interested in the allegories and parables of the Zohar than in its technical terminology or mythic symbolism. In a telling comment, he suggested that "the plurality into which the one divine manifestation is split symbolizes the state of imperfection into which God's relation to the world was thrown."[11] Heschel turned to those works of the mystical tradition that contain the most uncompromising defence of the unassailable unity of God, while arguing for the dialectic character of the world and everything within it.[12]

Of his overtly theological books, *God in Search of Man* is the most redolent with sources from the kabbalistic tradition. It is interesting to note a significant change in terminology between *Man Is Not Alone* and this later work. In *Search* there is much less "ineffability," far more "mystery," and a great rise of "insight." It appears that as he moved the discussion from universal generalities to the Jewish domain, the dimension of mystery could no longer be kept from his audience.

In *God in Search of Man* Heschel did warn against occultism, magic, divination, and necromancy.[13] However, the sources used to confirm this restriction on penetrating the veil and peering into the mysteries that lie beyond are themselves part of the mystical tradition. The ban on the priests seeing the holy things is explained by a commentary of Nachmanides and a reference to *Sefer Yere'im*, from the thirteenth and twelfth centuries, respectively. Heschel hinted at the power of esoteric teachings just as he rehearsed the traditional warnings against them.[14] Moreover, by juxtaposing these sources with the prohibition on occult practices, Heschel was implying that the essence of the Jewish mystical tradition related to something more profound than pyrotechnics.

None of the works extensively quoted in *Search* is more deliberately and intensively deployed than the Zohar. It is absent from whole chapters and sections, but in chapter 14, "Insight," it is quoted seventeen times. Heschel included particularly long sections from kabbalistic literature in the body of the text of *God in Search of Man*. In total, a quarter of the Zohar quotations and citations are long quoted texts used to bolster and illustrate the claims of the book. No other work is quoted in quite this way in *Search*. Such usage hardly supports the thesis that the Kabbalah is absent from Heschel's popular theological vocabulary.

The Zohar and Other Kabbalistic Works in Heschel's Canon

For Heschel the Zohar was the quintessential expression of Kabbalah. In a bibliographical note appended to his one essay explicitly on the theme, "The Mystical Element in Judaism," Heschel explained that since he considered it "proper to dwell primarily on one phase of the Kabbalah ... the *Zohar*, the authoritative book of the movement, was chosen as the basis for our chapter."[15]

Since this short essay is the only piece in which Heschel focused explicitly on the Jewish esoteric tradition, it is worth considering its content and structure. In explicating the essence of Jewish mysticism, Heschel set out his own theological agenda: beginning with questions of knowledge and perception, he proceeded to an assertion of the metaphysical significance and essential seriousness of human existence, establishing the principle of correlation between the human and divine domains. Pausing to sketch the broad contours of the sefirotic system, Heschel then proceeded to touch upon aspects of what he called "mystic experience," in particular *unio mystica* and some of its implications. After dwelling on the kabbalistic understanding of the Torah, Heschel propounded his understanding of the mystic way of life with reference to study, prayer, and ceremonies. In the closing section, "The Concern for God," Heschel discussed the notion of divine pathos and the holy dimension of existence and reflected on the relationship between prophecy and mysticism. I will return to this last point, a crucial aspect of Heschel's approach to mysticism, later in this chapter.

Beyond the essay dedicated to this theme, there is other evidence of Heschel's appreciation of the significance of the Zohar to Jewish culture. In an essay on the early Hasidic master Rabbi Pinhas of Korzec, Heschel quoted him as saying, "The Zohar sustained my soul … The Zohar helped me be a Jew."[16] The esoteric and mystical traditions of Judaism are fully integrated into the traditional Jewish canon. Indeed, as he observed in *Search*, "Up to the nineteenth century there were few outstanding Talmudists who were not stirred, for example, by the cravings and meditations of the Zohar. Beneath the calm surfaces of creed and law the souls were astir."[17]

In his earlier evocation of Ashkenazi Judaism, he noted that "every community had the Talmud and the Code of Law, the Shulhan Arukh, the legal system of Maimonides, and the classical work of Jewish mysticism, the Zohar."[18]

Heschel believed in an ultimate unity of purpose between the various genres, generations, and orientations within Jewish tradition. In this sense his approach was at odds with that trend within the *Wissenschaft* School which saw Kabbalah as "strange and repellent."[19] The literature of Kabbalah was integrated into the wider Jewish canon in the service of Heschel's own presentation of classical Judaism.

A striking example of this tendency can be found in the appendix to *The Sabbath*, in which Heschel asserted that "in the mainstream of Jewish tradition, the Presence of God in the world is not thought of as being static and permanently anchored to the world of space, but as being free, unfixed and conditioned on the attitude of man." The mainstream of Jewish tradition is then represented, with two sources brought in succession without commentary. The first is a quote from *Midrash Tehillim*; the second one is from *Tikkunei Zohar*.[20] The rabbinic and kabbalistic canons are cited together.

Elsewhere, too, other works of the mystical tradition are adduced as examples of the mainstream of Jewish thought. In his book on prayer and symbolism, for example, Heschel supported the sweeping statement that "to Judaism, the purpose of prayer is not to satisfy an emotional need" with a reference to the great sixteenth-century figure, the Maharal of Prague, who exemplified the blurring of distinctions between Jewish law, communal leadership, and mystical engagement.[21]

In order to get a sense of the scope and range of Heschel's kabbalistic canon, it may be helpful to compare his work with what has been described as the "internal bibliography" of S.Y. Agnon. Elchanan Shiloh has listed the kabbalistic works mentioned in Agnon's fiction. Almost all of the works on that list are also in Heschel's own internal bibliography. Of all the genres listed, it is the literature of Lurianic Kabbalah that is least reflected in Heschel's work, although some examples can be found.[22] By any criteria, the range of kabbalistic works cited in Heschel's works is extensive.

Kabbalah is not suppressed in Heschel's theological works. Rather, it advances to the foreground and then recedes. Its presence and absence is a mirror of the divinity towards which it strives: "God is within the world, present and concealed in the essence of things. If not for His presence, there would be no essence; if not for His concealment, there would be no appearance."[23]

Kabbalistic Imagery in *God in Search of Man*

Unlike *Man Is Not Alone*, where virtually all metaphor and allegory were of Heschel's own devising,[24] in *Search* Heschel built many of his key images, be they allegories or symbols, through extensive quotation of kabbalistic material. Compared to many of his other works, particularly in English, *Search* is relatively free of grandiloquent Heschelian imagery.[25] Metaphors employed in *Search* with reference to a classical source come, in virtually all cases, from the literature of Kabbalah.

Two highly significant and well-known images are extensively quoted in chapters 26 and 27, respectively. Heschel quoted at length the Zoharic parable of the Torah as maiden[26] in order to illustrate his claim that the Bible "is not a book to be read but a drama in which to participate."[27]

The longest quotation of the entire book is to be found in chapter 27 entitled "The Principle of Revelation." Following the assertion that the Bible has more than one level of meaning. While most of it is open to unambiguous understanding, much of it remains locked to the literal-minded,"[28] Heschel quoted a source from *Midrash on Psalms* and then proceeded to fill more than an entire page with a quotation from the Zohar, III.152a, in which the stories of the Torah are likened to outer garments, which must be stripped off if the main principles are to be understood.[29]

Heschel's critique of literalism was couched in Zoharic terms, and given thereby the authority of a traditional Jewish opinion, in contrast to the Liberal Jewish version of this same idea. Rather than invoke a distinction between the ethical kernel and the ritual husk, and in preference to some dry presentation of the various layers of the text posited by the Documentary Hypothesis, Heschel found internal Jewish expression for his belief that it is foolish to read the Bible tales only literally.

In the final part of *Search* Heschel introduced key tensions: between Halakhah and Aggadah, regularity and spontaneity, good and evil, the self and the non-self, and more. Kabbalistic terminology offered him a means of expressing this dialectic approach: "Tension, contrast, and contradiction characterize all of reality. In the language of the *Zohar*, this world is called *alma deperuda*, 'the world of separation.'"[30]

As noted above, the one explicit reference to the literature of the Zohar in *Man Is Not Alone* relates to the notion that true unity lies beyond the discord and incoherence of this world. The Zohar is employed to express a similar ambiguity in *Search*, where the polarity that characterizes everything does not extend to a dichotomy within God.[31] Zoharic metaphors and expressions help further Heschel's own theological agenda.

Deployment of Kabbalistic Literature in *Torah min Hashamayim*

References to kabbalistic works are to be found throughout *Torah min Hashamayim*.[32] It is possible to give a sense of the range and function of works cited in Heschel's Hebrew masterwork with one example from each of its three volumes.

In a short chapter in the first volume Heschel traced the Ishmaelian notion of biblical metaphor to various medieval scholars. He then went on to contrast this notion with the system of "masters of the Aggadah and kabbalists." Menahem Azariah da Fano and Isaiah Horowitz are quoted at length in this regard.[33] Here, then, these Kabbalists of the late sixteenth and early seventeenth centuries are presented as heirs of the Aggadah.

In the second volume Heschel noted a radical idea found in the Zohar for which he could find no precedent: that Moses uttered the Book of Deuteronomy from his own mouth, of his own volition. He understood this to mean that in some sense Deuteronomy was the beginning of the Oral Law, and he supported this bold notion with reference to another medieval mystical work, *Ma'arekhet ha-Elohut*. Here is Kabbalah in the service of radical theology.[34]

In the posthumously published third volume, Heschel raised another volatile theological question: would the mitzvot be cancelled at some future time? Following a familiar pattern, he devoted one chapter largely to rabbinic literature.[35] The subsequent mini-chapter traced the echoes of this debate into the Middle Ages, referring to an assortment of Sages. Sources from Zoharic works are brought to promote the notion that in the future one aspect of the Torah, that represented by the Tree of Knowledge, will no longer exercise control over the people Israel. The views of three masters of Kabbalah from the sixteenth and seventeenth centuries – Moses Cordovero, Isaiah Horowitz, and Avraham Azulai – on this issue are then summarized, before the conversation moves on to the Hasidic masters.[36]

In this way the esoteric tradition is deployed in Heschel's presentation of Jewish theological speculation through the ages.[37] By blurring the distinction between categories, he promotes a portrayal of Judaism that integrates various strands and approaches. In the first chapter of this book we noted that T.S. Eliot's ideal poet construes the whole tradition of great literature as possessing "a simultaneous existence" and composing "a simultaneous order."[38] While Eliot was referring to a European literary tradition, the essential thrust of his critique can be applied to Heschel's approach to his formative tradition. While some Jewish modernists eschewed Kabbalah, Heschel saw it as an integral part of Judaism.

Mysticism and Prophecy

In Heschel's life and work, the mystical and the prophetic domains are inextricable. "One cannot grasp the innermost thought of the holy men of Israel without remembering that in their eyes, prophetic inspiration hovered over human reason, and, at times, heaven and earth would meet and kiss."[39] This comment comes at the end of a long description of the prophetic ambitions of men, most of whom are associated with the kabbalistic tradition.

While we have demonstrated that this tradition is not as all-pervasive in Heschel's work as in the Bible or the literature of the Rabbis, it nonetheless plays a significant supporting role throughout much of his writings. In those rare cases in which mystical sources are centre stage, there is one issue which preoccupied Heschel: prophecy.

This is the case in the essay on the mystical element, which veered from mysticism to prophecy at its conclusion. The connection between mysticism and prophecy is also a major theme of the Hebrew essays on the continuation of prophecy into the Middle Ages and also of key sections in *Torah min Hashamayim*. Indeed, in that work he also presented the Sages of the Talmud as heirs of the prophets.

Another fundamental source for understanding Heschel's conception of the link between mysticism and prophecy is the aforementioned fourteenth chapter of *God in Search of Man*. Heschel opened the chapter with an auditory metaphor: "The voice of God is not always inaudible. 'In every generation didst Thou make plain parts of the mystery of Thy name.'"[40]

The opening quotation is from a *piyyut* attributed to Saadia Gaon.[41] In an extended footnote to the Saadia excerpt, the focus of his remarks is clearly on the question of prophecy, as understood from Second Temple Literature through to Heschel's own scholarly work.[42] He contrasted a Talmudic opinion[43] – the light of creation is to be revealed only to the righteous, at the end of days – with a significantly different view ascribed to the Zohar. Here, the primordial light of creation has been transformed into a world-creating seed. From the chapter's opening declaration of the potential audibility of the divine voice, we have now moved to a visual metaphor in which the light is transformed into a seed and stands as a constant ontological necessity.[44]

At the end of this footnote the reader is referred to Heschel's Hebrew essays about prophetic inspiration in the Middle Ages. It appears, therefore, that "the whole problem" to which he referred is that of the continuation of prophecy after the last of the biblical prophets. In both essays Heschel raised the question of the persistence of prophecy after Haggai, Zechariah, and Malachi,[45] implying that this was a version of the debate about the primordial light and the divine voice.

The essay on inspiration actually ends with a teaching, also to be found in *Search*, relating to the biblical expression "a great voice that goes on forever."[46] The verse from Deuteronomy and its various interpretations play an important role in a number of Heschel's works.[47] A section of the third volume of *Torah min Hashamayim* is dedicated to the phrase, and several kabbalistic and other interpretations are listed there.[48]

Heschel quoted approvingly one of Rashi's interpretations, prefer-ring "it did not stop" over "it went on no more."[49] In *Search* and the Hebrew essay on prophetic inspiration, the sources of this reading are Rashi, Onkelos, and the Talmud. In the parallel chapter in *Torah min Hashamayim*, Heschel cited the Zoharic reading of the verse, and then quoted other kabbalistic sources on the theme of innovation. In the sec-ond volume the teaching is used as part of the discussion of the in-complete transmission of the Torah to Moses. Following Rashi's two interpretations of the Hebrew expression from Deuteronomy, ולא יסף, Heschel quoted a discussion from Isaiah Horowitz's *Shenei Luhot ha-Berit*, according to which this issue contains within it a deep secret im-plying that both of Rashi's interpretations are true.[50] In contrast to the notion that at some time in history – be it after the Days of Creation, at Sinai, or at the end of the biblical period – the light disappeared and the voice fell silent, Heschel espoused the view that the light is preserved in a kernel; the voice goes on forever. A panoply of sources covering eras and genres is employed to press home the idea that divinity calls out to humanity; that God is in search of man.[51]

However, the voice is not heeded. In the second paragraph of chapter 14 of *Search* Heschel quoted a teaching from the Zohar that cites the rab-binic tradition according to which a voice issues forth daily from Mount Horeb. The Zohar comments that, "The Torah calls on man, and none pay regard."[52]

The Zoharic understanding of the constant voice and human inatten-tion to it helped Heschel solve a theological dilemma. If at this point in *Search* Heschel was at pains to emphasize the perpetual availability of the divine voice, elsewhere in this same work he cited what appears to be a diametrically opposed opinion:

> The historian Ranke claimed that every age is equally near to God. Yet Jewish tradition claims that there is a hierarchy of moments within time, that all ages are not alike. Man may pray to God equally at all places, but God does not speak to man equally at all times. At a certain moment, for example, the spirit of prophecy departed from Israel.[53]

This statement was important enough for Heschel to quote it verba-tim from his earlier *The Sabbath*.[54] It seems, however, to stand in direct contradiction to the aforementioned position.

The overwhelming evidence is that for Abraham Joshua Heschel, prophecy did not end with the last of the biblical prophets. Consistently throughout his work, and particularly in *Search*, he took issue with the modernist urge to understand all in terms of processes and constant forces of nature. He defended the primacy of the special moment and, indeed, of the special individual.

Heschel established the concept of a divine voice left unheard. Using sources from the Talmud, Hasidic literature, and the Zohar, he argued that the voice is uttered not in sounds but in signs. These signs are considered to be the latent source of religious longings and "inner awakenings of either joy or fear."[55] Contrary to the modern conception of the human subject, Heschel propounded the notion of the human as an object of divine concern.

While the mass of humanity ignores the divine voice, there are some who can indeed perceive the daily message of Horeb. The section entitled "Hear, O Israel" concluded with what purports to be a quotation from the Zohar:

> The acts of God are eternal and continue for ever. Every day he who is worthy receives the Torah standing at Sinai; he hears the Torah from the mouth of the Lord as Israel did when they stood at Sinai. Every Israelite is able to attain that level, the level of standing at Sinai.[56]

This is an uncharacteristically imprecise quotation. The source from the Zohar to which the readers are referred contains no more than the kernel of this teaching;[57] other unquoted sources also contain further elements of this message,[58] but the last sentence appears to be a Heschelian interpolation, redolent with Hasidic influence.

The last section of the chapter, "Doors for the Soul," comprises one long quotation (over a page in length) from the first part of the Zohar. In order to make the passage suit the thrust of the chapter, Heschel made a significant change to the Soncino translation, which he tended to follow in quoting the Zohar. Where the printed translation reads "But of a truth the Holy One makes Himself known to every one according to the measure of his understanding," Heschel's version reads "But of a truth the Holy One makes Himself known to every one according to the insight of his heart."

There is a brief footnote attached to this quotation, and it is arguably the key to understanding the entire chapter. It directs readers to kabbalistic sources, bringing the chapter full circle back to the theme of prophetic insight.[59]

When read in light of the sources that underpin it and the footnotes that accompany it, the chapter on insight constitutes an argument for the relationship between prophecy and mysticism. Rather than regarding them as two discrete realms, Heschel used kabbalistic insights to describe the conditions necessary for prophecy: God perpetually suing for human attention; human initiative and capacity for inner sight; and the reward of gradual divine self-exposure.

A traditional teaching – namely that at a certain moment the spirit of prophecy departed – is adduced in order to counter the notion that prophecy is an ever-present feature of nature. But just as that spirit departed at a certain time, it can return, as Heschel's Hebrew essays on the theme make abundantly clear. He preferred the immediacy, unevenness, and drama of the event to the inexorable predictability of the homogenized process. The Sabbath, the festivals, the lives of great people, the extraordinary events of remarkable epochs, the possibility of spiritual surprise in prayer and study, the unique moment in the life of the individual – all of these speak against a monotonous and symmetrical world view.

Prophecy versus Mysticism?

On two occasions in *Search*, Heschel appears to compare mysticism with prophecy to the disadvantage of the former:

> Unlike the mystic act, revelation is not the result of a quest for esoteric experience. What characterizes the prophet is, on the contrary, an effort to escape such experience ... From the mystic experience we may gain an insight of man into the life of God; from the prophetic act we learn of an insight of God into the life of man.[60]
>
> Unlike the mystic experience, the significance of prophecy lay not in those who perceived it but in those to whom the word was to be conveyed.[61]

Note that the references here are to the mystic experience and the mystic act, and as a footnote to the chapter in which the earlier excerpt appears explains, Heschel was relating to his phenomenological study of prophecy, *Die Prophetie*. In the first forty pages of that work, the distinction between ecstasy and prophecy is considered at some length,[62] and I would suggest that the "mystic experience" here is close to "das private Erlebnis der Ekstase" as discussed in *Die Prophetie*.[63] If mysticism is absent from that early work, the category of ecstasy known from the apocalyptic tradition fulfils a similar role.

In an important essay on the relationship between mysticism and prophecy in Heschel's thought, Alexander Even-Chen analysed the evidence presented in *The Prophets* and *God in Search of Man*. In the course of his discussion, he provided a useful exposition of a theme already discernible in Heschel's German dissertation: the profound distinction between the mystic experience and the prophetic act. This distinction is made explicit in *Search*:

> The mystic experience is man's turning toward God: the prophetic act is God's turning toward man. The former is first of all an event in the life of man, contingent on the aspiration and initiative of man; the latter is first of all an event in the life of God, contingent on the pathos and initiative of God ... the mystic experience is an ecstasy of man; revelation is *an ecstasy of God*.[64]

Even-Chen rightly pointed out that Heschel's understanding of the relationship between these two concepts is not consistently categorical. He is sensitive to the undertones audible in the essay entitled "The Mystical Element in Judaism," wherein the prophet and the mystic are compared rather than contrasted.[65] Indeed, the inclusion of a discussion of prophecy at the end of that essay should be seen as a deliberate decision rather than an aberration. The "longing for the mystical" is "a part of the heritage of the psalmists and the prophets."[66] In the last section Heschel linked the mystic enterprise to his own key theological watchword – divine pathos – and pointed to the common assumptions of prophets and mystics, namely that "there is an inner life in God and the existence of man ought to revolve in a spiritual dynamic course around the life of God."[67]

The closing paragraph of the essay posits an identity of purpose between the mystic and the prophet: "to have an open heart for the inner life of God."[68] Divine pathos, the central characteristic of the prophetic sensibility and perhaps Heschel's most enduring contribution to the theological vocabulary, is equated with the *Middot*, the basis of the sefirotic system.

Between Prophetic and Apocalyptic

If the relation between the mystic and the prophet occupied Heschel, he also devoted attention to the relationship between prophecy and apocalypse. In *Torah min Hashamayim*, Heschel suggested that the tension between Rabbi Akiva and Rabbi Ishmael stemmed from a distinction between the prophetic and apocalyptic approaches prevalent at the time of the Bible and in the Second Temple period.

References to apocalyptic literature abound in *Torah min Hashamayim*.[69] In his highly perceptive introduction to the fifteenth chapter in his translation, Gordon Tucker contrasted prophetic with mystical/apocalyptic thought. In his reading

> Heschel sets out for us what he sees as the ambivalent nature of Jewish tradition when it comes to mystical speculation ... mystical speculation has potentially great value, and that value is at the same time counterbalanced by the dangers that it poses.[70]

Apocalyptic is in essence visual: in encounters with the Divine, there is no room for personal agency. The prophet, in contrast, is called to translate the voice of God into his own voice.[71] The persistence of visual and optic aspects of the mystical experience serves as evidence of residual traces of the apocalyptic tradition. Heschel regarded the debate about the inclusion of the Book of Ezekiel into the canon as a crucial moment in the integration of apocalypse into the mainstream: "The books were hidden, but the thoughts and the aspirations of the apocalyptic visionaries continued to exert their influence and did not disappear from the teachings of many Sages in the course of history."[72] In the Book of Ezekiel, these thoughts and aspirations found their way into the Jewish canon.

Unlike *Die Prophetie*, the starting point of the discussion of prophecy in *Torah min Hashamayim* is neither the biblical text nor Husserlian phenomenology but rather rabbinic literature. In one section of particular significance, Heschel developed the notion that prophecy was transferred to the Sages after the last of the biblical prophets.[73] In this way the contrast between prophecy and mysticism reappears as the dialectic tension between Rabbi Ishmael and Rabbi Akiva.

The relationship of mysticism to prophecy in Heschel's account of Judaism is complex. On the one hand, they are contrasted. On the other hand, the prophet and the mystic meet at a sublime level – each of them has "an open heart for the inner life of God."[74] The prophet, the sage, the mystic, the philosopher, the Hasid – all participate in this quest.[75]

There is an important political distinction between the political and the apocalyptic instinct. Rabbi Akiva and Rabbi Simeon bar Yohai, both heirs of the apocalyptic tradition in Heschel's typology, responded to their political context in ways that Heschel rejected – in his 1936 vignette on Rabbi Akiva, Heschel described him as possessing a "mystical romanticism," and claimed that tragedy struck when Rabbi Akiva "turned his mystical way of life into a political game."[76] Neither withdrawal from the affairs of this world nor involvement in messianic adventures are to be considered as responses worthy of emulation. While they appear to be in contradiction to each other, they have in common a rejection of the path of social amelioration and engagement with the quotidian realities of human existence.

Politically, Heschel was a devout Ishmaelian. Despite the fact that some historians have portrayed Rabbi Ishmael as a yet more fervent extremist than his counterpart,[77] Heschel's Ishmael is a pragmatic rationalist, not a dogmatic nationalist. Rabbi Ishmael is engaged in incremental deeds of social amelioration, focused clearly on this world. This is a world view far from the mystical and the messianic. In the Ishmaelian view, to love and cleave to God is to work for the betterment of society. This is far from the Akivan notion of intimacy between the divine and human realms.

Abraham Joshua Heschel rejected a political world view calling for either the abandonment of concern for the world or the abandonment of realism and plausibility. The development of a strident political extremism imbued with a mystical vision was the fulfilment of all that he feared about the destructive potential of an unbridled apocalypticism. His world view was prophetic, not apocalyptic. This orientation provided him (and may provide later readers) with a model of passionate non-fundamentalism.

Against Elitism

Both in his life and in his writings, Heschel remained open to mystery. Significantly, however, while he acknowledged this dimension of reality, he was at pains to emphasize meaning beyond the mystery. This meaning is not synonymous with science, which offers "merely explanations of greater puzzles."[78] Nor is this meaning synonymous with one religious creed or another – faith is a response to the mystery but not its resolution.[79]

For Heschel, human existence is beyond comprehension.[80] Biblical man knows that mystery is not a synonym for the unknown but a term which pertains to God.[81] Meaning itself may not be accessible but rather *"an intuition for a meaning that is beyond the mystery, an awareness of the transcendent worth of the universe."*[82] *Awe, wonder, amazement, surprise, embarrassment* – these key terms in Heschel's lexicon describe both a response to human inadequacy in the face of the ineffable and also the best chance of responding to the call of the sublime. The content of meaning is inchoate. The intuition that there is meaning and worth is at the heart of Heschel's understanding of humanity.

Heschel was an explicit adversary of esoteric elitism: "The grandeur and mystery of the world that surrounds us is not something which is perceptible only to the elect. All men are endowed with a sense of wonder, with a sense of mystery."[83]

He assumed that wonder and mystery were realities – "The pious man believes that there is a secret interrelationship among all events, that the sweep of all we are doing reaches beyond the horizon of our comprehension"[84] – yet he rejected the notion that this secret was accessible to only the select few.[85] In an article published in honour of Leo Baeck in 1954 he excoriated the axiom of complete divine unknowability as a form of arrogance and a vestige of paganism.[86]

For Heschel, sensitivity to wonder is no excuse for mystification or unbridled arrogance. Rather, men (and women) are encouraged to hone their sensitivity, and their alertness to the voice calling out to them. In his 1948 manifesto, *Pikuach Neshama*, Heschel expressed this privileging of the incommunicable:

> The whole honor of Judaism is internal, in the depths, in the small containers that are hidden from sight ... It is of the essence of spirituality to perceive the hidden transcendence which is in the habitual ... to hear the sound of the stone which cries out of the wall.[87]

The great and profound things of the world may be beyond expression, but they are not devoid of meaning. "The sense of the ineffable, the awareness of the grandeur and mystery of living, is shared by all men, and it is in the depth of such awareness that acts and thoughts of religion are full of meaning."[88]

Peshat and Sod

Polarity is a major Heschelian trope.[89] The distinction between *peshat* and *sod* – the plain sense and the esoteric teaching – is exemplified within the overarching Ishmael-Akiva distinction. Rabbi Akiva is a man of mystery, not satisfied with the realm of the rational. For him, the realm of *sod* predominates. Rabbi Ishmael relies on the eye of reason and steers clear of metaphysical speculations.[90]

The debate epitomized by Rabbi Akiva and Rabbi Ishmael had profound epistemological and hermeneutical implications. While Rabbi Ishmael assumed that the content to be learnt in the Torah was decipherable by faculties of reasoning, Rabbi Akiva suggested that meaning could be gleaned from the letters of the Torah in ways beyond reason. Discerning these mysteries superseded deduction through exegetical rules and formal reasoning.

Heschel presented both sides of this debate with vigour. In chapter 1, I noted that he cited the jibe that the word *peshat* is comprised of letters which form the word *tipesh*, "stupid."[91] Yet he also mounted a stirring defence of *peshat*:

> Jewish tradition insists that the Biblical commandment must not be divested of *peshat*, of its naked meaning; without the reality of the naked word the spirit is a ghost. Even the mystics who cherished the allegorical meaning of Scripture and regarded the hidden significance as superior to the plain, naked meaning, always insisted that the secret rests upon the plain.[92]

At the opening of his Hebrew article on Maimonides and prophesy, Heschel engaged in an enlightening discussion regarding secrets and hints. He suggested that the sages of Israel did not usually give public expression to the mysteries dwelling within their hearts, and thus, in order to know the essence of a person, it was their passions that should be examined.[93]

The two domains of the explicit and the recondite are connected to each other. The Torah, like all reality, is both concealed and revealed. "All things are both known and unknown, plain and enigmatic, transparent and impenetrable."[94] The Bible has more than one level of meaning, and "much of it remains locked to the literal-minded."[95]

The most direct reference to the interrelationship of these two domains can be found in the third volume of *Torah min Hashamayim* in a mini-chapter entitled "Concealed and Revealed." Here Heschel, in essence, denied the efforts of the literalist to steer clear from the realm of the esoteric, claiming that the two were inexorably linked. Indeed, the revealed is a veil covering that which is concealed.[96]

Given the centrality of the theme of revelation in Heschel's work, it is significant that the figure of Moses is employed in the fifth chapter of *Search* to describe the paradoxical relationship between the known and the unknowable. Even Moses, who had an unmediated encounter with the Divine, was unable to fathom "the mystery of God."[97] Moses is said to have had everything revealed to him, and yet there are teachings and insights of which he was not aware. This line of argument reaches its peak with a direct quotation from Numbers Rabbah suggesting that Rabbi Akiva knew certain things that were not revealed to Moses.[98]

The reader of *Torah min Hashamayim* is afforded an insight into the background to Heschel's inclusion of these sources in *God in Search of Man*. In the second volume he devoted a chapter to that which was not revealed to Moses, and in a footnote he set out the problem of Moses being given future knowledge and yet not knowing. He quoted at length a teaching from a foundational work of Lurianic Kabbalah, Vital's *Peri Etz Hayyim*, which explained the tradition according to which Moses did not understand teachings comprehensible to Rabbi Akiva. Vital suggested that while Moses was familiar with the essential secret, he did not know how to adduce this esoteric truth from every jot and tittle of the Torah.[99]

Abraham Joshua Heschel trawled rabbinic and medieval traditions to bolster his discussion of knowing and not knowing, the expressible and the ineffable, the explicit and the concealed.

The Renewing and Unfinished Torah

In *God in Search of Man* Heschel referred to "a theory in Jewish literature containing a profound parabolical truth which maintains that the Torah, which is eternal in spirit, assumes different forms in various eons."[100] "Every hour another aspect is unveiled."[101] The notes appended to these statements cited key works of the Jewish esoterical tradition such as *Pardes Rimmonim* and *Shenei Luhot ha-Berit*.

Heschel employed a wide range of sources spanning the thirteenth to the eighteenth centuries – di Trani's *Bet Elohim*, *Sefer Temunah*, Azulai's *Hesed Le-Avraham*, and the Hasidic *Teshuot Hen* – in support of the following statement, also in the spirit of this idea of a Torah whose meaning is revealed, and indeed changes, through time:

> In the end of days, it was believed, countless unknown rearrangements of the words and letters and unknown secrets of the Torah would be made known. Yet in its present form the text contains that which God wishes us to know.[102]

The selection of prooftexts for this statement reflects a range of esoteric traditions around the theme of the letters of the Torah.[103] The last of these, attributed to the Ba'al Shem Tov, suggested that it was only human weakness and sin that made it necessary for the Torah to be split up into discrete words rather than retaining its true undivided state.[104]

Lurianic Kabbalah is rare in Heschel's work.[105] Nevertheless, a commentary to Vital's *Peri Etz Hayyim* is one of the plethora of kabbalistic sources used to promote this idea of the "penultimate" significance of the Torah as we understand it today: "Now we have the Torah, in the messianic eon we will have the crown of Torah. Thus the wisdom open to us in this eon is but the beginning of its revelation."[106]

The thread common to these different texts is the image of a changeless Torah whose understanding is nonetheless ever-changing. In this way, Heschel pointed to a possible response to the challenges presented by a modern historical consciousness. If modern Jewish theology had tended to pit the sanctity of the Torah against its changeability, Heschel made ingenious use of Kabbalah to undermine this dichotomy.

Traces of Esoteric Writing in Heschel

Moshe Halbertal has made the sweeping assertion that the esoteric tradition has disappeared from modern Jewish thought, citing Heschel alongside Mendelssohn, Hermann Cohen, Buber, Rosenzweig, and Soloveitchik. This claim is unsupportable in light of the sources I have discussed in this chapter. Either Heschel must be seen as an exception to Halbertal's rule, or an esoteric tradition in modern Jewish thought is waiting to be discovered. Halbertal stated that none of the named thinkers ever claimed that they were engaged in the decoding of Torah mysteries or that they themselves used techniques of encoding. In my reading, Heschel's work demands precisely such a conclusion.[107]

Time and again in his work on prophesy in the Middle Ages we find references to discretion and absence of full disclosure. Heschel claimed that Maimonides had a prophetic urge that was not made explicit and that his practice was "to lay bare something and conceal much."[108] Heschel was well aware of this tradition of concealment, and one of his scholarly articles deals with a manuscript discussing esoteric traditions relating to prayer.[109]

Leo Strauss's suggestion that the conditions of a liberal democracy do not obviate the need for writing "between the lines"[110] may indeed be exemplified through Heschel's work. He did not believe that every opinion should be made explicit, and he would employ hints and allusions to act as a "word to the wise."

I want to bring a somewhat speculative example which relates not to the mysteries of revelation but rather to the practical question of Sabbath observance. It is not often noted that the publication of *The Sabbath* came directly in the wake of the debate within the Conservative Movement concerning the permissibility of driving on the Sabbath, particularly in order that Jews now living in far-flung suburbs could reach their synagogue communities. Anecdotally, we know that Heschel opposed this notion, although there is no explicit discussion of this topic to be found in his writings.[111] However, *The Sabbath* can be read as a contribution to this debate. It is true that the work was directed to many for whom Halakhic observance was far removed, and Heschel pitched the argument at an abstract level. However, it may be that the trigger that led him to write the work was the prospect of a religious mandate for use of the automobile, symbol of technology, on a day intended to place one beyond technology.

The following passage includes a famous Heschelian phrase. I believe it also contains a hint regarding his position on the driving controversy:

> What are the kinds of labor not to be done on the Sabbath? They are, according to the ancient rabbis, all those acts which were necessary for the construction and furnishing of the Sanctuary in the desert. The Sabbath itself is a sanctuary which we build, *a sanctuary in time*.
>
> It is one thing to race or be driven by the vicissitudes that menace life, and another thing to stand still and embrace the presence of an eternal moment.[112]

Even in the land of the free and among the generation of the explicit, Heschel preferred to bury or encode some of his views. In this case, his call to stand still rather than be driven may be read as an allusion to the controversy over driving. Here and elsewhere, in the body of the text and in footnotes, Heschel means more than he says, encouraging his reader to deduce his further meaning.

Was Heschel a Mystic?

The common thread uniting the sources we have examined in this chapter is the notion encapsulated within the phrase "divine pathos," an idea which Heschel developed and used over four decades. Just as this notion asserts the reality of God against various faithless critics, it also opens the way to the renewal of prophecy and the generation of new wisdom. It is not coincidental or trivial that Heschel acted to undermine the concept of Moses's ontological difference from the rest of humanity. It is a divine invitation that issues from Horeb every day, a voice which does not end – and prophesy has not passed from the world.

The profound secret to be revealed to the sceptics is that the God of Israel is the living God of the universe. The profound secret to be revealed to the believers is that the sages of our day are endowed with the potential to go beyond that which is contained in books, beyond the current configuration of the letters of the Torah.[113]

In Heschel's own words,

> Every approach continues the general and the specific, the revealed and the concealed, uprooting and planting. Indeed reality itself is coming and going, general and specific, presence and absence, yes and no bound together. The secret of reality – two rules in one.[114]

Both before and beyond the specific revelation of the Torah, there is a realm of mystery, paradox, and possibility. The sources of the kabbalistic tradition are used in order to convey these depths: for example, the Maharal of Prague (sixteenth century). He is quoted in *Search* in order to promote the view that faith can reach the realm of mystery; that the voice at Sinai was not physical but spiritual; and that not all of the Torah was received by Moses at Sinai.[115] Time and again Heschel used Kabbalah to imply that something lies beyond our current reality and our present understanding of God's will. It points to the mystery at the heart of prophecy and also to the potential for innovation beyond the confines of fixed interpretation.

Was Heschel a mystic? As Arthur Green observed, the answer to this question "will turn on definition."[116] If mysticism is "man's turning towards God," then Heschel may be said to have been a mystic. However one chooses to define his approach, his conception of Judaism certainly maintained an honoured place for the insights of the esoteric tradition. The demands of a popular and ecumenical theology in the spirit of democracy meant that the pursuit of mystical truth by an elite was not at the forefront of his concerns. Equally, there is no evidence that he had any personal interest in any theurgy other than the *via activa* that is at the heart of *God in Search of Man* and at the heart of his life's work. Experience without response is insufficient. For Heschel, the true ecstasy is the ecstasy of the deed.

Whether or not Heschel should be viewed as a mystic remains a matter for debate.[117] It cannot be contested, however, that in the course of his life he made extensive and significant use of sources gleaned from the Jewish mystical tradition.

One more dimension of *setim ve-galya*, the recondite and the revealed, should be mentioned before closing. There are some influences on Heschel's thought which have been rendered invisible or banished to the background when they are in fact of central significance. Arthur Green has recently argued that the influence of the work of Hillel Zeitlin (1871–1942) on such works as *God in Search of Man* is great, though unacknowledged.[118] Heschel did cite Zeitlin in his Yiddish work on Kotzk but only in passing.[119] Zeitlin is an example of an understated link, a subterranean influence.

There are others. The work of Meir ibn Gabbai (sixteenth century) is only rarely mentioned in Heschel's work, but its influence is far greater than might be thought. As a proponent of the notion of *tzorech gavoah*, God's need for human fulfilment of the commandments, ibn Gabbai may be seen as an important source for Heschel. *Tzorech gavoah* and divine pathos are one.[120]

At the conclusion of a 1944 essay on the philosophy of Saadia Gaon, having explicated the interrelation of reason and revelation in the work of the great medieval thinker, Heschel set out his own spiritual manifesto:

> Religious faith precedes and transcends knowledge. It is an ultimate force in man, lying deeper than the stratum of reason and its nature cannot be defined in abstract, static terms. It is a sense of the transcendent, a dynamic quality, the ability to envision the invisible, to be stirred by what lies beyond the reach of reason or perception. It is a manifestation of man's position on the verge of God.[121]

In the face of a thoroughgoing religious rationalism, Heschel embodies a different approach. Heschel's conception of continuity in Jewish history was predicated on the antiquity of the esoteric strand within Judaism. In his view the sensibilities epitomized by Rabbi Akiva and Rabbi Ishmael stretched back to the Bible and foreshadowed the mystics and Hasidim of later centuries. The mystical voice – a sense for that which lies beyond the rational – changes in form and emphasis. In essence it is always present.

"Neither a rationalist nor an irrationalist,"[122] Abraham Joshua Heschel refused to accept a dichotomy between reason and what lies beyond its reach. Heschel's man is perched precariously but tenaciously on the verge of God.

Chapter Six

A New Accent: Heschel and Hasidism

The tombstone erected in memory of Abraham Joshua Heschel does not include a verse from the prophets or a teaching from rabbinic literature. It makes no mention of his struggle for civil rights or his commitment to the cause of interreligious dialogue. Heschel's service to the Jewish Theological Seminary and his many publications all go unmentioned. Instead, the gravestone reads (in translation):

> Here is buried Abraham Joshua Heschel, the son of sainted Master Our Rabbi Moshe Mordecai and Reizel Heschel, the grandson of the holy Rabbi Baal Ohev Yisrael and the holy Rabbi of Ruzhin and the holy Rabbi of Berditchev and of great sanctity the Maggid of Mezritch.[1]

Heschel entered the world a descendant of Hasidim, was called to the Torah at thirteen wearing the phylacteries of Levi Isaac of Berditchev (1740–1809) and is buried under a stone proclaiming his provenance. In this chapter I will consider the extent to which his writings display signs of Hasidic influence and the nature of his contribution to the scholarly understanding of the Hasidic movement. In the course of the chapter, his unique connection with this movement should become apparent.

Heschel wrote about Hasidism in four quite distinct ways; some have no parallel in his approach to other phenomena within Jewish culture. First, he engaged in original historical research based on primary sources, designed to shed light on "the Circle of the Ba'al Shem Tov." His two books on Menahem Mendel of Kotzk comprise a second category: extended explication of the thought of a particular Hasidic sage. In this case the primary emphasis was not historical but rather conceptual. Third, there are Hasidic anecdotes, tales, and teachings included in Heschel's theological and other works. We find such traces at every stage of Heschel's literary output, from the early poems to the last talks and articles.

The last of the four genres is highly informative: Heschelian reflections on the nature of Hasidism. Of these, perhaps the most revealing is a short article written in the final year of his life, "Hasidism as a New Approach to Torah,"[2] as well as some autobiographical comments in interviews and further remarks on particular strains of Hasidism in his two works on the Kotzker Rebbe.

There is much to be learned by considering the ways in which Heschel deployed sources in each of these categories. Despite generic distinctions, the scholarly blends into the spiritual domain and the historical into the theological. To some extent this mélange is unique to Hasidism in Heschel's work. Towards the end of the chapter I will posit the existence of a fifth stratum – a Hasidic underpinning to Heschelian tropes bearing no explicit indication of Hasidic provenance.

The Circle of the Ba'al Shem Tov

Between 1949 and 1965 Heschel published essays in Hebrew and in Yiddish,[3] which have made a significant contribution to understanding the earliest years of the Hasidic movement.[4] The Hebrew articles are characterized by an interweaving of traditional accounts of the wonders worked by the subjects of his essays with historical insights based on close readings of manuscripts. Some of these primary sources were introduced into scholarly discourse by Heschel himself. This mixture of approaches reflects some of the methodological challenges inherent in the study of Hasidism, but Heschel did not regard this combination of methods simply as an unavoidable disadvantage. It also reflects his interest in eliding the distinction between the academically sound and the spiritually resonant.

For an example of such methodological blurring, we may refer to a section of his article on Rabbi Pinhas of Korzec. Heschel quoted a tale according to which the Maggid of Miedzyrzec sent for Rabbi Pinhas when his wife and children fell ill. Because the Maggid's wife was not brought into the room where Rabbi Pinhas was praying, she died. After recounting this legend, Heschel added a comment: "The year of her death was, it appears, considerably before 1773, the year of the maggid's death."[5] Hagiography and chronology are thus blended.

There was no divide separating Heschel's scholarly investigations from his theological speculations. Material that appears in the historical articles also found its way into other aspects of Heschel's work. In the 1965 Hebrew article on Rabbi Nachman of Kosov, for example, Heschel presented his subject as a man given to extended speculation on the divine Name. He then cited a teaching of the Ba'al Shem Tov (also known as the Besht), based on Psalm 32:2 and relating to such intensive meditative practice, and surmised that "it is possible that the Besht had Rabbi Nachman in mind" when he offered his interpretation.[6]

Setting aside the probability of this hypothesis and the method employed to reach it, this discussion helps uncover the source of a comment made in *God in Search of Man* a decade earlier. There Heschel stated,

> It was a requirement in Jewish piety to be constantly aware of His presence. As an aid to such remembrance, it was suggested that one constantly keep before the inner eye the four letters of the Ineffable Name. Paraphrasing the verse in Psalms 32:2, it was said, that blessed is he to whom not to think of God for one moment is a sin.[7]

God in Search of Man does not reveal the identity of this apotheosis of Jewish piety. It is in fact the Ba'al Shem Tov.

Kotzk

That Heschel devoted his dying energies to the completion of two works about Rabbi Menahem Mendel of Kotzk seems remarkable. Judging from the arc of Heschel's interest in the history of Hasidism, one could have expected him to devote himself to a biography of the Besht. Indeed, those close to him report that this had long been an ambition of his, but that his hopes had been dashed following a fire in the library of the Jewish Theological Seminary.

However dearly he may have yearned to produce the Besht's biography, it was in fact the Kotzker Rebbe to whom he dedicated two works, or perhaps two versions of the same work. This fact is all the more noteworthy in light of the fact that Rabbi Menahem Mendel of Kotzk represents the antithesis to the Besht tradition within Hasidism, as Heschel himself was keen to emphasize.[8]

In fact, however, neither of these works reads like a biography of Menachem Mendel Morgenstern. Rather, Heschel devoted much of the discussion to his distinctive views set in contrast to a number of foils

– the Besht, Kierkegaard (particularly in *A Passion for Truth*), Simhah Bunem of Przysucha, and others. It seems clear that as he moved into later life, Heschel found the sensibility evoked by the Kotzker Rebbe to be most conducive to his mood and concerns about the human condition.

The issue of language, which is an important theme in any consideration of Heschel's work, is of particular significance in relation to his writing on Hasidism.[9] Annette Aronowicz has pointed out "certain differences" between the Yiddish *Kotzk* and its English counterpart, *A Passion for Truth*. She noted, for example, that the chapters on the Kotzker and Job are "terser and darker" in the Yiddish version than in *Passion*. The Yiddish work is larger than, and in many ways the source of, the English parallel. Aronowicz was surely justified in asking, "Could not Heschel be saying, through his choice of language, that the continuity of the Jewish tradition requires a leap out of the world of American and Israeli culture?"[10]

In my view, the turn to the Kotzker can be seen as Heschel's equivalent to the turn to post-Holocaust theology in modern Jewish thought in the aftermath of the Six Day War. For him, the Kotzker Rebbe came to be emblematic of a post-Holocaust sensibility, pessimism without nihilism, and a profound concern about the prospects for American Judaism.[11] Note the typology in his introduction to *Passion*:

> Was it good to live with one's heart torn between the joy of Mezbizh and the anxiety of Kotzk? To live both in awe and consternation, in fervor and horror, with my conscience on mercy and my eyes on Auschwitz, wavering between exaltation and dismay?[12]

In each case the former term represents the Besht, and the latter Kotzk. Heschel finds it necessary to face a post-Auschwitz world with both sensibilities at work.

If the dark tones evoked by the teachings of Menahem Mendel of Kotzk particularly suited Heschel's mood in the early 1970s, we have evidence of the influence of these teachings in earlier decades. In *Man Is Not Alone* he quoted relatively few Jewish sources, yet the Kotzker appears by name on two occasions. Heschel also referred to these sayings in his last works.

Both traditions are concerned with the relation between reason and faith. Chapter 11 of *Man Is Not Alone* is entitled "Faith," and there we find Heschel returning to the teachings of his youth. The first of these occasions refers to the relation of reason to faith, where he suggested that reason alone would not allow for a genuine search for God,[13] a theme which had long preoccupied him.[14] This teaching appears in both of Heschel's works on Kotzk,[15] and in the English version it is followed by a comment on the nature of Judaism: "Reb Mendl interpreted Psalm 14:2 to mean: is it possible for a rationalist (*maskil*) to seek God? Faith cannot be won by speculation. Jewish faith comes about by doing, by living the commandments."[16]

Later in *Man Is Not Alone*, in a chapter called "The Hiding God," Heschel referred to a Kotzkian paraphrase of Psalm 37:3.[17] He returned to this teaching, quoting it in the Yiddish original, in a 1957 lecture[18] and again in both the Yiddish and the English versions of his last book.[19] The integrated character of Heschel's thought is emphasized. A teaching from his childhood appears in the middle of his life and then again shortly before his death. The Kotzker escorted Heschel throughout his life. In his final decade, this perpetual presence assumed a heightened resonance.

Hasidic Teachings

With the exception of the essays and books dedicated to Hasidic figures, the work of Abraham Joshua Heschel is not replete with Hasidic sources. In *Search*, for example, there are as many quotations from Maimonides as there are from the entire Hasidic canon.

A number of Hasidic masters, most of them from the early generations, are cited in various books and articles. Among those to be found scattered in Heschel's general works but not otherwise discussed in this chapter are a number of figures born no later than the eighteenth century: Rabbis Jacob Joseph of Polonnoye,[20] Jehiel Michael of Zloczow,[21] Nahum of Chernobyl, Gedaliah of Lunicec,[22] Shneur Zalman of Lyady,[23] Jacob Isaac ha-Levi Horowitz (the Seer of Lublin),[24] Raphael of Bershad,[25] Zevi Hirsch of Zhidachov,[26] Simhah Bunem of Przysucha,[27] and Nachman of Bratslav.[28]

Despite the relative paucity of citations, these sources often play an important role in Heschel's argumentation. Later I will argue that many key parts of Heschel's lexicon have Hasidic provenance. But before we relate to the implicit influences, we should discuss the explicit use of Hasidic materials. *The Sabbath* provides an instructive example. This short work is relatively rich in sources – fifteen pages of endnotes refer the reader to a range of books from across Jewish history. While the

Bible is quoted or cited almost one hundred times in *The Sabbath* and the literature of the Rabbis is all-pervasive, there are only five explicit references to Hasidic works and one other unattributed tale, which is clearly of Hasidic origin.

The first of these is a teaching which appears in the body of the text with no clue to its origin:

> What does the word "Sabbath" mean? According to some it is the name of the Holy One.[n20] Since the word *Shabbat* is a name of God, one should not mention it in unclean places, where words of Torah should not be spoken. Some people were careful not to take it in vain.[n21][29]

Note 20 refers the reader to the Zohar and note 21 to the *Benei Yissakhar* of Rabbi Zevi Elimelech Shapiro of Dynow. In fact, the whole quotation is a paraphrase of the very first teaching in that Hasidic work, including the quotation from the Bible. It is worth noting that in some sense this reference may be read as a compliment or homage to one of Heschel's closest associates, Rabbi Wolfe Kelman, who graduated from the seminary a year before *The Sabbath* was published. The account of the first encounter between the two men touches upon the issue of Hasidic pedigree. The meeting is described in Heschel's biography:

> While Heschel continued a telephone conversation, Kelman picked up a *sefer* (religious book in Hebrew) and started to read it, absorbed. A few minutes later, Heschel put down the telephone and asked, "So you know that book?" Kelman smiled, "I know that book very well. My grandfather wrote it." Heschel looked at him. "Excuse me young man, what is the grandson of the Dinover Rav doing at the Jewish Theological Seminary?" Kelman answered, "I will tell you, if you tell me what the grandson of the *Ohev Yisrael* ... is doing at the Seminary." Heschel jumped up from his desk and hugged Kelman, an embrace that inaugurated Heschel's closest American friendship.[30]

The meaning of the word *Sabbath* as understood by the great Rabbi of Dynow, the distinguished ancestor of one of Heschel's closest associates, found its way into *The Sabbath*.

Elsewhere in *The Sabbath* Rabbi Solomon of Radomsk (the *Tiferet Shelomo*) recounts testimony from the household of Rabbi Elimelech of Lyzhansk (the *No'am Elimelech*) illustrating the Sabbath's capacity to spread inner peace.[31]

Heschel also cited an unattributed story concerning a rabbi who was granted a glimpse of paradise in a dream. He saw *tannaim* seated round a table studying and sensed some disappointment, until a voice explained to him, "the Tannaim are not in Paradise. Paradise is in the Tannaim."[32] This teaching was close to Heschel's heart. He reproduced it in 1954 in *Man's Quest for God* and then again in 1965 in a speech. In each case his intention was to privilege interiority over external mechanisms and appearances.[33]

The last appearance of an overtly Hasidic source in *The Sabbath* was reserved for Rabbi Hayyim of Chernovtsy. He is in fact mentioned twice, first in an anecdote concerning the change of his visage during the Sabbath, and then in a relatively long quotation from his book on the Sabbath, *Siddur shel Shabbat*.[34] Here too the theme is the physical transformation which overtakes the saintly person who is caught up in the holiness of the day. This mixing of the biographical and literary aspects, Shabbat practice and Shabbat theory, is an echo of how Heschel, the latter-day Hasid, may have wanted to present the Sabbath to his readers.

Hasidism on the Theological Frontline in *Search* and Beyond

In *Search* there is a fairly equal division between quotation of theoretical works on the one hand, and parables and tales on the other. Very few of the Hasidic sources appear in the footnotes: the overwhelming majority are found in the body of the text. The way in which Heschel related to Hasidic literature recalls his approach to the Bible: it is kept in the foreground, rather than being consigned to the background.

Throughout this book we have noted Heschel's predilection for ending chapters and sections with quotations. One of the most remarkable examples appears in chapter 33 of *Search*, in a section entitled "The Tension between Halakhah and Aggadah." This represents the longest quotation from Hasidic literature, and indeed one of the longest quotations of any kind in the entire work. Heschel quoted four consecutive paragraphs from Rabbi Mordecai Yosef Leiner's *Mei ha-Shiloah* on the relationship between the tribes of Ephraim and Judah, who are understood as archetypes: Ephraim concentrates on the law, and Judah concentrates on God. Leiner, the Rabbi of Izbica, predicted a future rapprochement between these two archetypes when the normative Ephraim would accept that the approach of the inwardly focused Judah was also for the sake of heaven.[35]

In his last works on the Kotzker Rebbe, Heschel made reference to this teaching of the Izbicer in a chapter on the relationship between God and Torah. In *Kotzk* we find this chapter almost at the very end of the book, and the full teaching is quoted in the footnotes.[36] In *A Passion for Truth* the chapter is positioned at a much earlier point in the book: his interpretation of the Izbicer's teaching is not left open to doubt:

> Reb Mordecai Yosef of Izbica ... did not question the sanctity and exalted-ness of the Torah but accentuated that God's majesty was more sublime. It stood above Law, above Halakhah. He maintained that there was a dis-tinction between the Torah and the Lord, that one could not really compre-hend the Torah unless the thought of God was present. That was why at times the Torah had to be laid aside for the sake of God, as indicated in the Psalms: "There is a time to act for God; set aside the Torah" (119:126).[37]

The high standard of observance set by the Rabbis is not to be seen as an unreachable good but rather as that which lacks meaning without "the thought of God." In the eternal tension between Ephraim and Judah, both are essential – but Judah prevails.

This teaching of Rabbi Leiner of Izbica appeared in a draft chapter of *Torah min Hashamayim*, which did not find its way into the printed ver-sion, in the name of "Rabbi Mordechai Joseph of Izbica, a major figure in the history of the Hasidic movement."[38] In three different kinds of composition, over three decades and in three languages Heschel pre-sented this teaching, brimming with antinomian potential, as a man-date for theological daring.

One remarkable note in which a teaching is offered "in apposition,"[39]– with no explanation or embellishment in order to illustrate a point – is to be found in a discussion of faith in chapter 15 of *Search*. In the main body of the text, Heschel made a general remark: "Faith is not the same as belief, not the same as the attitude of regarding something as true."[40]

To this statement he added the following note:

> A thief while breaking into a home in order to steal calls upon God to help him, reminds Rabbi Shneur Zalman of Ladi; see *Berakhot* 63a.[41]

On at least two occasions this founding figure of Lubavitch Hasidism referred to the Talmudic aphorism and in both discussions he offered a distinction between two concepts both understood by the term *emunah*. When the perspective of *emunah* is from the outside in, then it is indeed possible that a person might believe the proposition of God's unity and yet still behave at variance with the implications of this insight.[42] Such *emunah* is higher than reason, but not as high as the inner or revealed *emunah*, where the paradox of the praying thief becomes impossible.[43]

In these ways, teachings of the Izbicer and Shneur Zalman of Lyady are used in *Search* and beyond to highlight radical ideas.

Heschel's Conception of Hasidism

In a small number of essays and interviews, as well as in the introduction to the two books on Kotzk in which the Ba'al Shem Tov and the Kotzker are compared, Heschel set out some of his personal views on the unique significance of the Hasidic movement. The picture emerging from these writings is of a movement that transformed the course of Jewish history, introducing new attitudes to prayer, honesty, humanity, individualism, and indeed to the very concept of innovation. In a highly significant paragraph in a late essay, Heschel delineated four key characteristics of the Hasidic phenomenon:

> Hasidism must be understood in terms of great insights and teachings. It is equally important to remember that Hasidism is preserved not only in the form of teachings but also in the language of stories, tales. Third, Hasidism can be properly understood only if one realizes its leaning upon classics, on interpretations of biblical or rabbinic texts. The most important aspect of Hasidism is that it lives in personalities; without the charismatic person there is no teaching of Hasidism.[44]

While acknowledging in that same essay that the Hasidic movement was differentiated by a number of phases, there is no doubt that for Heschel, the figure of the Ba'al Shem Tov loomed large as its founding charismatic presence.

In his twilight reflection on the Hasidic movement, Heschel considered the unique place in history to be ascribed to the Ba'al Shem Tov, who "took the tradition of Jewish learning, the Talmud, and Kabbalah and gave it a new lustre and a new meaning. He was very much influenced by and adopted quite a number of ideas from Jewish mysticism, but he gave them a new slant, a new accent."[45]

> What was there about him that was not to be found in other great Jewish personalities like Maimonides or even Reb Isaac Luria or Rabbi Akiva? This one man in a little town brought into the new world a new spirit, and

that spirit captured without the use of a modern media a major part of the Jewish people within twenty years.[46]

The assertion that the Ba'al Shem Tov was in some sense greater than all the great sages who preceded him is not the measured hypothesis of a scholar but the declaration of an adherent. Like the statement that "there has been no one like him for a thousand years,"[47] these judgments of the founder of Hasidism are more Hasidic than academic. In a Yiddish interview Heschel gave voice to this stance in a different way, presenting the Besht as a torchbearer for the Eastern European tradition as contrasted with the intellectual legacy of modern German Jewry: "I have great respect for German Jews, but for me personally, the Ba'al Shem Tov is much more important than Einstein."[48]

Moshe Idel has raised the possibility that Abraham Joshua Heschel saw himself as "the spiritual inheritor of the Besht."[49] It is certainly true that Heschel made extraordinary claims for the unique status of the Ba'al Shem Tov: "Other personalities contributed great works, they left behind impressive achievements; the Besht left behind a new people."[50] Further, Heschel was at pains to point out that his ancestor, the Rabbi of Apta, was almost a reincarnation of the Ba'al Shem Tov.[51] However, I see little evidence to substantiate the claim that Heschel accorded himself the same epoch-making significance. He may indeed have regarded himself as an heir to the prophets, but the claim that he saw himself as the reincarnation of the reinventor of Jewish life would need more than a scant foundation in order to be substantiated.[52]

Rather than a manifestation of the transmigrated soul of the Besht, Heschel saw himself as scion, scholar, and spiritual heir of the Hasidic revolution. Even-Chen and Meir have offered the counter-suggestion that in fact Heschel saw himself as the transmigrated soul of his ancestor Levi Isaac of Berditchev and of the Kotzker Rebbe.[53] I differ from them not in doubting this assertion but rather in extending it to many of the great figures of Jewish history. He believed himself to be an incarnation of the Jewish spirit – not unique or messianic but profound and prophetic. The great figures of the Jewish past came alive as he evoked them.

Scion

Abraham Joshua Heschel Heschel (for such was his full name; he was named for his ancestor) was a descendant of many of the greatest figures in the history of Hasidism. His maternal uncle, the Novominsker

Rebbe of Warsaw, was a dominant figure in his life following the death of his own father. "Heschel's adolescence was ... guided by this great zaddik whose entire life conveyed holiness,"[54] and it has been suggested that he provided the model of the pious man described in a 1942 essay and then reprised in *Man Is Not Alone*.[55]

The Perlow family of which Heschel's mother was a part traced its ancestry back to Rabbi Levi Isaac of Berditchev (1740–1809), who is mentioned on Heschel's tombstone. His teachings found their way into *Man's Quest for God* and *God in Search of Man*.[56] Three other great figures of whom Heschel was a direct descendant were also mentioned on the stone: his eponymous forebear the Ohev Yisrael (ca 1748–1825), the Rabbi of Ruzhin (1796–1850) and the Maggid of Miedzyrzec (d 1772). All three of them are quoted or mentioned by name in Heschel's work.[57]

In his essay on Rabbi Pinhas of Korzec, Heschel said of his subject's grandfather that he was an itinerant preacher who "whenever he received payment ... would keep for himself only enough for his minimal needs, contributing the rest toward maintenance of the synagogue." In a footnote appended to this comment Heschel recounted,

I have been fortunate to find four collections of manuscripts in the United States containing an abundance of rich material regarding the history of R. Pinhas ... (the last two are in the possession of my relative, the Admor of Monestrisht, Rabbi Isaac Joel Rabinowitz).[58]

Heschel (and his extended family) were acting here as preservers of a sacred tradition in danger of extinction.

The fact that Abraham Joshua Heschel was a scion of Hasidic dynasties is of great significance to an understanding of his core identity. It sheds light on his oft-expressed sense of alienation: at the *Hochschule* in Berlin, the College in Cincinnati and the Seminary in New York, he was in the minority as a Polish-born Hasid with roots in the Ukraine, and he faced ridicule and insensitivity as a result. Beyond this motif of displacement, Heschel's Hasidic provenance provides a key to understanding many of his passions, concerns and sensibilities.

His few written reminiscences about his early years tend to relate to their intensity: "Day and night we spoke only about 'prayer' and *kavanah* ... and about *Hakodosh Baruch Hu* ... and about *mesirat nefesh*." "I lived in the presence of quite a number of extraordinary persons I could revere." "I was trained to live a life, or to strive to live a life, which is compatible with the mystery and marvel of human existence."[59]

For reasons which have been described and discussed elsewhere,[60] Heschel left the milieu of his youth behind and never rejoined it. While he maintained strong links with his cousins, who perpetuated the Hasidic tradition close to his Manhattan home, he chose not to return, describing his transition to modernity as an irrevocable act. Nevertheless, he never abandoned his Hasidic roots.

Heschel did in fact leave Warsaw twice: once of his own volition in 1925 and again in 1939 in flight from Nazi persecution. The two departures help explain two strands in Heschel's later approach to the Hasidism of his youth and indeed to Hasidism in general. The first departure did not take the form of a rupture: contact with the family home was maintained, even as the now clean-shaven Heschel set off on his westward journey.[61] The second departure was from a world in the process of liquidation. This consciousness of the destruction and the resultant imperative to preserve that which had been lost is itself an important aspect of Heschel's approach to Hasidism. He described himself as perhaps the last Jew to come from Warsaw with his soul in Mezbizh and his mind in Kotzk.[62] He felt impelled to communicate this combination of soul and mind to the next generation.

The fact that Abraham Heschel (who returned to the Hasidic signifier Joshua after the Holocaust) was connected by birth to many Hasidic dynasties influenced the way in which he related to and cited Hasidic traditions. He noted in his preface to *Kotzk* that the usual canons of text-based scholarship do not do justice to the original orality of the traditions. In this case, books are a pale reflection of the power of the original verbal transmission.

Heschel's relation to Hasidism was more intimate and personal than his relation to any other period of Jewish creativity. He saw himself as heir to a rich oral tradition, only some of which had been committed to writing in the Hasidic literature.[63] In a note following a story about Rabbi Mendel of Kosov in *The Earth Is the Lord's*, Heschel noted revealingly, "This story, which I heard from Rabbi A.J. Heschel of Kopcsynce, is now narrated by B. Hager, *Oifn Weg*, Bucuresti, 1946."[64]

Heschel described Hasidism's tragedy as being that it is "essentially an oral movement, one that cannot be preserved in written form. It is ultimately a living movement. It is not contained fully in any of its books."[65] This "tragedy" is due not only to corruptions in the process of transcription. It is related to the project of Hasidism itself.

For Heschel the ineffability of the Divine, the unwritten nature of the Torah, and the orality of the Hasidic tradition were all facets of the same fundamental reality. "In the absence of the oral tradition and a proximity to Hasidic personages, one can scarcely describe Hasidism."[66] In his introduction to Dresner's *The Zaddik*, Heschel set out his view that there was something essential to be gleaned from the spoken voice of Hasidism: Hasidism withers when placed on exhibition. Its substance is not perceptible to the eye. It is not enough to read its written word; one must hear it, one must learn to be perceptive to the voice. Fortunately, there are words in many of its records which still ring with the passion and enthusiasm of those who spoke them. The problem is how to hear the voice through the words.[67]

In the case of unattributed Hasidic sources in Heschel's writing, there is a strong possibility that several quotations are not from literary sources but rather from an orally transmitted tradition, which was characteristic of the Hasidic movement from its earliest phase.[68] A number of the Hasidic sources quoted in *Search*, for example, do not receive the level of precision in citation that generally characterizes that work.[69]

One statement relating to the nature of truth is attributed in that work to the Kotzker Rebbe with no precise indication of its provenance:

> To say the obvious is not yet to speak truth. When the obvious and the Word stand in conflict, truth is the refusal to rest content with the facts as they seem. Truth is the courage to fathom the facts in order to see how they relate to the Word.[70]

This is a mildly paraphrased and edited version of a tradition which appeared in the Kotzker's *Emet ve-Emunah*,[71] and yet Heschel omitted any direct citation of the source. It is remarkable that in *Kotzk*, the tradition is quoted at greater length and in a manner more directly connected to the printed text, once again with no citation.[72]

It is possible, of course, that in both of these works, almost twenty years apart in their composition, Heschel omitted the citation in error. There is, however, another plausible explanation, which may go some way to clarifying Heschel's apparently slapdash citation of Hasidic sources. In his view, as explained early in *Kotzk* and discussed by Dresner, the Hebrew works in which the thought of the Kotzker and others were preserved were inferior in quality to the original Yiddish tradition, which Heschel heard in his childhood. Reading the traditions of Hasidic sages such as the Kotzker in their Hebrew form is bound to lead to confusion, because the process of transcription and translation leads to corruption:

That I understand them despite their ambiguous Hebrew formulation is due to the fact that in my youth I heard many of these aphorisms in their original Yiddish. It was my good fortune to have known Rabbi Ben Tzion and Rabbi Moses Judah, who had visited Rabbi Mendl, as well as a large number of Hasidim who were thoroughly imbued with the way of the Kotzk. From them I learned many of the aphorisms which I cite in this book ...[73]

The apparent loosening of standards of citation in the case of Hasidic literature testifies to Heschel's intimate acquaintance with the oral traditions of which the Hebrew books are an expression. When Heschel quotes the Kotzker's teaching that the Oral Law can never be contained in books, this is not only a statement of the primacy of the unmediated oral experience at the source of the Bible: it is a reflection on the chain of tradition as it has developed ever since. The text's significance is never more than penultimate.

This intimacy with the spoken traditions of Hasidism reaches back to the earliest phase of the movement. In *Search*, Heschel wrote, "When we think He is close, then He is remote; when we think He is remote, then he is near (the Ba'al Shem). The bridge to God is awe."[74]

It is possible to find this teaching, or one very close to it, in the speculative literature of Hasidism.[75] Heschel was at home in this literature, and yet he "believed that there was a reliable oral tradition going back to the earliest Hasidic period, if only one knew where to look and how to listen."[76] When Heschel referred in a non-specific manner to the teaching of a Hasidic sage he was expressing intimacy rather than inaccuracy, and he was appealing to the oral source of the literary creation.

Another passing comment in *Search* is even vaguer:

The mind is never immune to "alien thoughts," and there is no easy way of weeding them out. A Hasidic rabbi, asked by his disciples in the last hours of his life whom they should choose as their master after his passing away, said: "If someone should give you advice on how to eradicate alien intentions, know he is not your master."[77]

No hint is given either to the identity of the rabbi or the source of the tradition. In fact, the rabbi in question was the Ba'al Shem Tov himself.[78]

When Heschel cited the traditions of Hasidism, he was not merely deploying citations to bolster an argument or for rhetorical effect. He was sharing his heirlooms.

Scholar

Abraham Joshua Heschel published a number of essays and books, many of them informed by his prodigious knowledge of Jewish sources, which represented a contribution to theological discourse. Few of them, however, had pretensions to original historical scholarship. Exceptions to this general observation would perhaps include his Hebrew essays on the phenomenon of prophecy in the Middle Ages[79] and his presentation of an anonymous manuscript on prayer, probably from the Abulafian school of medieval Kabbalah.[80] Neither of these examples, however, constitute a systematic attempt to contribute to the understanding of historical events and biographical details relating to a particular period of Jewish history.

This distinction is reserved for Heschel's essays concerning the early history of the Hasidic movement. As Dresner wrote, "Heschel felt it vital that the historical basis for the rise of Hasidism be established to whatever extent it was still possible."[81] In a 1952 Yiddish article Heschel expressed his own sense of mission thus:

> It is we, the last generation of East European Jewry, who owe a debt to future generations: to save what we can and to investigate thoroughly both the historical facts as well as the actual spiritual character of Hasidism, one of the most glorious chapters in Jewish history.[82]

Although some contemporary scholars take issue with his judgments and methods,[83] there are still those who claim that "Heschel was not only engaged in random piecemeal work on this or that Hasidic sage but rather, he was involved in a systematic study of the earliest and most important phase of Hasidism" and that his monographs "constitute a major contribution to Hasidic studies."[84]

Heschel was sensitive to criticism of his historical essays, most particularly the piece on Gershon of Kutow,[85] and this sensitivity is illustrated in a defensive letter written to Gershom Scholem in response to Scholem's criticism of the article.[86] In that very article Heschel was himself critical of scholars who had either ignored or misinterpreted "important facts,"[87] yet another indication that he strove for scholarly precision.

Dresner portrayed Heschel as a pre-eminent scholar of Hasidism. He listed some of Heschel's achievements and discoveries, criticized the excesses and errors of other scholars, and concluded that "Heschel was perhaps the one scholar who might have given us the definitive work on Hasidism."[88] For Dresner, if there is any shortcoming in Heschel's approach it is his "tendency towards Hasidic apologetics,"[89] but this is not seen as a significant threat to his status as a prime scholar of Hasidism.

Such a portrayal of Heschel seems unsupportable, not because it overestimates Heschel's capacities but because it misrepresents his intentions. Heschel did indeed bemoan the state of Hasidic scholarship in the modern period, and the exception he held up to exemplify the desired approach was Eliezer Zweifel, a learned *maskil* who mounted what has been termed "an intellectual defense of Hasidism."[90] Heschel, too, was motivated by priorities other than the pursuit of academic precision, and it is these priorities, rather than an oversight or failing, which accounts for the relative lack of critical analysis in his writing on this subject.

Rather than agree with the hagiographic claim that Heschel was the ultimate scholar of Hasidism, we might do better to pay attention to the carefully judged conclusion of Seymour Siegel, who wrote, "Heschel's amazing mastery of the Hasidic sources, his enormous scholarly ability, and his natural sympathy and affinity bring him close to the 'scientific' study of that great movement."[91] He was indeed close to scientific study, and his contributions still play a role in that arena. This was not, however, his ultimate goal.

The most famous and perhaps the most significant contemporary debate on the meaning of Hasidism was the exchange between Martin Buber and Gershom Scholem.[92] Where does Abraham Heschel figure in relation to this debate?

Maurice Friedman has recorded two comments made by Heschel in the wake of Scholem's critique of Buber's approach: "Abraham Joshua Heschel was extremely distressed by the nature of these attacks. 'You know I do not like some of what Buber has done with *Hasidism*,' Heschel said to me, 'but whom else do we have like him?'" and [in response to a question from a group of African students whether they should study Scholem or Buber] "Heschel ... a scholar whose knowledge and understanding was second to none, said: 'No, if you want to know Hasidism as it was, begin with Buber.'"[93]

Inherent in these remarks is some of the complexity that characterized Heschel's relationship – both personal and intellectual – with each of these two figures. In both cases the preference for Buber is accompanied by a certain reservation; after all, one should *begin* with Buber but not necessarily settle for him.

Heschel's affinities with and differences from Buber regarding the essence of Hasidism have been well summarized by Even-Chen and Meir.[94] It is surprising that Heschel allowed his ambiguity towards the theology of Buber to be expressed in explicit form (quite a remarkable phenomenon, given Heschel's usual allusive style) in a Hasidic context. Towards the end of his last work Heschel launched this uncharacteristic frontal assault:

> Martin Buber's declaration "Nothing can make me believe in a God who punishes Saul because he did not murder his enemy" must be contrasted with the Kotzker's statement "A God whom any Tom, Dick, and Harry could comprehend I would not believe in."[95]

Heschel knew the insights of Hasidism at first hand and not through the prism of Buber's presentation. Steven Katz suggested that the differences between the two were not only a function of personal experience: "Buber's Hasidism, for all its splendor, is largely a this-worldly existentialism in Jewish dress. Alternatively, Heschel's Hasidism is something radically different, being closer to the authentic mood of Hasidic piety."[96]

Scholem believed that Martin Buber played a pivotal role in sensitizing a generation of Jews to the treasures of Hasidism. Heschel is hardly mentioned by Scholem in his published works, and there is evidence that in private he was less than complimentary about Heschel's gifts. Scholem's student Joseph Weiss criticized one of Heschel's essays on the grounds that while it was "unusually rich in material ... the author persistently [ignored] the principal questions first posed by G. Scholem."[97]

In his 1974 essay, "Reflections in Jewish Theology," Scholem applied a telling critique to both Buber and Heschel. He explicated a medieval kabbalistic approach to revelation as that which is constantly unfolding in history. This mystical theory builds upon the Talmudic motif of a voice calling forth from Sinai every day and ascribes to tradition the role of passing on the word of revelation throughout history.

Scholem asserted that "such a mystical conception of Revelation, which at the same time made possible an affirmation of Orthodox fundamentalism, was not something the nineteenth century could absorb or appreciate,"[98] and went on to claim that Kohler, Cohen, Rosenzweig, and indeed Buber all "polemicized against mysticism while borrowing its metaphors in case of need."[99]

In Scholem's reading, the advances of scholarship have forced modern Jewish theologians back to the old mystical language of an "inner word" or an "inner light" as the actual basis of all revelation, replacing the doctrine of Sinaitic revelation with the Holy Spirit. Scholem then commented that the existentialist theologians, "above all, Martin Buber and Abraham Joshua Heschel – employed their considerable eloquence for the purpose of evading this issue."[100] In placing Buber and Heschel in the same category, Scholem misread at least one of these thinkers. In both this and the previous chapter I argue that Heschel's engagement with the esoteric tradition was neither cursory nor evasive. He engaged with the theological challenges presented to tradition as a living part of that tradition.

Moshe Idel has suggested that Heschel represents a third sensibility, quite distinct from both Scholem and Buber, although closer to the latter in a number of ways. He set out a typological distinction between Buber and Scholem: the former's approach was phenomenological, the latter's historical; the former emphasized the experiential, the latter the theological. Buber related to the legends and Scholem to the homiletical writings. Buber's approach was more romantic, Scholem's, in essence, more critical.

Idel positioned Heschel within this Scholem-Buber schema:

> Though differing from these two schools in many ways, Abraham J. Heschel also emphasized the vital role of Hasidism for modern Judaism and portrayed it, sometimes in a way reminiscent of Buber, as representing the essence of Judaism. Less concerned than Scholem was with the historical aspects of the emergence of Hasidism, Heschel was more interested in it as a spiritual, rather than a mystical phenomenon; his expositions of Hasidism reflect a deep affinity both with the literary texts and with the Hasidic lived experience.[101]

It should be noted that Heschel saw himself as making a contribution to the history of the Circle of the Besht and was proud of the documents he had discovered.[102] He took issue, even if only implicitly, with some of Scholem's historical assumptions.[103] Nevertheless, Idel's judgment is fair: there needs to be another way of judging Heschel's own understanding of his project in researching the history of both early Hasidism and the Hasidic phenomenon in general.[104] Indeed, Moshe Idel's insight may be applied beyond the genre of Hasidism. His approach to scholarship offered a third way, blending profound textual affinity and expertise with a no less profound engagement with the immediate and the contemporary.

Spiritual Heir

So far we have paid attention to Heschel's explicit discussion of Hasidic teachings and sources. Surely, however, the impact of Hasidism on Heschel's thought extends far beyond these explicit references. Some attempts have been made to identify the areas in which Abraham Joshua Heschel's thought shows a particular debt to his Hasidic roots.[105] Drawing on his profound acquaintance with Hasidic literature and his reading of Heschel's prose and poetry, Arthur Green noted five areas where "Heschel's roots may be seen as significant."[106] He listed, first, a sense of "wonder as the key to religious consciousness," a central Heschelian trope. He proceeded to the notion of faith as a matter not of dry explication but rather of living testimony to the reality of faith; third, he mentioned the Hasidic emphasis on a "continuous unbroken relationship with the entire Jewish past"[107] rather than the notion of modernity as a radical break. His fourth insight was that the traditions of Hasidism brought to Heschel's work an emphasis on "charismatic leadership and its role in human religious community."[108] Finally, he emphasized Heschel's belief in the capacity of human activity to make a difference in the world, and indeed to affect God. Green demonstrated that Heschel empathized with an activist tendency to be found in certain Hasidic circles, and he linked that tendency with the prophets of the Bible.

This list of five dimensions of Hasidic impact – five ways in which Heschel was a spiritual (as well as genealogical) heir of Hasidism – is not exhaustive. A number of Heschel's theological terms also show evidence of their Hasidic origins. Moshe Idel suggested that some of these terms approximate Hasidic concepts, although a key to uncover these correspondences is not readily available.[109] He then went on to propose that the familiar Heschelian term *exaltation* might be identified with the Hasidic term *ha'ala'ah*. I want to consider this example and add some other terms that show traces of Hasidic provenance.

Exaltation

In the particular case of the term *exaltation*, Heschel did in fact offer a key. The chapter in *A Passion for Truth* entitled "Exaltation or

Self-Examination"[110] has a parallel in the Yiddish work in which exaltation is rendered as *hitpa'alut*.[111] In the theological lexicon he prepared
for his Cincinnati students in the early 1940s, the same term was translated as "affection, emotion," with no exaltation to be found. It is thus
evident that there was not a simple translation of terms at work.

Authenticity

Another important word for Heschel was *authenticity*. Typically, he understood the term very much in the tradition of Przysucha, Kotzk, and
Ger: to be witheringly honest with oneself, true to oneself in the fullest
sense.[112] There is a clear echo of this notion in *Who Is Man?*, a work almost wholly free of direct citations of sources: "Neither authenticity of
existence nor the equalities of being human are safe properties. They
are to be achieved, cultivated and protected. We often live pretentious-
ly, deceiving ourselves as others."[113]

Heschel clearly had this work in mind when he came to discuss the
Kotzkian conception of honesty. Quoting aphorisms from his earlier
book he stated,

> Truth is severe, harsh, demanding. We would rather hide our face in the
> sand than be confronted by it. "To live means to be indebted" – who wants
> to hear this? "I am commanded, therefore I am" – who knows how to cher-
> ish it?[114]

Here the distinction between Heschel's own theological voice and his
presentation of the concerns of the Hasidic master disappears.

Textpeople

Other terms and phrases common to Heschel's writings may be found
to have Hasidic origins or at least overtones. In a 1953 essay on Jewish
education Heschel declared, "What we need more than anything else is
not *textbooks* but *textpeople*. It is the personality of the teacher which is
the text the pupils read; the text that they will never forget."[115] Seven
years earlier a cousin of Heschel's, Rabbi Jacob Friedman of Husiatyn,
had declared that the teaching and the teacher form a whole and cited
the Ruzhin tradition according to which a person's deeds spoke more
than their teaching.[116]

Space and Time

There is significant disagreement on the influence exerted by Hasidic thought on Heschel's *The Sabbath*. Not all agree with the judgment of Reuven Kimelman that the "immediate precursors" of that work were *Kedushat Shabbat* of Rabbi Tzadok Hacohen of Lublin and the *Sefat Emet* of Rabbi Judah Leib Alter of Ger.[117] In an extended note at the end of an article about the approach of the *Sefat Emet* to the Sabbath, Yoram Jacobson took issue with the assumption that Heschel's thought grew out of Hasidic thinking.[118] Indeed, he employed the *Sefat Emet* as evidence of his assertion that Heschel's poetic rhetoric is profoundly at odds with Jewish tradition. He claimed that there is no basis in *Sefat Emet* (and by inference in the entire Hasidic tradition) for a key claim of *The Sabbath*: the superiority of the dimension of time over that of space.

It is a curious fact that the notes appended to Heschel's assertions of the primacy of time in Judaism refer to other comments made by Heschel himself.[119] For example, his statement that "Judaism is *a religion of history, a religion of time*"[120] is uncorroborated. In *Torah min Hashamayim* there is a hint that this preference for the dimension of time is an Ishmaelian perspective. In his attempt to interpret the notion that Moses saw the Divine Glory, Heschel's Ishmael translates the spatial concept of *Kavod* into the dimension of time, thus neutralizing the danger of rampant anthropomorphism.[121] However, this can hardly be considered a source for his sweeping statement that Judaism is a religion of time.

To the extent that Heschel invoked Jewish sources to bolster his axiom, these were not from the Hasidic or kabbalistic tradition. In a 1952 essay, written in response to criticism provoked by *The Sabbath*, he defended his thesis with (relatively scant) reference to rabbinic and medieval sources.[122] Of Hasidic prooftexts there are none. It is tempting to regard the privilege afforded to the dimension of time as a Heschelian innovation, a response to the conditions of modernity. Note, for example, Heschel's repeated insistence that "man transcends space, and time transcends man":[123] namely, that unlike the domain of space, time cannot be controlled or conquered; it can only be sanctified.

This is not the position stated repeatedly in *Sefat Emet*, in which time and space were regarded as two parallel dimensions, perhaps aspects of God, with the potential for certain individuals to exert their dominance over the realm of time.[124] The Children of Israel are above time; likewise, freedom is above time.[125] Time is not granted the unique status Heschel affords it.

If the primacy of time is not a motif drawn directly out of the Hasidic tradition, other aspects of his theory of time do imply such a provenance. Indeed, despite Jacobson's insistence that Heschel's views contradict those of the *Sefat Emet*, the very insistence on the significance of the Sabbath can be traced to Heschel's Hasidic background. The term "a palace in time" may be cited as an example of this influence. It certainly predated his experiences in North America, since we find the phrase, albeit in a different context, in a poem by Heschel published in 1933.[126] Reference to this same notion of the Sabbath as a palace can be found in Hasidic literature, for example in a teaching of Rabbi Tzadok Hacohen of Lublin, published in the year of Heschel's birth.[127]

The influence of Hasidism on the development of this particular tenet of Heschel's world view – namely Judaism as a religion of time – is not clear-cut or linear. I believe that in large part this emphasis was a corrective to the world of nationalism and capitalism in which Heschel found himself, and to which he wished to offer a counterbalance. Hence his insistence that

> the Bible is more concerned with time than with space. It sees the world in the dimension of time. It pays more attention to generations and events than to countries and things; it is more concerned with history than with geography. To understand the teaching of the Bible, one must accept its premise that time has a meaning for life which is at least equal to that of space, that time has a significance and sovereignty of its own.[128]

The phrase "at least equal" suggests the apologetic or corrective aspect of this remark. In a world in which domination of space, whether in the political or technological spheres, had the upper hand, Heschel was striving to emphasize the forgotten dimension – the holy dimension – of human existence.

The claim that Heschel's approach to time is foreign to the spirit of Hasidism is an exaggeration. In his championing of time, he implied the possibility of innovation and the potential of the sacred deed. It is an irony – but not a coincidence – that by the end of his life this champion of the eternal had become a hero of the contemporary.

The New

Another recurrent theme in Heschel's writings is *hiddush* (renewal or innovation), and in this case he left his reader in no doubt as to the source of his views on the subject. In a reflective mood, in the last year of his life, Heschel wrote,

> I seek to understand the present and the future while I disagree with those who think of the present in the past tense. I consider in my own intellectual existence that the greatest danger is to become obsolete. I try not to be stale, I try to remain young. I have one talent and that is the capacity to be tremendously surprised, surprised at life, at ideas. This is to me the supreme Hasidic imperative: Don't be old. Don't be stale. See life as all doors. Some are open, some are closed. You have to know how to open them.[129]

In a much earlier paean to Eastern European Jewry, Heschel had noted that in the Hasidic era the conservative notion of *yeridat ha-dorot*, the gradual descent of the generations, had been renounced. "Indeed ... there were Hasidim who believed that it was easier to attain the Holy Spirit in their own day than in the days of the *Tannaim*."[130] In *Search*, as was noted in the first chapter of this book, Heschel asserted "there are events which can never become past. Sacred history may be described as an attempt to overcome the dividing line of past and present, as an attempt *to see the past in the present tense*."[131] Heschel's own ancestor, Abraham Joshua Heschel of Apta, is quoted by his great-great-great-grandson in *Torah min Hashamayim* as saying that each person should see every day as if he himself were standing at Sinai. Future and past are human constructs, he wrote, but they are not properties of God, who gives the Torah to His people Israel on each and every day. God is described by the first Abraham Joshua Heschel as eternally present, and man is enjoined to relate to all time as the present. His descendant adopted and translated the teaching for his own purposes.[132]

The Self-Surpassing Individual

Unlike many of the leading voices in American Judaism in his day, Heschel emphasized the sphere of the individual: "The time has arrived to pay heed to the forgotten individual. Judaism is a personal problem."[133]

To a certain extent Heschel's emphasis on the individual was in response to opposite trends, such as Reconstructionism and Zionism, in the postwar Jewish world. His works on Kotzk devoted chapters to the theme of the individual, and it seems likely that the following reflection was deliberately laced with contemporary resonance:

Hasidism had become a mass trend, threatened with spiritual enfeeble-
ment, even trivialization. The only possibility of renewal, thought the
Kotzker, lay in the reinstatement of the individual's role. The movement
that had come into being through stress of the personal aspect of Judaism
could be reborn only by an emphasis on individualism.[134]

Heschel inherited from Hasidism a concern for the struggle of the
individual to overcome the challenges of the ego and to reach outward
and upward. Shai Held made this issue of personal transcendence a
central motif in a recent work uncovering a highly significant aspect of
Heschel's theology.[135] In my view this individualism is further evidence
of the profound impact of Hasidism on Heschel's world view.

Many of the Hasidic sources cited and quoted in *Search* relate to the
personal realm.[136] This theme of the struggle with the self runs throughout the book, and is most prominent in chapter 38, "The Problem of
Integrity." Towards the end of the book, having established the theory of
the mitzvah, Heschel turned his attention to the obstructions and challenges that confront any person who endeavours to practice mitzvot.

Considering the challenge of altruism, Heschel turned to the literature of Hasidism as he described the trap of pride, which can threaten
the pious man as he wrestles with his ego.[137] The Hasidic voice falls silent for the rest of the chapter until its final section, entitled "The Failure
of the Heart," where it assumes the dominant role: Jacob Aaron of
Zalshin, Jacob Joseph of Polonnoye, Isaac Meir of Ger, and Kalonymus
Kalman Epstein are all marshalled as part of Heschel's description of
the struggle against the ego. He closed the chapter with the following
teaching, in the name of another Hasidic sage, from Epstein's work:
"Moses' saying to Israel, "I stand between God and you" (Deuteronomy
5:5), was allegorically interpreted by Rabbi Michael of Zlotshov to
mean: *The 'I' stands between God and man*."[138]

A comment made in a 1962 paper on Jewish education offered a tan-
talizing clue to Heschel's indebtedness to the Hasidic tradition in his
understanding of the individual and the personal. "Personal meaning
is meaningless," he wrote, "unless it is related to transpersonal meaning." At the end of that paragraph he continued, "The problem of man
is the greatest problem, or ought to be the greatest problem of man
himself. The essence of Hasidism has consistently been misunderstood
in this respect. The essence of Hasidism is *arbeten oif zich*."[139]

The Yiddish term is left untranslated here. It means "to work on one's
self," and it is the subject of a fascinating chapter at the beginning of the

ch. 4

fourth chapter of Heschel's Yiddish work on Kotzk. That section also includes an extensive discussion of the notion of individualism as understood by the Kotzker. It is remarkable that very little of this section is to be found in the parallel English work.

In *Kotzk* Heschel develops the notion that a Hasid is constantly at work on his own person, constantly engaged in study and prayer, perennially occupied by the process of self-transcendence.

Heschel's concern for the issue of prayer is itself indicative of the influence of Hasidism, and here too the normative preference for the communal in preference to the individual is undermined in a manner highly reminiscent of Hasidic writing.[140] Each person is understood to be a protagonist in the great drama, the great struggle of prayer.

Not every aspect of Heschel's work can be read as a direct translation of Hasidic attitudes. The strident particularism of most Hasidic literature is at odds with Heschel's no less strident universalistic tendencies. In my reading, he broke sharply with the common Hasidic trope of the insignificance or insidiousness of the non-Jew. It is possible, however, that even here he found some inspiration within certain Hasidic approaches. For example, in the tradition of Ruzhin, part of his own pedigree, the *zaddik* of the generation is obliged to pray for all humanity.[141]

Abraham Joshua Heschel was born and buried as a Hasidic prince. In the intervening years he travelled far from the aesthetic, political, and cultural emphasis of Hasidism. But in important ways he never left. His unwavering self-examination and passion for truth, his unending quest for exaltation, his sense of being confronted by God at every moment, his capacity for surprise – in these and other important ways, he was always the man his tombstone proclaimed him to be, the man foreshadowed by the bar mitzvah boy wrapped in the phylacteries of his ancestor Levi Isaac of Berditchev: a scion, a scholar, an heir.

Chapter Seven

An Affinity of Strangers

In his very last work Abraham Joshua Heschel suggested a startling link between the Danish thinker Søren Kierkegaard (1813–1855) and the Hasidic sage Menahem Mendel Morgenstern, the Kotzker Rebbe (1787–1859).

Describing this connection as an "affinity of strangers,"[1] Heschel did not posit a line of influence running from one of these contemporaries to the other. Rather, he claimed that the comparable elements in the work of these two men "must have been elicited by requisites inherent in their respective traditions."[2] The affinity between Kierkegaard and the Kotzker is an expression of commonalities between Christianity and Judaism rather than evidence of spiritual plagiarism.[3] By the same token, differences in their understanding of human existence were "rooted in the fundamental differences between Judaism and Christianity."[4]

Heschel's decision to highlight the parallels between two religious figures who, though roughly contemporary, inhabited distinct and unrelated universes of discourse, was not intended to imply that the traditions from which these two men emerged were identical. Heschel maintained that there was "not one but many philosophies, and the divergence between Aristotle and Augustine, the Stoics and the thinkers of India is just as real as the divergence between Moses and Buddha."[5]

However, he also asserted that there were "many creeds but only one faith."[6] Rather than seeing these statements as contradictory, he maintained that both were true. Citing "profound differences in perspective and substance" between Judaism and Christianity, he nonetheless asserted that "parochialism [had] become untenable."[7] Arguing for a core resonance between Kierkegaard and the Kotzker, of for that matter between Reinhold Niebuhr and himself,[8] Heschel asserted affinity not identity.

The comparison of two figures divided by culture and religion was not only a statement of faith. It was also a strategy. By pointing to a link between two men not usually thought of in the same context, Heschel created an analogy. He assumed that most readers of his English works would have more prior acquaintance with the Dane than with the Pole.

In this particular case it is not difficult to demonstrate the tactical or rhetorical dimension of the inclusion of Kierkegaard. Heschel wrote two works about the Kotzker Rebbe in the final months of his life. The Yiddish version mentions the Danish thinker only in passing;[9] the work leans on Hasidic literature and compares the Kotzker with other giants of the Hasidic movement. We might imagine that Heschel was looking for a parallel within Western culture to help him explain the often brusque and misanthropic tone of the Kotzker to a Westernized audience.

There are thus both substantive and rhetorical dimensions to the inclusion of non-Jewish thinkers and their works and concepts in Heschel's work. In a variety of citations, quotations, and mentions, he uncovered parallels and highlighted differences. We will examine some key examples of this phenomenon to be found in his writing, most particularly in *God in Search of Man*. Our primary question is this: To what ends does he marshal an array of references and allusions from Buddha to Berdyaev, and from Lucretius to Schopenhauer?

Before we embark on an examination of Heschel's extensive receptiveness to non-Jewish authorities, it is instructive to note that one of his major works, though replete with citations from Jewish literature, is all but devoid of non-Jewish voices. The three volumes of *Torah min Hashamayim* span more than 900 pages and include thousands of references. Almost all of them are from within Jewish literature, and the rare exceptions are themselves revealing. In some cases, scholars like G.F. Moore are cited by dint of their expertise in the field of classical Judaism.[10] A number of references to the New Testament are to be found scattered throughout the work, although their role is in essence historical – they illustrate the views of early Christianity, usually as a contrast to Rabbinic Judaism.[11] More frequently, experts in Christianity, Islam, and Hellenistic thought are cited in discussions peripheral to the main emphasis of the book.[12] To an overwhelming extent, however, one is struck by the absence of these sources in the Hebrew work.[13] It is designed to be a *sefer*, a book of Jewish learning in the traditional mode, and the wisdom of other peoples is consigned to the margins. Elsewhere in his writing, a different picture emerges.

As examples of the opposite tendency in Heschel's writing, the two iterations of his work on prophecy are instructive. Already in *Die Prophetie* Heschel introduced a pantheon of thinkers and scholars from around the world, most of whom offered a contrast to the peculiar contours of the Hebrew spirit. Either in this capacity, or occasionally in a different context, there is frequent mention of Aristotle and Plato as well as great modern German scholars such as Hugo Gressmann and Max Dessoir. In the same pages we also find Diogenes Laertius, Goethe, William Blake, Dante, Descartes, Homer, Plutarch, and a host of others. This trend is continued and accentuated in *The Prophets*, published almost thirty years later, where many of these sources are repeated along with many new references.

In *God in Search of Man* there are almost two hundred quotations and citations of a range of non-Jewish thinkers and scholars from antiquity to modern times. Only the Bible and rabbinic literature are more intensively quoted. The presence of non-Jewish texts is particularly strong in the early parts of the book; the more pronounced the Jewish message of the work becomes, the less prominent these other sources.

It is interesting to reflect on the wider phenomenon of reference to non-Jewish sources in the canon of modern Jewish thought. A comparison of *Search* with a later work of liberal theology, Eugene Borowitz's *Renewing the Covenant*, reveals that Borowitz, both here and elsewhere, referred to thinkers from outside Jewish tradition more frequently than those from within.[14] The same could certainly not be said of Heschel, whose work is suffused with Jewish texts from every era. The philosophers and scholars of the West and elsewhere are neither the benchmark by which the veracity of Heschel's statements is measured nor their inspiration.

Support and Polemic

Heschel's use of sources from beyond his core canon of normative Jewish literature took different forms and served different purposes. On occasion, he invoked scholars and sages from outside Jewish tradition, either as support for his original assertions or as a complement to Jewish authorities. His observation, for example, that "to believe is to remember" appeared as an unelucidated aphorism in some of his early works,[15] while in *Man Is Not Alone* this statement is amplified and even justified by the inclusion of a quotation from Carl Jung.[16] A section on beauty in *Search* is crowned by two excerpts from poems by Wordsworth.[17]

Some hermeneutical latitude was occasionally needed to suit a source to his purposes. For example, in the chapter "The Problem of Evil" in *Search*, Heschel argued for the existence of "a supreme distinction" between good and evil which "counts as much as the distinction between life and death."[18] In support of this contention, he quoted three paragraphs from Henri Bergson's *The Two Sources of Morality and Religion*, the nub of which is that in contrast to the impotence of mere philosophy, the indignant resistance of the Hebrew prophets to injustice reaches down through the generations.

In its original context, however, Bergson saw the Hebrew prophets as the precursor to the coming of Christ.[19] Bergson's idea has been altered radically and made to conform with Heschel's approach to the question of prophecy. The second stage of this historical process (which Bergson considered crucial), namely the universalizing of the prophetic quest for justice, which he attributed to Christianity, is quite absent from Heschel's presentation of Bergson's insight. Thus is Bergson "Judaized" and rendered appropriate for Heschel's purposes.

Here and elsewhere the function of the non-Jewish reference is to shore up Heschel's argument, but in some cases, individuals are mentioned and works cited with the opposite purpose. For example, in the introduction to *Torah min Hashamayim*, he lambasted the opinion that the Jews of old were incapable of abstract thinking and in a footnote censured the approach of the theologian Paul Fiebig. Here is an explicit case of mention for polemical purposes.[20]

Nowhere is the polemical application of non-Jewish sources more explicit than in the chapter entitled "Comparisons and Contrasts" in *The Prophets*. Expanding on *Die Prophetie*, this chapter propounds the notion that the prophetic theology of pathos is unique, using counter-examples from Greek, Roman, Hindu, Tao, Buddhist, Mesopotamian, Egyptian, and Muslim traditions. The chapter represents an example of apologetic polemics of a traditional kind.[21]

Mainstream Christianity is notable for its absence in this litany of unflattering parallels, but elsewhere Heschel presented Christianity in a polemical light. In a telling section towards the end of *Search*, he discussed a motif running from Paul through Luther, Ritschl, Barth, and Kierkegaard (who, as previously noted, was later to appear in spiritual affinity with the Kotzker). All of these men promoted a notion antithetical to the spirit of Judaism. They proclaimed that faith alone was the path to redemption, while "Judaism [stressed] the relevance of human deeds."[22] While Heschel's contribution to interreligious dialogue has been justly celebrated, it can be seen that Heschel populated his works with a broad range of thinkers and scholars from outside Jewish literature, not only as supporting witnesses but also as polemical foils.

Shorthand Points of Reference

On occasion Heschel brought short quotations from a variety of sources in order to evoke an entire literature or to provide a taste of the approach being described. An example from *Search* has Heschel quoting from two plays by Sophocles and Seneca's *Hippolytus*, as well as Shakespeare's *King Lear* and *Cymbeline*.[23] He used these literary references to exemplify an attitude to nature, which he contrasted with that evinced by biblical man. The literature of the world is presented here as a foil and perhaps also as evidence of Heschel's mastery and appreciation of Western tradition. By citing these sources he honoured them, just as he expressed his opposition to them.

As well as such use of the short evocative quotation, Heschel displayed a tendency to mention great figures from Western culture in passing rather than reference their work. This practice served to situate the author within a certain cultural milieu and to have the individuals cited serve as what Martin Jay has described as "convenient shorthand points of reference."[24]

An extreme example of this can be found in *Man's Quest for God*, where Heschel warned the reader to "beware lest we reduce Bible to literature, Jewish observance to good manners, the Talmud to Emily Post,"[25] thus contrasting the sublime with the trivial. The twentieth-century doyenne of etiquette is used as a symbol, not because Heschel harboured an animus towards her, but rather in order to criticize the tendency of urbane and sophisticated Jewish circles to disembowel and sanitize Judaism.

At the other extreme are references to Beethoven in *God in Search of Man*. Discussing the relationship between process and event he wrote,

A process occurs in the physical order. But not all events are reducible to physical terms. The life of Beethoven left music behind; yet valued in physical terms its effects on the world were felt less than the effect of a normal rainstorm or an earthquake.[26]

When questioning whether the prophets could be taken seriously by the contemporary person, Heschel commented, "An aspiring composer would not compare Beethoven with himself but compare himself with Beethoven."[27]

By his own admission, Heschel took music very seriously.[28] And Beethoven is used here as an exemplar of excellence and profundity. Be it Emily Post or Ludwig van Beethoven, the purpose of this technique of mentioning would seem to be the demarcation of common cultural ground between author and reader.

Whether it be in a mention en passant or a more substantial referential gesture, some giants of world culture are employed by Heschel to underline his assertions, while others are presented as undermining them. One might imagine that particular thinkers would consistently play either a positive or a negative role in Heschel's work, but this is not always the case. His Schopenhauer, for example, is he "who made popular the idea that the Bible had no awareness of the problem of evil."[29] It would be reasonable to assume that Heschel would not use Schopenhauer, an enemy of the Bible in his description, to support any of his arguments. However, he quoted from the Supplements to *The World as Will and Representation* in support of his contention that wonder was an essential part of the philosophical enterprise.[30] With very rare exceptions, there are no unmitigatedly negative figures in Heschel's pantheon; that distinction goes in fact to a Jew, whose case will be discussed below.

Philosophers from Plato to Dewey

Some individuals played a particularly important role in Heschel's work. They loom large in his landscape, either as blights or landmarks, or both. As noted above, he was capable of adducing a thinker as both a buttress for his own argument and a butt of his disapproval.

It is informative to consider some of the appearances made by Plato and Aristotle, both separately and as a pair, in Heschel's work. There are certainly cases in which these giants of classical thought filled a supporting role. Plato was adduced as an additional reference to illustrate a point made in *Search* with recourse to Maimonides's *Guide* and the Zohar. In that note[31] Heschel directed the reader to one of Plato's Epistles, the same one quoted earlier in the main body of the text.[32]

Earlier in the same work, however, Heschel stated, "Hebrew thinking operates within categories different from those of Plato or Aristotle."[33] Examples of this tendency to present these Greek philosophers as the epitome of a non-Hebraic approach can also be found in *Who Is Man?*, where Aristotle is presented as the source of the tendency to define man in relation to the animal kingdom. An array of sources is cited in support of this assertion.[34]

Aristotle's notion of God as the *primum movens immobile* is employed by Heschel in *Die Prophetie* and thereafter in order to emphasize the profound distinction between the Greek and biblical world views. As Fritz Rothschild observed in his introduction to Heschel's theology, "The pathetic God as distinguished from the God of Aristotle is not the Unmoved Mover but the *Most Moved Mover*."[35]

The fluidity displayed in the marshalling of Plato and Aristotle both for and against Heschel's understanding of the spirit of Judaism is best exemplified by Plato's Socrates.[36] *The Apology* is mentioned in *Search* to illustrate a verse from Job on the theme of human ignorance.[37] If Socrates is in tune with Job here, we later find him at loggerheads with Moses:

> Greek philosophy began in a world without God. It could not accept the gods or the example of their conduct. Plato had to break with the gods and to ask: What is good? Thus the problem of values was born. And it was the idea of values that took the place of God. Plato lets Socrates ask: What is good? But Moses' question was: What does God require of thee?[38]

In *Search*, Plato is used to embellish a Heschelian phrase on at least one occasion,[39] and both Plato and Aristotle are mentioned prominently and frequently early in the book.[40] These references later taper off, indicating that they have already served their function.

The use of Immanuel Kant furnishes another example of Heschel's willingness to invoke a thinker for various purposes and not simply as a friend or foe. Kant appears most frequently in a polemical light. Heschel rarely expressed vigorous opposition to Kant, but he was not slow to point out what he considered to be the crucial differences between Kantianism and normative Judaism.[41] For example, "'What ought I to do?' is according to Kant the basic question in ethics. Ours, however, is a more radical, a meta-ethical approach."[42]

Elsewhere in *Search*, Kant's *Critique of Aesthetic Judgment* is quoted extensively in order to depict an approach to the sublime which Heschel considered inadequate;[43] the Kantian axiom "I ought, therefore I can" is rejected or reformulated by Judaism;[44] and the emphasis by "Kant and his disciples" on pure intention with no regard for deeds or outcomes is ascribed in origin to Paul and emphatically rejected by Heschel.[45]

In fact, most of Heschel's references to Kant are in a critical or polemical context. In the section entitled "The Sublime and the Beautiful" in *Search*, Heschel devoted some time to expounding the views of Burke and Kant on the nature of the sublime. He subsequently baldly stated that the "meaning of the sublime and its perception, we believe, was not adequately described in these theories."[46] Later in the same work, Kant's attempt to undermine the ontological proofs for the existence of God is referenced, as Heschel reframed the Kantian discussion of the idea of having one hundred dollars.[47]

If in these examples, Kant's views are the object of Heschel's critique, elsewhere in *Search* he quoted Kant with enthusiasm. A long quotation from the preface to *The Critique of Pure Reason* appears in the first chapter in direct support of Heschel's contention that religion must not be excused from the rigours of critical examination.[48] Similarly, the chapter "Wonder" concludes with an entire paragraph from *The Critique of Practical Reason*, containing the famous formulation "the starry heavens above and the moral law within."[49]

In *God in Search of Man*, then, as indeed elsewhere in Heschel's work, Kant is a significant figure. There is little surprise in this. After all, the modern world, which both attracted and distressed him, was in large measure a world imagined by, or at least ushered in, by Kant. In *A Passion for Truth* Kierkegaard is lauded for turning away from the notion of the abstract self, a concept which Heschel associated with Descartes and Kant.[50] Kant, I believe, came to represent a certain philosophical sensibility for which Heschel held respect, but about which he also harboured doubts and fears.

Later thinkers also feature in Heschel's web of citations and references. The case of John Dewey is instructive in this regard. An allusion to the thought of Dewey was already to be found in one of Heschel's earliest English essays, his 1942 article "The Quest for Certainty in Saadia's Philosophy," a play on the title of Dewey's 1929 work, *The Quest for Certainty*. Heschel's discussion of the shortcomings of medieval religious rationalism can also be seen as a broadside aimed at a leading non-metaphysical philosophical approach. In *Search* he was more explicit still, quoting Dewey's view that rationalism precludes religious faith in order to ridicule this form of extreme rationalism.[51]

In his work on prayer Heschel launched an assault against the curricula of institutions such as the Jewish Theological Seminary, his own place of employment, and here the technique of mentioning characters in order to evoke a certain mindset is exemplified to good effect:

In the modern seminaries for the training of rabbis and teachers the art of understanding what prayer implies was not part of the curriculum. And so it is not the Psalmist, Rabbi Jehudah Halevi, Rabbi Isaiah Horovitz or Rabbi Nachman of Bratslav; it is Hegel, Freud, or Dewey who have become our guides in matters of prayer and God.[52]

Later in the same work he remarked that we are not ready to amend the beginning of the silent prayer to read "Blessed be It, the Supreme Concept, the God of Spinoza, Dewey and Alexander."[53] In both lists we find John Dewey linked with thinkers about whom Heschel displayed ambivalence at best. Dewey is also implicated in the attempt to undermine the philosophical bona fides of such giants as Philo and Bergson.[54] The overall impression is that John Dewey represents an approach that Heschel acknowledges as highly influential – but firmly rejects.

Jews outside the Canon: Einstein and Freud, Spinoza and Mendelssohn

In 1958 Heschel offered the following reflection, in which he mentions several harbingers of modernity who hailed from a Jewish background:

> We are proud of our contributions to modern civilization. But many of these were contributions we made as men of the Western world. Where are the contributions of Judaism itself to modern civilization? How different the world would have been if Heine had been imbued with the spirit of the psalmist, Marx with the spirit of the prophets, and Freud with the spirit of the Ba'al Shem.[55]

In this statement Heschel bemoaned the levels of alienation from Jewish culture exemplified by these great modern Jews. Elsewhere he was engaged in more explicit polemical encounter with Jewish symbols of modernity. In September 1940 a paper by Albert Einstein entitled "Science and Religion" was read at a conference held at the Jewish Theological Seminary in New York. Heschel was not yet a member of the seminary faculty, and he had no formal role in the conference. Nevertheless, so scandalized was he by Einstein's rejection of the notion of a personal God that he took issue with the scientist. As Heschel's biographer has noted, Heschel's response to Einstein "initiated his lifelong campaign against secularized religion."[56] Challenged by critics to defend some of the key notions of *The Sabbath*, Heschel published an essay in 1952 in which he discussed some of Einstein's concepts, albeit less severely. Rather than attacking Einstein, he was keen to demonstrate that "space and time mean something totally different in philosophy and religion from what they mean in physics."[57]

However much respect Heschel displayed towards the great scientist, his true colours were on display in a 1963 Yiddish interview in which he declared that "for me personally, the Baal Shem Tov is much more important than Einstein."[58]

There is only one figure who was consistently presented as an adversary and for whom more disdain than respect was displayed: Baruch Spinoza. Heschel's overt opprobrium towards Spinoza was unparalleled, and it deserves close attention. In *God in Search of Man* he is named in only two chapters, and in both he is accused of spurning the Bible and discrediting Judaism: "The father of the depreciation of the intellectual relevance of the Bible is Spinoza, who may be blamed for many distorted views of the Bible in subsequent philosophy and exegesis."[59]

Heschel argued that Mendelssohn had adopted many of Spinoza's key assumptions, despite being "a zealous opponent of Spinoza's metaphysical theories and profoundly different from him in motivation and intention."[60] As a result, Spinoza's view of Judaism came to dominate both in influential non-Jewish circles and within the Jewish world itself. The influence of Spinoza and Mendelssohn is seen by Heschel as the root cause of the retreat from the Bible in secular society and the disproportionate emphasis on Judaism as law within Jewish circles.

When did Heschel's attitude to Spinoza crystallize? It is important to remember that he was taught in Berlin by Julius Guttmann, whose 1931 essay on Spinoza and Mendelssohn is credited in *Search* as proof of Spinoza's influence on Mendelssohn.[61] Already in *Die Prophetie* the figure of Spinoza is represented as an opponent of the integrity of the prophets. After all, if Spinoza's understanding of the affects as confused ideas is correct,[62] then the insights of the prophets are nothing more than errors, and the Heschelian notion of pathos and sympathy has no validity.

The role played by Mendelssohn in *Search* is worthy of note. He is presented as an unwitting cause of the spread of Spinoza's approach to the Bible and Judaism, particularly in the non-Jewish world. The work of Julius Guttmann on this theme is credited as proving the influence of the *Tractatus* on Mendelssohn, despite the efforts of Isaac Heinemann to argue otherwise.[63] This thesis enabled Heschel to portray Mendelssohn as an unwitting accomplice to the crime against Judaism perpetrated by Baruch Spinoza. There is no engagement with the thought of Mendelssohn beyond this characterization, and indeed there is compelling evidence to suggest that Heschel quoted him from a secondary source: it seems clear that he copied the *Jerusalem* quotation from the *Jewish Encyclopaedia*.[64]

All in all, in the brief appearances made in *Search*, Mendelssohn features as a foil or an accomplice, rather than as a thinker with whom Heschel engaged on a profound level. The reasons for Mendelssohn's presentation of Judaism as law are not discussed by Heschel.[65] In short, while Mendelssohn is represented in *Search* as something of a dupe, Spinoza appears throughout Heschel's work as nothing but a rogue.

It is possible to chart a progression in Heschel's writings on Spinoza, although it is unclear if his opinion changed,[66] or if rather he became bolder in articulating that which he had always believed. As mentioned in the chapter on Maimonides above, in a 1948 essay Heschel described Spinoza as the best modern exemplar of the Sephardi mentality. He cited Spinoza's "aristocratic intellectualism" as an example and continued,

> God is conceived of as a principle of mathematical necessity, a sort of logical shell in which all things exist; logical thinking alone can bring men into a relation with God. Personalism of any kind is excluded. It is remarkable how limited was the influence of Spinoza's philosophy even upon those Jewish thinkers who departed from religious tradition.[67]

Given the nature of this critique, it is all the more remarkable that Heschel should see in Spinoza the modern embodiment of the Sephardi sensibility. The emphasis on the soulless pursuit of logic is continued in *The Sabbath*, where Spinoza appears to deprecate time: "time to Spinoza is merely an accident of motion, a mode of thinking. And his desire to develop a philosophy *more geometrico*, in the manner of geometry, which is the science of space, is significant of his space-mindedness."[68]

Bearing in mind that in this work the time-space distinction is used to delineate the boundary between Jewish and non-Jewish thinking, it is no surprise that in an essay appearing shortly after *The Sabbath* Heschel asserted that Spinoza would have been quite aware he was placing himself beyond the pale of traditional Jewish thought: it was Spinoza who taught that space or extension was an attribute of God, in other words, that God was not immaterial. He knew well that in this he was breaking with the views of his predecessors and with the authoritative Jewish sources.[69]

It is in *God in Search of Man* that the presentation of Spinoza as a major factor in the de-biblicization of the West first appeared in Heschel's writings. Crediting Hermann Cohen and Julius Guttmann, he argued in *Search* that Spinoza's view of Judaism as Law spread to Mendelssohn and from him to Kant and beyond. In a 1958 essay he attributed the general perception that Judaism has no theology to Spinoza:

> In his effort to discredit Judaism, Spinoza advanced the thesis that the Bible has nothing to say to the intellect. It was in the spirit of Spinoza that the slogan was created: Judaism has no theology. As a result, modern Jewish scholarship, with very few exceptions, neglected the field of inquiry into the world of Jewish thought.[70]

Some ten years later, in a conversation with school principals, Heschel told his audience that when he was working on *Man Is Not Alone*, a "very distinguished Jewish scholar" warned him off any involvement with divinity or theology. The unnamed scholar told him that a Jew does not touch such material. This is how Heschel explains the "very typical" response of his interlocutor:

> Historically this goes back to Spinoza. Spinoza was the man who attempted to destroy Jewish theology. He found many admirers and they followed him. I discuss this in the early part of *God in Search of Man*. He claimed that the Bible, as such, has nothing relevant to say regarding philosophy and ideas. The Bible was not theology. It is law. And his concept was, paradoxically, taken over by Moses Mendelssohn. He must have grasped the situation existing in the Western world, that throughout the seventeenth and the eighteenth century there was only one book written about Judaism, and that was the *Tractatus*, by Spinoza. Since it was the only book available on Judaism in the Western language, it has had the most profound impact on Christians and on Jews alike. It is evident when studying Kant or Hegel, that whatever they have to say concerning Judaism was derived from the *Tractatus*. Paradoxically, Moses Mendelssohn was profoundly influenced by this book and by its approach. Moses Mendelssohn's influence upon Jews, in turn, was enormous. Thus, a system was developed whereby Judaism was Halakhah, Law – nothing else. This tremendous importance place [sic] on Halakhah, I heard not in Warsaw where I grew up, but suddenly, in Berlin. Here was a kind of system based only on Halakhah, as if Halakhah could exist by itself – without Aggadah, without Jewish theology.[71]

Heschel's Spinoza is held responsible for a multitude of misdemeanors. He represents the triumph of Sephardi symmetry over Ashkenazi passion; the accusation of prophetic error over the acknowledgment of prophetic authenticity;[72] the dissemination of an inaccurate picture of Judaism to Western culture; the domination by Western European intellectuals of the Eastern European sensibility; the deprecation of the realm of Aggadah, understood as inwardness or as theology; and more.[73]

There is evidence that Heschel saw traces of the Spinozan heresy in Mordecai Kaplan. In order to uncover this link, we need to consider an example of Heschel's technique of hinting. In a section on agnosticism in *Man's Quest for God*, Heschel launched a barely concealed assault on the rising popularity of Kaplan's views in the American Jewish community in the 1950s: "There are some people who believe that the only way to revitalize the synagogue is to minimize the importance of prayer and to convert the synagogue into a social center."[74]

The footnote to this comment instructs the reader to see *Shabbat* 31b. No further information is added, and it is reasonable to assume that most of Heschel's audience passed over this somewhat enigmatic reference. At the start of the first volume of *Torah min Hashamayim*, there is a similar Talmudic reference, but the object of his disapproval is different:

> It was Spinoza who established in Israel the rule that Judaism is not a law but rather law, halacha. This "rule" has circulated in the bloodstream of modern thought like a snakebite ... It is not only Derekh Eretz which precedes the Torah – it is also faith.[75]

Here Heschel quoted a saying from the very end of *Shabbat* 31a and the beginning of 31b. It is this saying that Heschel had in mind in his attack on Jewish agnosticism, and it appears again in *God in Search of Man* in the section entitled "Torah Is More Than Law":

> The Persians had no way of distinguishing between religion and law. In Judaism even the word Torah is not all-inclusive. "A man who has Torah but no *yirat shamayim* (awe and fear of God) is like a treasurer who was given the keys to the inner chamber but not the keys to the outer chamber."[76]

In *Torah min Hashamayim* Heschel continued the quotation to include Rabbi Yannai's declaration: "Shame for the person who has no courtyard but makes a gateway for the courtyard!" Perhaps this is Heschel's judgment on a synagogue without prayer: it is a gateway to nowhere. By charting the deployment of this Talmudic saying, a subterranean link between Kaplan and Spinoza is revealed, at least in Heschel's consciousness. They each lack an essential prerequisite – faith in God above nature – and for this reason their views are to be rejected. Kaplan and Spinoza may possess keys to the intellect, but they lack keys to the spiritual dimension. In fact, the personal relationship between Heschel and Kaplan was devoid of hostility, and their personal correspondence shows evidence of warmth. Nevertheless, the theological position adopted by Kaplan was sharply (if indirectly) rejected.

Ciphers, foils, symbols, exemplars, and bugbears – these and other roles are played by the figures from outside Heschel's Jewish canon who populate many of his works. He read broadly and regarded spiritual classics and scholarly masterpieces as indispensable. Nonetheless, in almost all of his writings these works are relegated to one or other of these secondary roles. He did not believe that his readers were in need of his invitation to taste of the riches of world culture. Heschel's role was to bring the many layers of Jewish tradition into the conversation.

The attitudes he adopted to some Jewish voices outside normative Jewish tradition, sometimes subtly polemical or overtly combative, fits into a long tradition of discourse between Jewish traditions. His animosity towards Spinoza was more tribal than it was philosophical. Spinoza had misrepresented the essence of Judaism to Jews and Christians alike, and in opposing him, Heschel was opposing the tendency to a reductionism which might leave Judaism desiccated, caricatured, and abandoned.

Where Heschel differed from much of the tradition which preceded him was in his openness to an experience of what he termed "depth theology," which transcends dogmas and labels. In his encounters with theological students, meditative communities, activists, and others, Heschel's sense of deep connectedness to persons capable of sympathizing with the divine pathos went beyond denominational demarcations. While he set for himself the task of promoting the unique voice of "biblical man" in the wider world, the notion of the chosenness of the Jews was also one that was severely downplayed, and even occasionally contradicted, in his writings.[77]

The Amber and the Bee: Tradition and Immediacy

At the start of this book, a question was posed: What is the relationship between Heschel's repeated emphasis on elemental unmediated human responses to God's call on the one hand and his intensive references to the sources of Jewish tradition on the other? I hope that the ensuing chapters have demonstrated the depth and richness of Heschel's engagement with almost every era of Jewish literature. In this chapter we have observed that he was motivated by both affinity and a sense of contrast to extend his world of references to include sources from beyond the contours of Jewish culture. However, no text from outside Jewish tradition serves a role comparable to that of the Bible, the Talmud, Maimonides, or the Hasidic masters.

The intensity of citation has been demonstrated, but its motivation is more elusive. Why, indeed, did Heschel feel the need to evoke immediacy through reference? He posited a reciprocal relationship of dependence between the tradition and the individual. Each needs the other to be sustained and enhanced. The idea of unbridled, unmediated, unreflective self-expression and encounter was not an ideal for him. Nor was the prospect of adherence to a dry creed.

In *Man Is Not Alone*, Heschel offered a metaphor designed to illustrate the relationship between the immediacy of faith and the solidity of doctrine. I believe it may also offer an insight into his understanding of the relationship between the encounter of the individual and the referential framework offered by tradition:

> Are dogmas unnecessary? We cannot be in rapport with the reality of the divine except for rare, fugitive moments. How can these moments be saved for the long hours of functional living, when the thoughts that feed like bees on the inscrutable desert us and we lose both the sight and the drive? Dogmas are like amber in which bees, once alive, are embalmed, and which are capable of being electrified when our minds become exposed to the power of the ineffable. For the problems we must always grapple with are: How to communicate those rare moments of insight to all hours of our life? How to commit intuition to concepts, the ineffable to words, communion to rational understanding? How to convey our insights to others and to unite in a fellowship of faith? It is the creed that attempts to answer these problems.[78]

In order to communicate rare moments of insight to ourselves and to others, we turn to tradition in which the inspiration of generations is encased, as amber embalms the bee. Is it a coincidence that the Greek term for amber is *elektron*? The immediacy and power of an encounter with the ineffable can activate the fossilized material, since it is of its essence. Heschel shrouded most of his writing with texts and allusions for a variety of reasons, including his wish to establish his own bona fides. Above all, in so doing he was expressing his approach to the interplay between the present and the past. Asserting the essential identity of current spiritual events with the experience of our ancestors allows them to be released from their embalmed state, and our own experience can reach out beyond its evanescence.

It should not be forgotten that in the latter years of his life, men and women of many faiths who displayed spiritual depth and moral courage became Heschel's friends and allies. Men like Reinhold Niebuhr and Martin Luther King became more than comrades. He identified their encounter with the challenges of the age, while expressed through the prism of different creedal commitments, as comprising the same purity and the same essence he saw in his own tradition. Through his affinity with these men, they were transformed from abstract strangers to living prooftexts.

Having considered Heschel's reading of sources in a systematic way, we turn now to examples of tradition in action, of the past in encounter with the present, of the interplay between the bee and the amber.

Chapter Eight

Heschel's *Aspaklaria*

"Heschelisms" and Why They Matter

Abraham Joshua Heschel is famous for a string of expressions with which he is uniquely associated. A partial list of these expressions would include many of the titles of his books – "God in search of man," "an echo of eternity," "a passion for truth," "the insecurity of free-dom," and more – as well as a number of phrases which have made their way into the vocabulary of contemporary spirituality and Jewish thought: divine pathos, radical amazement, a palace in time, the inef-fable, diversity as the will of God, the guilt of some contrasted with the responsibility of all, moral grandeur and spiritual audacity, and a host of others.

In this chapter I want to consider the ways in which Heschel found his own voice, including by quoting himself. Particular attention will be paid to an outstanding example of Heschel's own rhetoric: a range of optical allusions and references to be found throughout Heschel's work, and above all the term *aspaklaria*, which plays a central and re-current role in his imagery and thought. Sight, insight, perspective, reflection, refraction – all these feature prominently both through the prism of quoted and cited sources and in their direct and unreflected form. Scrutiny of this web of related terms will hopefully bring to light some important aspects both of Heschel's poetics and his theol-ogy and help to gauge to what extent Heschel's *aspaklaria* – his per-spective and the prism through which he viewed the world – was uniquely his own, and to what extent it was coloured by the multiple lenses of tradition.

The Sounds of Silence

Throughout this book I have analysed the use Heschel made of different sources in his work. It may therefore seem odd to include in such a
discussion an analysis of their distinct absence. However, there are so-
norous silences in Heschel's work that deserve some consideration.

For one, the question arises why some of his books are full of quoted
sources while others have so few. His biographer recorded that
Heschel's younger colleague Fritz Rothschild implored him to add
sources to the sequel to *Man Is Not Alone*, since their paucity in that
work had left him open to "the charge by careless or malicious critics
that Heschel's thought was idiosyncratic or more compatible with
Christianity than with Judaism."[1]

Why, then, had Heschel written *Man Is Not Alone* with so few sources
attached? This was not the only kind of popular English writing in
which he was engaged. *The Sabbath*, published the very same year, has
many more sources both in the text and in the endnotes. It would appear that when it came to making his great personal philosophical and
theological statement, Heschel's first thought had been to free it of the
great weight of references.

On occasion Heschel felt the need to give expression to his spiritual
intuition without mediation or embellishment. If the sources of Jewish
tradition are the constant accompaniment to many of his works, there
are instances when Heschel chose to sing a cappella; to speak his truth
in his voice alone. In *Torah min Hashamayim* he quoted biblical passages
on more than 3,400 occasions; in *Who Is Man?* fewer than ten.

Just as some of Heschel's books take on this unaccompanied style, so
do a number of chapters in a book otherwise replete with references.
Each chapter of *God in Search of Man* has on average over eleven notes
attached, as well as numerous biblical verses and other sources quoted
in the body of the text. A small number have virtually no endnotes, and
of these there are five that are also almost devoid of sources quoted in
the foreground.

It might be argued that there is a special quality of originality in those
chapters in which quotations and citations play little or no part.
Certainly, Heschel's choice to make the chapter on freedom the pre-
penultimate chapter of the entire work implies that he ascribed particular significance to his treatment of the theme. Like the other "unaccompanied" chapters, it is not wholly lacking in sources,[2] but with the
exception of a brief paraphrase of Maimonides, no classical Jewish

sources are quoted. In the main, the conception of freedom advanced in the chapter is based solely on Heschel's own reasoning.[3] In this sense, the chapter on freedom is itself free.

There are other kinds of silences in Heschel's work. He made very little reference to his contemporaries among the great figures of modern Jewish thought. The only modern Jewish thinkers to be mentioned in *Search*, for example, are Hermann Cohen and Will Herberg. Cohen appears in a supporting role and not primarily because of his own theological voice.[4] The two references to Will Herberg are the closest Heschel came to engagement with a contemporary Jewish thinker.[5] Franz Rosenzweig's name is mentioned only once, and not in relation to *The Star of Redemption* but rather for an epigram of Friedrich Leopold von Stolberg, quoted in his work on Judah Halevi.[6] The only Buber mentioned in the entire work is Solomon Buber. Mordecai Kaplan does appear, thanks to his edition of Luzzatto's *Mesillat Yesharim*,[7] but not as a thinker in his own right (and in the previous chapter something of his ambivalence towards Kaplan was highlighted). Indeed, throughout his work, references to contemporaries and colleagues are sporadic and usually inconsequential.[8]

Heschel devoted an essay to the theology of his friend, the Protestant theologian Reinhold Niebuhr – no contemporary Jewish philosopher was afforded comparable attention.[9] Here is another silence in his work. W.Z. Harvey has suggested that such disregard was typical of medieval Jewish thinkers, who seemed more at ease in conversation with interlocutors long dead than with their more obviously accessible contemporaries.[10] Nonetheless, the silence is loud.

In many cases, these silences reflect implicitly on Heschel's understanding of his own role. If in most cases he substantiated claims about the spirit of Judaism with chapter and verse, in some chapters he is the only verse needed.

Self-Quotation: From Heschel to Heschel

While Heschel rarely quoted from his contemporaries, he often quoted himself. In *Search* alone, there are at least forty-five examples of such quotations and citations: from *Die Prophetie*, *Maimonides*, the Hebrew essays on prophecy in the Middle Ages, *Man's Quest for God*, *The Sabbath* and predominantly *Man Is Not Alone*.

In some cases the quotations are precise,[11] while in others Heschel felt no compunction about altering the quoted text either for felicity of style or relevance of meaning.[12] Such alterations demonstrate Heschel's approach to his previous writings: rather than quoting them as he would any other source,[13] he moulded them to suit his current purpose. Some of the changes had at root a theological motivation. In a section entitled "A Leap of Action" in *Man's Quest for God*, Heschel grappled with the modern Jew's

> inability to sense the presence of Divine meaning in the fulfillment of the law. Let us never forget that some of the basic theological presuppositions of Judaism cannot be justified in terms of reason. Its conception of the nature of man as having been created in the likeness of God, its conception of God and history, of prayer and even of morality, defy some of the realizations at which we have honestly arrived at the end of our analysis and scrutiny.[14]

Heschel returned to this list of "basic theological presuppositions" in *Search*, reproducing it with only one addition: the election of Israel.[15] It may be that this was merely a correction of an original oversight. Perhaps, however, it was a response, conscious or otherwise, to Mordecai Kaplan's critique of the doctrine of election.

At times Heschel preferred to paraphrase his own earlier work, while crediting it in the notes.[16] Elsewhere, a sentence or paragraph from Heschel's previous works appears, but with no attribution. A notable example of this latter phenomenon is to be found in a note in *Search*, which appeared first in Heschel's 1937 monograph *Don Jizchak Abravanel*,[17] but there is no indication of this in the note. Heschel cut and pasted from his own work at will.

Not All Ages Are Alike: Self-Quotation in Action

All these varieties of Heschelian self-quotation come to expression in at least one case. At the end of a section on "The Uniqueness of History" in *God in Search of Man*, Heschel took issue with Ranke's claim that every age was equally near to God, asserting that not all ages were alike and stating that "at a certain moment ... the spirit of prophecy departed from Israel."[18] The relevant footnote directed the reader to *The Sabbath*, where indeed this entire passage (and the preceding sentences on the diversity of time) appeared word for word. Since the chapter in *Search* in which this paragraph appeared was in a sense a reprise of some of the major aspects of *The Sabbath*, it is no great surprise to find this material reproduced.

Both the contention that not all ages are alike and the statement that prophecy departed from Israel at a certain time resonate within Heschel's other writings. The phrase "not all ages are alike" is Mishnaic, as Heschel was to note in the third volume of *Torah min Hashamayim*,[19] and it had already been employed by Heschel in his 1946 Hebrew essay on Maimonides and prophecy.[20] Given the thrust of that essay and the companion piece on the notion of the Holy Spirit in the Middle Ages, it is remarkable to find such a bald assertion that at a certain time the spirit of prophecy ceased. After all, these essays were designed to show that the declared end of the period of prophecy by no means put an end to the question of divine inspiration in the post-biblical era.[21]

It has been noted that the Heschelian trope by which no two moments are alike appears in the epilogue to *The Sabbath*. This phrase is also employed early in that work as part of the construction of its key argument: the primacy of time in the Jewish imagination.

> Judaism is a *religion of time* aiming at *the sanctification of time*. Unlike the space-minded man to whom time is unvaried, iterative, homogeneous, to whom all hours are alike, qualitiless, empty shells, the Bible senses the diversified character of time. There are no two hours alike. Every hour is unique and the only one given at the moment, exclusive and endlessly precious.[22]

Used in this way, the phrase is not a quotation but rather a slogan or a motto, and we find it here in the service of one of Heschel's most influential claims. An appreciation of the uniqueness of particular moments is at the heart of what Heschel regarded as an essential component of Judaism and part of his call for a corrective to his age's infatuation with the dimension of space. Every time he re-employed this phrase it carried traces of its former usages.[23]

The fluidity with which Heschel related to his own previous writing suggests that for Heschel all parts of his oeuvre were interconnected. By relying on self-quotation he presented his own voice as a legitimate component of the continuum of Jewish creativity. Also, by referencing his own thought he was indicating that his current opinions rested on an established conceptual foundation and inviting the curious reader to explore more of his arguments and ideas.

His Own Voice

Abraham Joshua Heschel effected a transition into modernity while steadfastly refusing the temptation to rebel against the culture of deference and citation into which he was born. While his arsenal expanded, nothing was decommissioned. His copious references and allusions make this clear. Despite the dearth of self-reflective comments to be found in his work, Heschel can nonetheless be read as a man in search of his own voice: his own response to what he experienced as God's urgent call.

In the case of a man such as Heschel, the distinction between his own voice and the voices of tradition is not easily drawn. A prime example of this can be found in a motif rooted in Judaism which he employed in his own distinctive fashion. As behooves such a blurring of the personal and traditional horizons, this motif will subsequently be considered in both its wider Jewish setting and its specific context. In order to inquire into the provenance and resonance of this example of Hechelian imagery, it is appropriate not only to look at excerpts in which this term is employed, but also relate to its origins in Jewish literature.

Aspaklaria

Reading Heschel, the imagery of perception is inescapable. Throughout his work phrases, metaphors, and references to seeing and hearing prevail. Already in a Yiddish poem he described his own sense of purpose through the use of daring optical imagery:

> Everything demands of me: "Feel us!"
> Everyone begs of me: "See us!"
> God lend me Your eyes!
>
> I've come to sow seeing in the world –
> To unveil God – Who has disguised himself in the world –[24]

Some of the ways in which Heschel sought to "unveil God" will be examined below with the aid of one optical allusion which played a central role in Heschel's work:[25] the *aspaklaria*, or in its anglicized form, the speculum. So central a term was this in the Heschelian lexicon that he coined a neologism, "the *aspaklaria* of the generations," and used it in the title of his Hebrew magnum opus, *Torah min Hashamayim be-Aspaklaria shel ha-Dorot.*

To suggest that this term and other optical allusions exemplify Heschel's own voice is not to imply that this usage is free of his usual practices of quotation and reference. Indeed, some eighty biblical sources relating to optic metaphors are deployed in *God in Search of Man.* But alongside these citations, Heschel's unique voice is clearly audible.

The word *aspaklaria* made its way into Hebrew via Greek and Latin, and we find it used most prominently to describe the ways in which the prophet encounters the Divine.[26] In Numbers 12:8 it is said of Moses that he communicated with God mouth to mouth, ומראה ולא בחידות, which the Jewish Publication Society edition translates as "plainly and not in riddles." This translation is based, however, on an exegetical tradition that does not reflect the synesthetic dimension of the image – the deliberate blurring of the distinction between the senses, the confusion of seeing, speaking, and hearing implicit in the phrase.[27]

A rabbinic tradition plays up the optical dimension of the Mosaic revelation, based on a reading of this verse in Numbers and also on Moses's wish to see God directly. A Midrash states that the difference between Moses and the rest of the prophets is to be found in the way they looked and what they saw. While the other prophets of the Bible saw through many speculums, or cloudy or unilluminated ones, Moses saw through a single, clear, or shining optical instrument.[28]

This tradition has parallels in the New Testament,[29] and its later role in Jewish thought has been chronicled and discussed at length in the scholarly literature, of which Elliot Wolfson's *Through a Speculum That Shines* is an outstanding example.[30]

The nature of the *aspaklaria* has itself been a matter of debate and speculation. For our purposes four different interpretations of the term will help to bring into focus the various uses of optical imagery in Heschel's work. Heschel's *aspaklaria* will be considered as a mirror, a lens, a perspective, and a screen or barrier.

Self-Reflection and Depth Theology

Aspaklaria can be interpreted as a mirror:[31] a device for looking back at oneself. Heschel made use of this image time and again. In *The Earth Is the Lord's,* for example, he lauded the Ashkenazi legal code, the *Turim,* commenting that "Maimonides' system is logical, but the Arba Turim is a mirror reflecting life as it is," while just two pages later the synagogue services of the Sephardi rite are described as being "like silent mirrors of the ancient rite."[32] There is something pejorative about this latter image, as if a mere reflection is less vital than the thing itself. Indeed, later in the same work he opined that "man is no mere reflection of the above,"[33] but rather carries within him something of the Divine. Thus for Heschel in this 1950 book a mirror represented both a true and a pale reflection.

Heschel always saw a close connection between self-perception and perception in general. His religious humanism was predicated on the notion that the capacity to see the other is linked to our ability to see ourselves:

> A thing I perceive in the light of my knowledge: a human being I perceive in the image of my own being ... There is agreement of being, concurring of existence, a self beholding a self. I see what I am ... There is only one way of comprehending man's being-there, and that is by way of inspecting my own being.[34]

In his last work he contrasted self-reflection with speculation to the distinct advantage of the former:

> This book is a study in depth-theology. It discusses moments, battles, situations, rather than doctrines or beliefs; confrontations of the conscience with God rather than summaries of theology; involvements and appropriations rather than rituals or recollections. In short, this study will deal with self-reflection rather than speculation.[35]

The contrast between depth theology and regular theology is portrayed here as the contrast between a gaze fixed upon oneself for the purpose of profundity and the speculative gaze of an onlooker.

Forty years earlier he wrote a poem in Yiddish in which the act of self-reflection takes place in an interpersonal encounter:

> Often I glimpse Myself in everyone's form,
> Hear my own speech – a distant, quiet voice – in people's weeping,
> as if under hundreds of masks My face would lie hidden.[36]

This is the Heschelian person, fully engaged with the Other, both human and divine. And this is also the Heschelian conception of God, who appears to be the subject of this poem:

God is indeed very much above man, but at the same time man is very much a reflection of God. The craving to keep that reflection pure, to guard God's likeness on earth, is indeed the motivating force of Jewish piety.[37]

Heschel's God holds up a mirror to the world, and the ensuing reflection is the truth that the prophets are capable of perceiving: "reality reflected in God's mind."[38]

Holding up a mirror to reality is not just a prophetic imperative. Our contemporary reality forces us to look into ourselves to see if the image of God is to be found there. The alternative, as Heschel wrote during the Nazi years, was to find a beast lurking within.[39]

Prism and Pluralism

The *Sefat Emet,* a work of great significance for Heschel's own development, suggests that the ability to see oneself as in a mirror was the genius of the biblical prophets: this is the speculum which does not shine. Only Moses was blessed to know an even higher level of seeing and to look out as if through a window.[40]

An heir to Polish Hasidic traditions and fully acquainted with the rich vein of tradition linking introspection and insight with true sight, Abraham Joshua Heschel related extensively to such motifs. Leaving that milieu and coming eventually to the United States, Heschel encountered a culture in which self-reflection assumed great significance. He called for God-centred self-examination in which insight into the self is kept distinct from narcissism.

If the mirror stands for the virtue of self-reflection and the danger of self-infatuation, what is the significance of the window, the prism through which one looks? Heschel was aware that the term *aspaklaria* had both reflective and refractive connotations. In his Hebrew work containing the word *aspaklaria* in its title, Heschel noted that there was some difficulty in deciding whether the term related to a device that returned light or something through which one looked.[41]

Refraction is an imprecise business, and rarely do we see as through a clear glass. As Heschel reflected in a 1953 essay, "Spiritual meaning is not always limpid; transparency is the quality of glass, while diamonds are distinguished by refractive power and the play of prismatic colors."[42]

In his writing Heschel pointed to various prisms through which reality might be perceived. Judaism, he wrote, turned the individual into the *aspaklaria* of the nation;[43] Aggadah is described as involvement in the problems of life through the *aspaklaria* of faith, while Halakhah is the *aspaklaria* through which the permitted and forbidden is considered. Divine pathos was the *aspaklaria* through which Rabbi Akiva looked upon the world,[44] while Rabbi Ishmael looked at history through the *aspaklaria* of compassion.[45]

Heschel's most striking use of *aspaklaria* as a lens or prism is in his phrase "the *aspaklaria* of the generations," which appears in the title of *Torah min Hashamayim be-Aspaklaria shel ha-Dorot*. Gordon Tucker showed a clear understanding of this optical dimension in his decision to translate that work as *Heavenly Torah as Refracted through the Generations*. There seem to be no direct parallels to this term elsewhere in Jewish tradition. This is Heschel's terminology.

The image epitomizes the central thesis of this long and significant work: the theophany undergoes a transformation of understanding throughout history. It is possible to find a vocabulary for historical change and development from within Jewish culture. Indeed, the only way in which the heavenly Torah may be seen in the earthly realm is through the *aspaklaria* of the generations.

A highly revealing section in the second volume of *Torah min Hashamayim* sheds light on Heschel's understanding of this key term. He quoted the third-century sage Rabbi Bena'ah, according to whom the Torah was written one scroll at a time. He proceeded to explain that this Sage represented a rationalistic and historical approach to the sacred and sublime process of Mosaic composition of the Torah. Rabbi Bena'ah saw this process through the *aspaklaria* of time and appreciated that Scripture was composed in history and over time.[46]

The passage of light through a multidimensional surface leads to multiplicity and diversity. Evoking the culture of learning of prewar Eastern Europe, Heschel wrote:

> Ideas were like precious stones. The thought that animated them reflected a wealth of nuances and distinctions, as the ray of light passing through a prism produces the colors of the rainbow. Upon rotation, many-faceted ideas shed a glittering brilliance that varied in accordance with the direction in which they were placed against the light of reason.[47]

This complex metaphor provides a mandate for both specificity and plurality – as the light of reason passes through precious stones it receives a special lustre, while it also reaches out into different directions.

Ideas bearing the quality of precious stones through which the light of reason may refract in various directions – here something of

Heschel's pluralism finds its voice.[48] It can be suggested that his instinctive pluralism was prismatic in nature: he believed that the light of reason should be directed at ideas and beliefs. He certainly reserved the right to reject opinions and practices as wrong-headed or simply wrong. Nonetheless, he did not presume that the light of truth would lead to one incontrovertible truth. Rather, he celebrated the play of prismatic colours.

Perspective and Prophecy

Another meaning of the term *aspaklaria* is perspective.[49] Heschel described faith as, first and foremost, a perspective[50] and prayer as a point of view.[51]

It is possible to demonstrate that Heschel himself translated the term *aspaklaria* as perspective.[52] In *Israel: An Echo of Eternity*, he paraphrased ideas developed more fully in *Torah min Hashamayim* when he wrote, "Jewish thinking was essentially shaped by two different perspectives each of which suggested a different way and approach to reality."[53]

In this paragraph Heschel was in fact translating a paragraph from his Hebrew work, and there the word used for perspective was *aspaklaria*.[54]

Heschel maintained that the "perspective from which we look at reality determines our way of formulating our problems."[55] He spoke approvingly of the capacity to shift perspective, and yet he also believed that culture and language constituted a prism through which the world might be perceived. His emphasis on "a Jewish way of thinking"[56] was another aspect of his search for *aspaklaria*.

There is much to suggest that he was aware of the dangers of perspectivism, namely the notion that the valence of concepts is purely a function of the viewpoint of the spectator. He stated, for example, that the core value of all religions was peace, from whatever perspective one looked at them.[57] On the other hand, he celebrated the blessings of diverse viewpoints:

> Most people think only once in their lives, usually when they are at college. After that their minds are made up ... Views, just as leaves, are bound to wither, because the world is in flux. But so many of us would rather be faithful to outworn views than to undergo the strain of reexamination and revision ... A human being must be valued by how many times he was able to see the world from a new perspective.[58]

Rabbi Ishmael and Rabbi Akiva epitomized the lower and higher *as-paklaria,* respectively. (While higher *aspaklaria* has its origins in Zoharic literature,[59] lower *aspaklaria* would appear to be another neologism.) They were the embodiment of ways of looking at the world. Heschel's introduction to the first volume of *Torah min Hashamayim* included a presentation of two essential perspectives: one immanent, one transcendental.[60] A remarkable chapter in the third volume presented these two perspectives, which he termed the perspectives of Reason and Vision, and it employed a bold visual metaphor: in order to see clearly, it is necessary to allow for both points of view, to see from both angles. Indeed, he wrote, in order to see clearly it is necessary to change perspective from time to time.[61]

For Abraham Joshua Heschel, perspective was not only a human category. On several occasions he referred to the divine perspective, describing the Torah as "a vision of man from the point of view of God."[62] Accordingly, prophesy is the interpretation of existence.[63] In his introduction to *The Prophets,* Heschel explained, "The prophet's task is to convey a divine view, yet as a person he *is* a point of view. He speaks from the perspective of God as perceived from the perspective of his own situation."[64] And later in the book he wrote, "The prophet does not see the world from the point of view of a political theory; he is a person who sees the world from the point of view of God; he sees the world through the eyes of God."[65]

Heschel's term *sub specie dei* [66] is without doubt an alternative to Spinoza's *sub specie aeternitate.*[67] Given that, as noted in the previous chapter, Spinoza was the subject of Heschel's unique disapproval, it is hard to imagine that this fact is either trivial or accidental. To see the world from the perspective of a God of pathos is quite different from a disembodied view from the perspective of eternity.

The *aspaklaria* tradition, distinguishing between Moses and the other prophets, is quoted in *Torah min Hashamayim.*[68] In introducing the *Yevamot* text, Heschel averred:

> No-one can understand the Talmudic conception of prophecy without going deeply into the hints to be found in their teachings on the status of Moses and the way of the Sovereign of the Universe.[69]

In *Torah min Hashamayim* Heschel indicated that the Ishmaelian perspective is to be associated with the prophetic urge, while Akiva is the bearer of the apocalyptic tradition. In *Israel: An Echo of Eternity*, in the discussion of the contrast between pragmatic and messianic views of redemption, he effected a surprising shift in his attribution of the provenance of these perspectives:

> Jewish thinking was essentially shaped by two different perspectives each of which suggested a different way and approach to reality. One perspective may be called rational, historical, realistic, stressing the concreteness of things, human values, natural order. The other perspective, which may be called prophetic or apocalyptic, looks at the world from the perspective of heaven – its concern is with supernatural events, the miraculous, the indescribable, and the paradoxical. Basic issues were conceived and defined in accordance with the perspective ...[70]

In the following chapter, Heschel exemplified the political implications of these contrasting perspectives, preferring the sober views of the Amora Samuel and Maimonides to "apocalyptic overstatements." In a highly revealing statement he explained his enthusiasm for multiple persectives: "A central concern in Jewish thinking is to overcome the tendency to see the world in one dimension, from one perspective, to reduce history exclusively to God's action or to man's action ..."[71]

Heschel made little use of the methodological tools offered by psychology or the social sciences. Nonetheless, his exposure to phenomenological methods did leave a mark on both his thinking and his writing. He was aware that matters of great import to one individual might seem banal and uninteresting when regarded in generalized abstraction. In *Who Is Man?* the language of perspective (along with other optical metaphors) is used to describe this dichotomy:

> It is the notability of my existence that becomes elusive when looked upon from without, from the perspective of society, from the viewpoint of generalization. In other words, although my singularity is a matter of personal certainty to me, it looks like a conceit from the perspective of statistics or manpower administration. Luminous from within, my notability seems opaque if not absurd from without.[72]

These examples should suffice to demonstrate the importance of perspective in Heschel's imagery. It figures prominently in both his understanding of prophecy and his notion of polarity.

Screens and Obstructions

A fourth interpretation of the term *aspaklaria* renders it as a screen or barrier.[73] This has its roots in one of the rabbinic versions of the Midrash, contrasting Moses with all other biblical prophets. While the former saw through one *aspaklaria*, the others saw through nine.[74] In *God in Search of Man* Heschel noted that for Rashi and others, the difference between Moses and the other prophets was that "the prophets believed that they had seen God but did not, whereas Moses, who looked through a lucid speculum, knew that he did not see Him!"[75]

Maimonides played up this sense of the term, both in his commentary to the Mishnah and in his introduction to Tractate Avot.[76] The word itself is given a fascinating etymology – *aspaklaria* is understood as *safek re'iyah*, that which is viewed only in a doubtful manner. Human faults such as anger, lust, and pride are barriers that separate us from unmediated encounter with the Divine.

Moses's unique and exalted status as archprophet is due to his capacity to divest himself of these corrupting interferences.[77] It is in this spirit that Heschel defined prophecy as "a moment of unshrouding, an opening of the eyes, a lifting of the curtain."[78]

Heschel discussed the process of human refinement leading to the status of prophet in his Hebrew essay on Maimonides and prophecy. He noted the need for divine grace if the veil of sense perception was to be removed from the heart, and true prophetic insight was to be attained.[79]

Heschel acknowledged that every lens was also a screen and related to the challenge presented by this division. When the optical device is anachronistic or unsuitable, the conduit to insight can become an impassable barrier:

Not through our own eyes but through lenses ground by our intellectual ancestry do we look at the world. But our eyes are strained and tired of staring through spectacles worn by another generation. We are tired of overlooking entities, of squinting at their relations to other things. We want to face reality as it is …[80]

Here is the radical voice of Heschel, the opponent of spiritual nepotism and fossilized thinking. This position was not rooted in an antinomian urge but rather in the sense that true continuity demands change.

In this fourth reading of the *aspaklaria*, Heschel highlighted the difficulty – indeed, the impossibility – of confronting reality as it is. With Kant, he appreciated that the very act of perception necessitated a corruption of some kind. In Heschel's conception and in his reading of Maimonides, intuition takes over where perception can no longer help. In the next chapter of this book we will see how this favouring of the role of intuition helped lay the foundation for Heschel's own political activist stance.

As for the obstructions to true untrammeled vision, they come in a variety of forms. In a recent article, Einat Ramon portrayed Heschel as an impassioned opponent of modern secularism which, in her view, he equated with idolatry. In the title of her Hebrew article she made use of a remarkable optical metaphor to be found in Heschel's writing, which translates as "dazzled by the lights of the metropolis."[81] Towards the end of *The Earth Is the Lord's* Heschel propounded the idea that a great light emanated from East European Jewry, but that the stark glare of modernity obstructed our view of that more fragile glow:

> In the spiritual confusion of the last hundred years, many of us overlooked the incomparable beauty of our old, poor homes. We compared our grandfathers, our scholars and rabbis, with Russian or German intellectuals ... Dazzled by the lights of the metropolis, we lost at times the inner sight. The luminous visions that for so many generations shone in the little candles were extinguished for some of us.[82]

Ramon's thesis, however controversial, offers an important corrective to the common liberal reading of Heschel by emphasizing his strong resistance to the blandishments of modern secularism. She rightly points out that for Heschel the glare of the new was a barrier to true vision.

Veils and obstructions of various kinds recur in Heschel's imagery. Waxing lyrical about Jerusalem, Heschel suggested that the inner force of the city could be perceived only by blocking out the apparent and the visual: "I try to use my eyes, and there is a cloud."[83] Here again, the actual and the contemporary obscure the view of the true and the eternal.

Not every obstruction to clear sight is caused by modern foibles at the expense of traditional values. In the opening address of the 1963 Conference on Religion and Race, Heschel railed against racial prejudice: "a deadly poison that inflames the eye, making us see the generality of race but not the uniqueness of the human face."[84] Here the image is deliberately external. That which keeps us from appreciating the humanity of the other is not an innate quality of sight but an infection to be treated.

Elsewhere, however, Heschel suggested that reality was never wholly apparent to the human eye. In a highly revealing paragraph in the third volume of *Torah min Hashamayim*, he provided a conceptual basis for appreciating both the apparent and the recondite realms of existence rooted in this notion that barriers to unmediated perception are inevitable:

> The purist tends to believe that his reason corresponds to reality and forgets that reason is to reality is as a dwarf is to a giant. The visionary knows that truth is expressed only in fractions and is revealed only through the lens of metaphors and parables. Is it really possible to see what is concealed without a veil? Or to peek past our bounds without metaphors?[85]

If obscurity is inevitable, why criticize those whose vision is obstructed? In a comment buried in an endnote in *God in Search of Man* Heschel commented, "To the wicked, the spiritual light that is hidden from the eyes of the body is indistinguishable from darkness … They do not even know that they walk in the darkness."[86] Heschel was pushing against the arrogance of those critics of the spiritual realm who assume that what they cannot see cannot exist.

As discussed, this fourth interpretation of the *aspaklaria* emphasizes the veils, screens, and obstructions that prevent clear vision. What these various usages have in common is a suspicion of modern confidence in the possibility of total clarity. As Heschel wrote in 1968, "The task is to deliver the mind from the illusion that availability and transparency are the exclusive attributes of being. False lucidity misguides us more than plain obscurity."[87]

The Eye of the Heart

Ken Koltun-Fromm argues that in *The Sabbath* Heschel promotes the concept that "Jewish authenticity requires a visual capacity to see beyond material things to their spiritual wonder."[88] In Koltun-Fromm's highly suggestive reading, Heschel is calling his readers to look through things in the dimension of space and see through to their essence: "Jews must envision time rather than gaze at things in space."[89] He suggests that Heschel "seeks to awaken in his readers a 'spiritual eye' that sees through rather than gazes at objects."[90]

Koltun-Fromm discerns in *The Sabbath* a specific example of a broader phenomenon – a concern with issues of perception and most particularly sight, which characterized his work. There is a recurrent call to face up and see beyond that which is presented on the most facile level. Already in 1943 Heschel set out his critique in its most basic form: "Modern man seldom faces things as they are."[91]

In order to see beyond the surface, a different kind of eye is needed, and here Heschel turned to medieval thought to identify the appropriate organ. A brief section in *God in Search of Man* is devoted to the eye of the heart, where he cited Maimonides's use of this term, which Heschel calls "a medieval name for intuition."[92] The attached note refers the reader to another part of the *Mishneh Torah*, as well as to Judah Halevi's *The Kuzari*, a commentary by Abraham Ibn Ezra, two essays about Ghazali, and lastly the concept of the "divine eye of the soul" from *De Mundo*, attributed to Aristotle. Kabbalistic sources are also pressed into service to advance the notion of spiritual sight, which is one of the great implicit themes of *Search*.[93]

At the end of the section, Heschel wove a number of references into the paragraph and concluded with a long and significant quotation:

> Yehuda Halevi maintains that just as the Lord gave all of us a bodily eye to perceive external things, he endowed some people with an "inner eye" or "inner sense."[n19] In his poems he speaks of himself having seen God *with the heart* (rather than with the bodily eye).[n20] "My heart saw Thee and believed Thee."[n21] "I have seen Thee with the eye of the heart."[n22]
>
> > The Creator who discovereth all from nothing,
> > Is revealed to the heart, but not to the eye ...[94]

This is a remarkable concentration of references by Halevi to this idea of the inner eye, and yet another reference to *The Kuzari* is found in an earlier footnote in the same chapter.[95]

Why did Heschel turn to Halevi on this point when he is hardly to be found in any other context in *Search*? Elliot Wolfson discussed Halevi's concept of the "inner eye" and its connection to the imaginative faculty of the prophet and suggested that the expression "the eyes of the heart" or simply "the heart" became current among the Geronese

Kabbalists through Halevi's influence.[96] Halevi stands at the juncture between the philosophical and mystical traditions, and perhaps for this reason Heschel paid particular attention to his terminology of prophetic insight.[97]

It is evident that this concern with non-corporeal sight was part of Heschel's vocabulary decades earlier. In his unpublished "Concise Dictionary of Hebrew Philosophical Terms," prepared for students at the Hebrew Union College in the early 1940s, the entry for *ayin* reads, "substance, essence, being, entity; color; 'inner eye.'"[98]

In Heschel's lexicon, God searches for us as we go out to encounter God. Humanity is engaged in a quest for God, and the Torah of Heaven is perceived through an *aspaklaria*. This kind of vision requires special vision, capable of seeing with insight, in contrast to the overwhelming amount of visual stimulations and motes to trouble the mind's eye. In an age in which everything is on view, Heschel feared that matters of significance were rendered invisible. The traditions of Judaism offer not only a point of view, but also a way of seeing.

Insight

There is mystery at the heart of existence, and many rabbinic texts are used to evoke this mystery, its impenetrability, and the occasional glimpse of its resolution. As Heschel writes in *Search*,

> To Jewish thinkers of the past, the evidence for their certainty of the existence of God was neither a syllogism derived from abstract premises nor any physical experience but *an insight*. The eye of the body is not that of the soul, and the soul, it was believed, does at times attain higher insights.[99]

The note appended to this comment is itself worthy of mention:

> The concept of insight seems to be contained in the Talmudic expression, *ovanta deliba*. It is an act in which a perception of the mysteries of the Merkaba is attained, see *Megillah* 24a, and *Tosafot, Avodah Zarah*, 28b.[100]

The term *ovanta deliba* is understood by the Tosafists in the sense of "the understanding of the heart."[101]

One of the most significant terms in Abraham Joshua Heschel's work is *insight*. Heschel's prophets see with insight: "The characteristic of the prophets is not foreknowledge of the future, but insight into the present pathos of God."[102]

The term *insight* appears on several occasions in *Search*, in addition to an entire chapter dedicated to the term. Bemoaning the fact that Jewish tradition is under siege, Heschel observed in Hebrew that the illuminated *aspaklaria* was becoming more and more blurry.[103] In his English translation of this expression, Heschel wrote that the "authenticity of insight is being corroded."[104]

To see through the *aspaklaria* of the generations is to combine a capacity for self-reflection with openness to the multiplicity of refraction. It involves a willingness to adopt a particular point of view, while remaining ready to shift perspective. The *aspaklaria* is influenced by history and change, but it also helps avoid the risk of being dazzled by the bright lights of the city, the glare of the faddish and the evanescent.

Here Heschel speaks in his own voice. It is a voice which resounds with echoes and cadences from many eras of Jewish tradition, and yet it is unmistakeably and uniquely his. He gathered many of these sources and threads and created imagery, which he hoped would guide his contemporaries through the sensory overload of the modern condition. Judaism can serve as a multigenerational speculum, an instrument of insight.

We have traced a Heschelian image from its ancient roots to its deployment. In this way Heschel's particular vocabulary developed, and his distinct voice came to be heard. To return to the metaphor cited at the end of the last chapter, here is an example of Heschel's project – electrifying the amber, liquefying the solid tradition. Without the immediacy of authentic experience, the amber will not glow. Without the prisms and perspectives of tradition, the immediacy of the moment dissipates. In Abraham Joshua Heschel's life and thought the dynamics of tradition were constantly unfolding. In our last chapter we will consider the role played by tradition in his involvement with the most pressing challenges of his day. In optic terms, we are in search of his perspective, his unique insight refracted through the *aspaklaria* of the generations. In oral terms, we are listening for his voice.

Chapter Nine

Heschel and the Call to Action

Heschel's Last Decade

The last decade or so of Heschel's life saw a pronounced change in emphasis. To be sure, the years from the publication of *The Prophets* in 1962 to his death were not devoid of literary and scholarly activities – he published five books and over thirty articles during those years. But the nature and tone of most of those publications demonstrate a change of approach. In these years we find Heschel expressing opinions on a wide array of social issues and current affairs, among them interreligious dialogue; the plight of Soviet Jewry; health, youth, and aging; the theological basis for the State of Israel; the Civil Rights movement; and American involvement in Vietnam.

In these years Heschel moved out of his study and onto the barricades. In Selma, Alabama, protesting racial segregation; at the Arlington Cemetery, protesting Vietnam; at public meetings large and small, Heschel changed the venue and emphasis of his activities. He did not, however, abandon the passions and commitments of a lifetime.

In an explicit statement made in a short article published posthumously, "The Reasons for My Involvement in the Peace Movement," Heschel offered an explanation for this turn. He noted that for many years he had lived a life of scholarly seclusion, convinced that his "destiny [was] to serve in the realm of privacy." He cited three "events" which changed his attitude:

One was the countless onslaughts upon my inner life, depriving me of the ability to sustain inner stillness. The second event was the discovery that indifference to evil is worse than evil itself. Even the high worth of reflection in the cultivation of inner truth cannot justify remaining calm in the face of cruelties that make the hope of effectiveness of pure intellectual endeavors seem grotesque …

… The third event that changed my attitude was my study of the prophets of ancient Israel, a study on which I worked for several years until its publication in 1962. From them I learned the niggardliness of our moral comprehension, the incapacity to sense the depth of misery caused by our own failures. It became quite clear to me that while our eyes are witness to the callousness and cruelty of man, our heart tries to obliterate the memories, to calm the nerves, and to silence our conscience.[1]

In my reading, the first two "events" described here relate to the experience of a man who had been exposed to many of the most horrific upheavals of the twentieth century. It is not in fact clear when in his life Heschel was able to achieve the inner stillness described above. In the 1930s he published a poem in which he described himself as perhaps the guiltiest person of his generation.[2]

The first of Heschel's three reasons for his turn to activism is perhaps less an event and more a personality trait. As he grew up, he realized that the hope of attaining stillness through withdrawal from the world was futile and unworthy.

The second "event," the realization of the immorality of the bystander, must be seen in terms of his years in Germany and beyond. The events through which he lived made silence impossible. Heschel had experienced a profound sense of impotence during the years of the Holocaust when, by his account, he attempted to mobilize members of the American Jewish community but "nobody listened to me."[3] This non-response was perhaps the key event that gave rise to Heschel's theology of response. The slogan Never Again, which became the watchword of exponents of Jewish sovereignty and mundane power, was understood by Heschel as a moral imperative to refute indifference.[4]

As for the third factor in his move to activism, there seems to be little doubt that Heschel drew solace, succour, and inspiration from the example of the prophets of Israel and was thus moved to reach out beyond the confines of his study. With the prophets as his guide, the road leading from the Upper West Side of Manhattan to Selma, Alabama, and Washington, DC, was a short one.

In this chapter I will examine the ways in which Heschel employed precedents to bolster and underpin his own engagement with contemporary issues. The simple tripartite explanation for his activist turn

– personality, history, and the example of the prophets – is insufficient. When we examine the different genres of Jewish creativity noted in each of this book's chapters, a picture emerges of a man who drew upon every era of Jewish history and indeed upon inspiration outside Judaism. His move to action can be seen as a culmination of his life of study and struggle with the meaning of tradition. In Heschel, the perennial and the temporal are intertwined.

The Bible as a Licence for Social Engagement

It is not simply a quirk of publication that *The Insecurity of Freedom*, a 1966 collection of essays by Heschel on some of the burning issues of the day, ends (as do almost all his works) with an index of biblical passages. Heschel the social commentator did not stop being Heschel the exponent of Biblical Man. Indeed, in the very first essay in the book he proclaimed that a meaningful relationship between religion and the free society "can be established only if we succeed in rediscovering the intellectual relevance of the Bible."[5]

Not only the Bible in general but specific biblical episodes and characters featured prominently in the articulation of Heschel's social vision. An outstanding example is the opening to the speech he delivered in January 1963 in Chicago at the National Conference on Religion and Race, a conference which was to contribute much to Heschel's rise to public prominence:

> At the first conference on religion and race, the main participants were Pharoah and Moses ... The outcome of that summit meeting has not come to an end. Pharoah is not ready to capitulate. The exodus began, but is far from having been completed. In fact, it was easier for the children of Israel to cross the Red Sea than for a Negro to cross certain university campuses.[6]

Here was the mouthpiece of the tradition of the Hebrew Bible placing contemporary events in biblical perspective.

Above all, it was the prophets of Israel who were charged with the task of bearing moral witness, rendering barriers of history and geography irrelevant. In *The Prophets* Heschel placed his key slogan of political activism upon the lips of the ancient prophets of Israel: "Above all, the prophets remind us of the moral state of a people: Few are guilty, but all are responsible."[7] He returned to this slogan in his essay concerning his decision to become a peace activist, once again linking it explicitly with both "the thinking [and] ... the lives of the prophets."[8]

Through the prophets, the tribulations of a modern activist came into perspective.[9] Heschel's description of the risks that the biblical prophets were prepared to run was to provide inspiration to activists in the civil rights and antiwar movements: "To the patriots, they seemed pernicious; to the pious multitude, blasphemous; to the men in authority, seditious."[10]

During his final years, preoccupied by social activism, Heschel invoked the example of the prophets time and again. When asked why he did not stick to spiritual matters, he responded that the prophets "mixed into social-political issues," and that if political involvement was to be regarded as inimical to religion, then God must also "be a non-religious person."[11] It has been noted in some recent studies that Heschel's enthusiastic blurring of the lines between religion and politics resonates differently in a post–9/11 world than it did in 1967,[12] but in Heschel's time and context, his call for a politics rooted in the example of the prophets was unambiguous:

> What is the essence of being a prophet? *A prophet is a person who holds God and men in one thought at one time, at all times.* Our tragedy begins with the *segregation of God*, with the bifurcation of the secular and the sacred. We worry more about the purity of dogma than about the *integrity of love. We think of God in the past tense* and refuse to realize that *God is always present and never, never past*; that God may be more intimately *present in slums than in mansions, with those who are smarting under the abuse of the callous.*[13]

In 1966 Heschel published a short piece entitled "The Moral Outrage of Vietnam." The article is highly polemical in nature and relates in the main to the policies of the American government with no reference to the texts or values of Jewish tradition. In one paragraph, however, Heschel's rage at the use of military force is amplified with recourse to the prophet: "Militarism is whoredom, voluptuous and vicious, first disliked then relished. To paraphrase the prophet's words: 'For the spirit of harlotry is within them, and they know not the Lord.'"[14]

The paraphrase here is not of the words but rather of the context. While Hosea used the language of adultery and harlotry to excoriate the moral degradation of the people, Heschel turned his fury on the use of state power in the pursuit of what he believed to be an unjust war.

Similar usage can be found in other contexts. Leviticus 18, Deuteronomy 21, Psalm 91, Isaiah 49, Jeremiah 31, Amos 5, and other biblical chapters are employed in an article on the plight of the Jews of the Soviet Union, which finishes by placing the contemporary challenge in a biblical light with the words: "If I forget thee, O Russian Jewry ..."[15]

There is no reason to doubt Heschel's statement that his return in the early 1960s to the study of the prophets was an event that triggered his turn to social activism. The prophets stood in stark contrast to those calling for conformity: "The prophet Amos was forbidden to appear in Bethel and Jeremiah was imprisoned because their message shocked those in power."[16] Spurred into action by the events of his day, Heschel found in the ancient prophets of Israel a model for stubborn insistence on moral absolutes, regardless of the immediate cost.

As the chapter on Heschel's reading and deployment of the Bible argued, appealing to the common patrimony of the monotheistic religions was also a good way of assuring the resonance of his teaching beyond the confines of the Jewish community. It is remarkable to think of Heschel in the early 1960s, working more or less simultaneously on his theology of the Rabbis and the reworking of his book on the prophets, just as he was finding his voice in the great issues of the day.

Beyond Biblical Prophecy: The Literature of the Rabbis

While the centrality of the prophets in the construction of Heschel's social vision cannot be doubted, the notion that the Bible stood alone in providing a licence to act cannot be supported. As has been demonstrated throughout this book, for all of his radicalism, Abraham Joshua Heschel was deeply entrenched within the literary and religious traditions of Judaism in every generation. He is not usually to be found leapfrogging the rabbinic tradition or sidestepping the codes and tracts of the Middle Ages. On the contrary, Heschel's work is replete with references to Jewish sources from the Bible to Will Herberg. In Heschel's construction of Judaism, there are no Dark Ages.

In an earlier chapter I argued that Heschel's emphasis on the sacred deed was rooted in his reading of rabbinic literature, and thus the latter sections of *God in Search of Man* relied heavily on rabbinic sources. The final part of that work, entitled "Response," opened with a chapter on deeds. It is clear that the Heschelian "leap of action"[17] involved the fulfilment of sacred deeds, but he was at pains not to define the nature of

these deeds. The following description of the mitzvah, taken from the
same section, may apply to preparing a kosher kitchen or to opening a
soup kitchen:

> Mitsvot are not ideals, spiritual entities for ever suspended in eternity.
> They are commandments addressing every one of us. They are the ways
> in which God confronts us in particular moments. In the infinite world
> there is a task for me to accomplish. Not a general task, but a task for me,
> here and now. Mitsvot are *spiritual ends*, points of eternity in the flux of
> temporality.[18]

Near the end of *Search* Heschel included a chapter entitled "The Deed
Redeems," in which almost all of the supporting sources were taken
from rabbinic literature.

To be sure, Heschel's extension of the rabbinic emphasis on the sacred deed to the social domain involved a particular reading of these
sources. In his 1963 paper on the plight of the Soviet Jews, he demonstrated the lengths to which he was prepared to go in pursuit of this
goal: "According to our tradition, whoever forgets even one fragment
of the Torah commits a great sin. How much more so is a person guilty
if he remains callous to the agony of one human being."[19]

The first sentence is supported with reference to the third chapter of
Tractate Avot, while the second statement has no such supporting citation. It should not be inferred, however, that Heschel believed the
Rabbis to be concerned only with the spiritual and ritual domains. He
looked to the legacy of Rabbi Ishmael, which he read as a direct continuation of the prophetic impulse in Israel, to provide the theological
foundation for a stance privileging social amelioration.

The way in which Abraham Joshua Heschel rooted his social activism in the sources of Judaism can be illustrated with reference to one
verse, Psalm 119:126. Given the difficulty of rendering this verse in
English, it is appropriate to bring the text in the original Hebrew:
עת לעשות לה' הפרו תורתך. As Heschel pointed out in a small chapter devoted to this verse in his work on rabbinic theology, it is susceptible to
a variety of interpretations: It is time to act for the Lord/for the Lord
to work; make void Your Torah/ they have made void Your Torah.

While some biblical verses seem to have stayed in the forefront of
Heschel's consciousness throughout his life,[20] this verse was introduced
explicitly into his repertoire only in the 1960s, and it may be seen as a
biblical foil to his growing political activism. Following his various

interpretations and applications of this verse may afford a glimpse into his approach to activism.

He devoted a mini-chapter of his work on rabbinic theology to this verse, noting that it "served as a firm foundation for a modest measure of flexibility in the legal construction of mitzvoth."[21] As the chapter proceeds, the interpretations seem less and less modest. In the last of them, Heschel brought a number of bold legal decisions predicated on the notion, to quote Rashi on Berakhot 54a, that "there are times when one cancels the words of Torah in order to act for the Lord." Having mentioned some of the classical applications of the legal principle, such as greeting on the Sabbath and committing the Oral Law to writing, Heschel then brought a tradition from Mishnah Keritot, according to which Rabbi Simeon ben Gamaliel changed the price and scope of a bird sacrifice in the Temple in a year when prices were prohibitively high, explaining his social intervention by reference to this same verse.[22] Here is an example of a classic Sage engaged in issues of economic justice and ritual probity.

In Heschel's view, Rabbi Ishmael, one of the two great protagonists of Heschel's epic rabbinic theology, understood the commandments to love God and to cleave to Him in the social domain alone. Heschel quoted a locus classicus of the religious social justice tradition as being "in the style of Rabbi Ishmael":

> The verse says, "You shall follow the Lord your God" (Deuteronomy 13:5). Is it possible for man to follow Divinity? It means, therefore, that man must imitate the divine attributes of the Holy and Blessed One. Even as he clothes the naked, so you shall do likewise; even as He visits the sick, so shall you, etc.[23]

When it came to his social philosophy, Heschel expressed a clear Ishmaelian preference. Rabbi Akiva lauded the salutary effects of poverty, while Rabbi Ishmael bemoaned its destructive effects.[24] To love and cleave to God should not mean to be carried away in ecstatic throes, but rather to act in the world in a way which expresses this love for the betterment of others.[25]

If Heschel drew strength from Rabbi Ishmael's no-nonsense approach, he looked to his counterpart for theological inspiration. He found within the teachings of the Rabbis a strong expression of the belief that human agency is a divine need. In *Torah min Hashamayim* Heschel made clear that the origins of this belief are to be found in the prophetic notion he called divine pathos. But the Rabbis, and most particularly Rabbi Akiva, were responsible for a remarkable development of this notion, according to which human redemption is a need of God.[26]

The second volume of *Torah min Hashamayim* has a chapter dedicated to the expansion of this Akivan idea and its impact on later generations of Judaism; the Shekhinah went into exile with the people Israel. For all who engage in prayer and good deeds, it is as if they redeem God; redemption is to be found in the partnership between the human and the Divine.[27]

Heschel brought to the barricades not only the rage for justice of Hosea and Amos, but also an Ishmaelian commitment to social amelioration coupled with an Akivan belief in the divine need for human initiative.

A conversation Heschel had with Jewish educators in 1969 will serve to conclude this discussion of the literature of the Rabbis in service of Heschel's social vision: on discussing the embarrassment felt by blacks towards whites he described it as a religious problem and referred to a teaching from Berakhot 43b concerning the shaming of a fellow human being. His strident approach to the social issues of his day was rooted in his reading of classical Jewish sources.[28]

Maimonides and Heschel

For Heschel, the prophetic prompt to effect change in the world and the rabbinic notion of divine need and exile were not the end of the unfolding imperative to act in the world. In 1945 Heschel published a highly significant essay on the question of Maimonides's self-understanding as a prophet and in 1950 another on the concept of the Holy Spirit during the Middle Ages up until the Maimonidean period.[29] There is evidence to suggest that he wrote a piece on a similar theme dealing with the rabbinic period.[30] Together, these works cover the notion of a continuation of Hebrew prophecy spanning thirteen centuries. Heschel was keen to emphasize the belief of Maimonides and others that prophecy was an ever-present possibility, dependent on the moral excellence of an elite in each generation.

Maimonides played a surprising role in the formation of Heschel's own social conscience. It is by no means coincidental that he chose to end *The Insecurity of Freedom* with a piece entitled "The Last Days of Maimonides."[31] This is a translated version of the chapter "Imitatio

Dei" with which he concluded his 1934 biography of Maimonides, and at its heart it is a description of the change which came over Maimonides towards the end of his life. As discussed in chapter four, Heschel did not read Maimonides's late engagement with the quotidian tasks of a working physician as a concession to economic reality but rather as a sublime metamorphosis "from metaphysics to medicine, from contemplation to practice, from speculation to the imitation of God."[32]

Heschel read this example of the progression from the seclusion of study and reflection to engagement with people in society as a potent source of personal inspiration. Just as he saw the prophet as "*a person who holds God and men in one thought at one time, at all times*," so he described Maimonides's use of a similar bifurcation: "It took a life-long dedication to intellectual pursuits to be able to attain simultaneity of involvement with people and being absorbed in the contemplation of God."[33] In describing a process leading from intellectual endeavour to strident engagement with contemporary ills, it is clear that, Heschel saw his own journey mirrored in that of Maimonides.

In the previous section mention was made of the chapter in *Torah min Hashamayim* relating to Psalms 119:126. In that chapter, Heschel cited two of Maimonides's responsa in which the principle of *'et la'asot* was employed. In the first, Maimonides ruled that the silent recitation of the Amidah prayer should be suspended since the dignity of prayer was being undermined; while in the second, he offered a lenient ruling to allow a man to wed his former maid "with gentleness and dignity."[34] Heschel found in these examples a precedent to take bold steps with a view to the greater good of the community.

Kabbalah and Hasidism

As previously noted, Heschel saw in the thought of Rabbi Akiva an important development of the prophetic concept of divine pathos. From several of his writings, it is clear that for Heschel the mystical tradition was the full efflorescence of this notion: "Jewish mystics are inspired by a bold and dangerously paradoxical idea that not only is God necessary to man but that man is also necessary to God, to the unfolding of His plans in this world …"[35]

While Heschel did not cite the Zohar as a playbook for his social activism, he did regard it and other works of the esoteric tradition as an important expansion and fulfilment of ideas that reached back to the Rabbis and earlier. Two paragraphs from chapter 14 of *God in Search of*

Man illustrate this point: in the first, the teaching from the sixth chapter of Avot regarding the heavenly voice resounding daily from Mount Horeb is followed by a Zoharic statement: "But there is no one who inclines his ear. The Torah calls on man, and none pay regard."[36] The reader is directed to eight different excerpts from the Zohar.

In the second of the two examples, once again a text from the Zohar completes an idea presented from rabbinic literature. God calls out to humanity, but it is up to human initiative to respond to the prompt: "Open to Me, my sister, because thou art the door through which there is entrance to Me; if thou openest not, I am closed."[37]

In the earlier chapter on the literature of Kabbalah, it was argued that Heschel was particularly drawn to the radical potential inherent in several teachings to be found within the esoteric tradition. New aspects of Torah, new ways of constructing meaning, come to light at different times in the unfolding of history. To judge from the last decade of his life, Heschel decided that his times called for a new facet of revelation to be expressed. In these and other ways the literature of Kabbalah found its way into Heschel's activist theology.

The aforementioned chapter in *Torah min Hashamayim* on the principle of *'et la'asot* will serve to illustrate the role of Hasidic thought in the development of Heschel's theological approach to social activism. Having brought the Halakhic discussion in the chapter to a climax by referring to the Maimonidean application of our verse, he appended two paragraphs suggesting quite different readings offered by the Ba'al Shem Tov and the Kotzker Rebbe, respectively.[38] In each case the implication seems to be that there is more to be found in discussion of this principle than had been so far discussed.

Another chapter, purportedly from an original version of *Heavenly Torah* although not to be found in the original published text, discussed the relationship between God and Torah. Here Heschel cited the verse from Psalm 119 in order to assert the principle "Sometimes one should annul parts of the Torah to act for the Lord."[39]

The tension between the dictates of Torah and the demands of God came to a crescendo in Heschel's last works, his books in English and Yiddish on the Kotzker Rebbe. In some ways, devotees of the militant pacifist and indomitable activist may have had cause to be disappointed by these works. The two-volume work in Yiddish was written in a language indecipherable to most young Jews in America in the 1960s, while the English one-volume *A Passion for Truth* holds little of direct application for budding antiwar activists. True, there is a section comparing the Kotzker and Kierkegaard on the subject of radicalism, but it is their souls that are on fire, not draft papers.[40]

In these last works, and most particularly in the Yiddish *Kotzk*, Heschel was engaged with a search for a mandate from within Jewish tradition for his highly non-traditional approach. It is not so much the misanthropic Kotzker to whom Heschel turned in this case but rather the radical antinomianism of Rabbi Mordecai Joseph Leiner of Izbica. As argued above, Heschel saw in the Izbicer a mandate, or at least an inspiration, for theological radicalism. Here it is my contention that such daring helps explain how Heschel concluded that it was time to man the barricades.

Before briefly analysing these sources, it is worth mentioning that Heschel's growing involvement, towards the end of his life, with life outside his study forced him to confront any numbers of issues relating to his commitments as a traditional Jew. One example, discussed in his biography, may prove instructive. Heschel was pictured next to Rabbi Maurice Eisendrath of the (Reform) Union of American Hebrew Congregations carrying a Torah scroll in an antiwar mobilization at Arlington Cemetery. Many Orthodox Jews protested that this represented a clear infraction of Jewish law. Heschel was at pains to offer a defence for his actions, using both Halakhic and other criteria.[41] In his last works Heschel struggled with exactly this question of how to deal with a conflict between the word of God and the demands of Torah.

Early in *Kotzk*, Heschel entitled a chapter "Torah and God." Towards the end of the book, he included a chapter called "God and Torah." In the former, the verse from Psalm 119 is mentioned, along with a teaching of the Rabbi of Izbica to the effect that a Jew may employ intuition to decide how to act in matters not covered by the 613 commandments.[42] In the latter, the penultimate chapter of the book, Heschel made a much bolder and more challenging statement. Here he asserted that on occasion a person who is fully acquainted with the demands of Torah will act against its injunctions for the sake of God. God opens our eyes anew to His will, and we are impelled to act.[43] Heschel then referred his reader in a footnote to a tradition of the Izbicer which he had quoted years earlier in *God in Search of Man*, concerning two archetypes – Ephraim, the strict legalist, and Judah, the spiritual adventurer:

Judah refuses to be content with routine observance or perfunctory faith. Not content to do today what he did yesterday, he desires to find new light in His commandments every day. This insistence on fresh light sometimes drives Judah into doing actions for the sake of God which are against the strict law.[44]

How is a follower of Judah to know when God's will demands a break with traditional norms? Here Heschel employed a particularly significant teaching of the Izbicer:

"In time it is said unto Jacob and unto Israel, what God has wrought." (Numbers 23:23) In every moment, every Jew, from the smallest to the greatest, knows what the Creator of the World wants now. The Jews know "intuitively" that the will of God is thus.[45]

Arnold Eisen charted a course in Heschel's life "from Hasidism to Prophecy."[46] Here, however, at the very end of his life, Heschel reverted to a rich particularistic tradition in Yiddish to express a radical idea he only hinted at in English, namely that there is an ever-present possibility to act according to one's intuition in order to do what God demands at this time. So conscious was Heschel of the dangers inherent in this position that he employed the scepticism of the Kotzker with regard to human motivation, as a kind of dampener to the Izbicer's antinomian enthusiasm. Nevertheless, here is a theology of radical innovation for the sake of God, even if this innovation be at the expense of Torah.

As mentioned above, in a conversation with Jewish educators Heschel quoted a rabbinic source to explain why one should get involved in the issue of racial injustice. Tellingly, a teaching of Reb Aaron of Karlin was also cited in this regard followed by his own interpretation that toleration of another person's poverty is a "threat to my existence."[47] While it may seem unlikely to evoke the sources of Hasidism in the struggle for civil rights in America in the 1960s, this is in fact what Abraham Joshua Heschel Heschel, scion and heir of Hasidic dynasties, chose to do.

Universalistic Tendencies

Heschel reread particularistic Jewish sources in a universalistic light, occasionally presenting these sources in contradiction to their plain meaning. His own intuition drew him to this interpretation.

A striking example of Heschel's way of reading sources in such a way that their exclusivist claims are played down or muted can be found in *Search* in a quote from Moses Almosnino's sixteenth-century apologetic work, *Tefillah le-Moshe*: "The divine Torah should become the very essence of man, so that a person can no longer be conceived as man without Torah, as little as he can be conceived as man without having life."[48]

Almosnino did indeed make this assertion, but he based it on a profound ontological distinction between the people of Israel and the other nations: only the Jews are to be considered truly human, since only with Torah can man merit the name Adam.[49] In Heschel's treatment of this teaching, the original distinction has disappeared.

Another example of a universalistic rendering of a kabbalistic source can be found in both *Search* and an essay considering the thought of Reinhold Niebuhr. In both pieces, authored in the mid-1950s, Heschel quoted a tradition from the Zohar concluding with these words: "So, too, from good issues evil and from mercy issues judgment, and all are intertwined, the good impulse and the evil impulse ..."[50] The Zoharic excerpt continues the list of polarities to include right and left, Israel and the other peoples, and black and white. Clearly, the particularistic bent of this teaching encouraged Heschel to leave the sentence incomplete.[51]

There are cases in *Search* in which a rabbinic source is presented in such a way that it seems to promote universal humanistic values, while the text itself has a quite different emphasis. In a note on the first words of the Decalogue, for example, Heschel described the divine voice dividing itself into the seventy tongues of man. Thus presented, this teaching is the epitome of transnational fraternity. There is, however, only one distinction which Heschel chose not to bring into his paraphrase of the source: whereas all the other nations of the earth would sense their souls depart when they hear the words of Torah in their own language, Israel would hear the voice and be unharmed.[52]

However, not all of the rabbinic sources employed to promote the brotherhood of all peoples under God are the results of creative editing. To cite yet another example from *Search*, Heschel declared,

> There is a grain of the prophet in the recesses of every human existence. "I call heaven and earth for witnesses that every man, whether gentile or Jew, whether man or woman, whether manservant or maidservant, according to the measure of his good deeds, the spirit of holiness rests upon him."[53]

This is an accurate and apt quotation from Seder Eliahu Rabbah.[54] Here the contemporary agenda of multidenominational, postwar America is complemented by the sentiments of an ancient text.

It would be mistaken to suggest that Heschel interpolated a universalistic agenda. Rather, he cited a variety of Jewish sources in order to show that the meaning of the Torah changes from era to era.[55] Although not naive about the chauvinism to be found in some sources, he believed that the characterization of Judaism in universalistic terms was not an external accretion but rather an expression of Judaism's essence. He offered ethical criteria according to which the authentic divine derivation of a teaching could be shown: "If a thought generated pride, separation from other people's suffering, unawareness of the dangers of evil – we know it is a deviation from His way."[56]

Heschel ended a 1957 paper called the "Sacred Image of Man" with a vision of the future based on Isaiah 19:23–25. He read the prophecy concerning Assyria, Egypt, and Israel as evidence that these three peoples would live together when they worshipped together, adding that "all three will be equally God's chosen people."[57] In a speech given to an ecumenical conference Heschel offered a reading of the prophet that compromised the unique status of Israel as chosen people.

Abraham Joshua Heschel did not believe that he was adding a universalistic gloss to inhospitable texts. Rather, he was motivated by a profound religious intuition that the present eon was exposing an aspect of these sources which had been previously been downplayed. His statement that racial prejudice was the antithesis of true religion should not be read as an historical thesis. Rather, it was a declaration of faith.

Addressing a group of Jewish educators, Heschel set out something of a particularistic manifesto:

> We are essentially trained in a non-Jewish world. This is where we obtain our general training. We are inclined to think in non-Jewish terms. I am not discouraging exposure to the non-Jewish world. I am merely indicating that it is not biblical thinking. It is not rabbinic thinking. It is not Hasidic thinking. It is non-Jewish thinking. A non-Jewish philosophy is fine. But we would also like to have in our thinking a Jewish view of things. We would also like to apply the Bible and *Hazal* …
>
> This has been my major challenge, ever since I began working on my dissertation; that is: How to maintain a Jewish way of thinking? This was the major concern and the major thesis of my dissertation *Die Prophetie*. Since that day I consider this to be my major effort.[58]

Heschel's universalism was couched in Jewish terms. Applying "a Jewish way of thinking" to the great problems of the day was not a strategy for garnering acceptance by the host society. Rather, in Heschel's view it was the fulfilment of the promise of Judaism in the current era. By bringing a biblical-rabbinic-Hasidic sensibility to bear, two simultaneous acts of preservation were in play: both a world in crisis and Judaism in danger of spiritual extinction were changed for the better by the development of "a Jewish view of things."

External Influences

It has been suggested that external influences provided the catalyst for Heschel's universalistic emphasis. Eugene Borowitz highlighted two factors that help to explain Heschel's emergence in the area of social ethics and activism. These are neither strictly textual nor traditional but rather a product of context and contact. In Borowitz's view, the first factor was what he termed "the reality of American life in the early 1950s,"[59] by which he appeared to refer to undercurrents in contemporary Christianity. He argued that Heschel's friendship with Reinhold Niebuhr both was sparked by and gave rise to an engagement with the theological zeitgeist. The milieu of the Union Theological Seminary, in contrast to that of the Jewish Theological Seminary, served a significant catalyzing role. Second, Borowitz noted the rise of the slogan "prophetic Judaism," which became "the mantra of Reform Judaism" during Heschel's early years in America.[60] If the first environmental factor was the political and cultural mood of America preparing to face the struggle for civil rights, the second related to processes playing out within the Jewish community.

There is certainly some truth to Borowitz's insight. Niebuhr was only one of a range of Protestant and Catholic progressives with whom Heschel developed a deep and mutually influential bond. To give an historic example, Heschel's relationship with Martin Luther King, Jr. was founded on profound theological affinities.[61] There is ample evidence to suggest that Heschel's work on the prophets influenced King and his circle: King referred to Heschel as "a truly great prophet," just as Heschel compared King's voice to "the voice of the prophets of Israel."[62]

The crusading zeal for social change that characterized some parts of the American Reform Movement also had an impact on Heschel. Newly arrived in Cincinnati in the early 1940s, he came into contact with Abraham Cronbach, a radical pacifist professor at the Hebrew Union College.[63] Cronbach held up the prophets as the archetype for contemporary social involvement, stating, for example, that "Amos makes short shrift of white supremacy."[64] While baldly asserting that concepts such as divine retribution, denunciation, antiritualism,[65] and prognostication were "prophetic ideas to which we do not subscribe," he lauded "the soaring idealism and the ravishing loveliness of many a prophetic utterance [which] makes that utterance veritably an approach of the Divine unto our souls."[66]

By all accounts Heschel was struck by Cronbach's personality and admired his integrity. However, his own approach to Jewish tradition, and his way of reading the sources of that tradition differed sharply from Cronbach's.[67] While admiring and learning from the best of Reform activism, and while engaging in partnership and dialogue with progressive Christians, Heschel's own path to social engagement was distinct from both of these approaches.

A Time to Act

In the previously mentioned chapter on *'et la'asot*, Heschel suggested that the most radical reading of the verse in Psalms 119 "should not be entrusted to any but the wisest of Sages, who truly understand contemporary times."[68]

The risk inherent in the provision of a mandate for overruling the strictures of Halakhah is self-evident: who is to decide when a particular situation justifies the abrogation of norms? A special capacity to fathom the times in which we live, specifically bestowed upon the elite of each generation, is necessary to ensure that this Halakhic flexibility does not lead to licentiousness. Heschel looked to *yod'ei ha'itim*, those who read the times, in order to make such judgments.

A crucial component in Heschel's theology of social action was a reading of time. It is well known that Heschel was preoccupied by the relationship between time and space, but it seems that his understanding that the times speak to us has been obscured by the brilliance of his theory of the Sabbath. To understand the centrality of time for Heschel, we must look to not only to the Sabbath but also the six days of action which precede and follow it. For Heschel, the times spoke. An example of this is a famous statement from his essay "No Religion Is an Island": "Perhaps it is the will of God that in this eon there should be diversity in our forms of devotion and commitment to Him. In this diversity of religions is the will of God."[69]

Elsewhere Heschel quoted a mystical tradition according to which the eternal Torah "assumes different forms in various eons."[70] Our particular situation demands a response of us, which must be new if it is to avoid the pitfalls of spiritual nepotism. God's word is communicated to us in the specificities of this time.

Abraham Joshua Heschel was wary of any talk of impersonal processes unfolding in history. Instead, he was fascinated by those events that mould our lives. Faith itself is an event, and our most important decisions happen likewise as events:

> Man lives in an order of events, not only in an order of processes. It is a spiritual order. Moments of insight, moments of decision, moments of prayer – may be insignificant in the world of space, yet they put life into focus.[71]

Returning to Heschel's description of the causes of his involvement in the antiwar movement, it is by no means trivial or coincidental that he described the three main reasons as events: the twentieth century spoke to him in all its tumult, and he was commanded to respond.

Niebuhr and King, napalm and Nagasaki – the personalities and issues of Heschel's times – were not the *sources* upon which Heschel based his activist response; rather they were the prompts which awakened this response. Drawing on a range of traditional sources, Abraham Joshua Heschel described the divine call to humanity as a daily event: each day a voice issues forth from Horeb. Each day a ceaseless call asks to be heard.[72]

God in Search of Man ends in true Heschelian style, with an unexplained biblical excerpt:

> Upon thy walls, O Jerusalem,
> I have set watchmen,
> All the day and all the night
> They shall never be silent.
> Ye that stir the Lord to remember,
> Take no rest,
> And give Him no rest till
> He establishes Jerusalem,
> And makes a praise in the earth.   Isaiah 62:6–7[73]

The verses from Isaiah strike a note of activism and ceaseless vigilance that challenge the reader to respond. Heschel left the words of Isaiah reverberating in the ears (perhaps even the hearts) of his readers.

Isaiah 62:6 had been quoted earlier in the work as part of a Zoharic consideration of the role of human initiative.[74] Years later Heschel quoted the first nine verses of Isaiah 62 at the opening of his work on Israel. In both cases the verse reads as a human response to a divine prompt.[75]

The words preceding the excerpt from Isaiah at the end of *Search* were a slight reworking of sections of a Hebrew piece he published in the late 1940s. Following a familiar pattern, Heschel quoted himself, but at the climax of what was arguably his most important work, he turned to the words of the prophet. Human beings are enjoined to remind God to continue His perpetual search. Calling out to God, they find God calling out to them.

The day, the contemporary situation, is not just the date when this divine call takes place; it is also in some sense the content of that call. In Heschel's understanding, it is in the circumstances of the day, with its horrors and beauties, that the insistent invitation to respond can be heard. The human task is to heed that call and respond to that daily event. It is not just that the divine call issues forth every day. It is that every day is a call from the divine.

Abraham Joshua Heschel invoked the prophets of the Bible as archetypes of protest and engagement. Not willing to privilege these figures at the expense of the rest of Jewish tradition, he emphasized the continuation of the prophetic urge beyond the biblical period, and he read out of some rabbinic and Hasidic sources a mandate for radical response to new realities. He spoke in passionate defence of the Deed, both in its ritual and social manifestations, and he developed a theology of time, according to which our contemporary situation, understood through the filter of our honest intuition, may intimate God's will to us.

Eternity utters a day, as Heschel wrote at the end of *The Sabbath*,[76] and each day utters eternity. He called upon his audience to hear the utterance and to see the signs. Every time, and especially this time, is a time to act.

The *Aspaklaria* of the Generations

Heschel was steeped in Jewish sources in a way that set him apart from most of the major figures of modern Jewish thought. As noted in the first chapter of this book, in his 1937 monograph on Abravanel, when he described his subject as being at home in all fields of religious literature – in Halakhah, Aggadah, religious philosophy and exegesis, as well as in Christian theology and Islamic philosophy[77] – he was in fact describing the range of his own learning and interests. Jacob Neusner, contrasting the depths of Heschel's Jewish knowledge with that of Buber and Rosenzweig, concluded that "Heschel knew everything he had to know to do what he wanted to do,"[78] while Pinhas Peli attested that Heschel, "more than anyone else I know in recent generations, represented the totality of what Judaism is."[79]

Rooted in these sources, Heschel advanced a picture of contemporary Jewish existence in which, despite profound differences, our present-day discourse would be discernible to the great figures of the Jewish past in every generation. To this extent, Heschel was a conservative. His radicalism was predicated on the idea, however, that the current era demands a new response.

In the last chapter I noted that Abraham Joshua Heschel coined the expression "the *aspaklaria* of the generations." Just as authors of previous eras were referred to as "an illuminated speculum" (we find this honorific applied to Heschel's ancestors, such as Levi Yitzchak of Berditchev), so might we bestow on Heschel the term he himself invented. He was a speculum of the generations. He aimed to hold up the traditions and attitudes of thirty centuries to the light of contemporary realities.

To *be* an *aspaklaria* rather than to *use* one is parallel to the Heschelian ideal of a textperson rather than a textbook.[80] It is parallel to the rabbi (in an anecdote Heschel recounted) who asked a student who claimed to have gone through the Talmud three times, "Yes, but how much of the Talmud has gone through you?"[81] To be an *aspaklaria* is not to aspire to be the single authoritative source but rather to offer a set of perspectives, to be a prism through which various ideas can be refracted.

Heschel experienced the call of time. Time, he believed, was "eternity in disguise";[82] "it is the dimension of time wherein man meets God, wherein man becomes aware that every instant is an act of creation, a Beginning, opening up new roads for ultimate realizations."[83] Heschel held himself up to the dimension of time. Some of the resulting insights were in opposition to the ravages of change – the loss of seriousness and learning, the rise of the trivial and the grossly material. Other insights were radical and challenging – the call to social responsibility, the refusal to submit to indifference.

The image of a human transgenerational *aspaklaria* has serious educational implications. Liberals and traditionalists alike might ask how the

combination of intensity and sensitivity can be achieved. In an unpublished conversation Heschel himself expressed doubt that had he
been raised in postwar America he would have remained an observant
Jew,[84] and already in 1948 he bemoaned what he called "the banaliza-
tion of Judaism ... the tumult of arrogant not-knowing and not want-
ing to know."[85] Heschel's lenses were formed in intense conditions.
From Poland in the 1920s to the United States in the 1960s, Heschel
found a remarkable way of looking at and casting light on the pressing issues of the day, both spiritual and political. He once suggested
that a goal of Jewish education should be "that every Jew become a
representative of the Jewish spirit."[86] Abraham Joshua Heschel was
one such representative.

Perhaps the critique of Heschel that most offended his understanding of his own project was that he espoused a view foreign to the true
spirit of Judaism. This was the nub of Eliezer Berkovits's 1964 reading
of the theology of pathos: "While it is utterly unknown to Judaism, it
has a long history in Christian thought."[87] For Heschel this must have
been a scandalous claim, not because he harboured disdain for Christian theology, but rather because he believed his approach to be a thoroughly Jewish response. *Torah min Hashamayim* was intended to demonstrate that a bold theological stance could find its mandate within the
sources of Judaism.

This book began with a person, a question, and a phenomenon. We
have attempted to shed light on the person, Abraham Joshua Heschel,
by considering the sources of tradition that are to be found explicitly or
otherwise in almost every word he uttered and wrote. As for the question of his emphasis on immediacy while surrounding himself and his
reader with a cascade of sources, we have presented a Jew committed to
the notion that "only he who is an heir is qualified to be a pioneer."[88]

Returning to Emerson's thought, quoted at the start of this work,
that "only an inventor knows how to borrow, and every man is or
should be an inventor,"[89] we may suggest that Heschel offers a distinct
approach to the broad question of the dynamics of tradition in modern
times. He sought a basis for radical immediacy and activism in rapture,
not rupture.[90]

Committed to the notion that Judaism was of urgent relevance to the
contemporary world, Abraham Joshua Heschel put Jewish tradition to
work, applying it in a variety of ways to the urgent spiritual and political issues of the day. Biological heir of Hasidic masters, he was heir to

millennia of Jewish teachings, few of which were foreign to him. His core experience was that of being confronted by God's concern. His responses – wonder, piety, insight, sympathy, and more – did not bypass the sources of Judaism; rather they were infused with these sources. The light of the contemporary was refracted through the *aspaklaria* of the generations. That this intensely Jewish reading of contemporaneity through the prism of posterity resonated so widely, and that this legacy continues to grow decades after Heschel's death, these too are sources of wonder.

Notes

1 Abraham Joshua Heschel: Heir and Pioneer

1 The Heschel literature is voluminous. For a survey of this literature up until 2006, see Michael Marmur, "In Search of Heschel," *Shofar* 26, no. 1 (2007): 9–40. Between 2006 and 2013, over sixty new articles and books were added to the bibliography, and there is no sign of this flood abating. For an account of Heschel's life, see Edward K. Kaplan and Samuel H. Dresner, *Abraham Joshua Heschel: Prophetic Witness* (New Haven: Yale University Press, 1998) (hereafter *Prophetic Witness*); and Edward K. Kaplan, *Spiritual Radical* (New Haven: Yale University Press, 2007). Among special editions of journals dedicated to Heschel, two are particularly noteworthy: *Conservative Judaism* 50, no. 2–3 (1998) and *Modern Judaism* 29, no.1 (2009). Important articles by a number of leading Heschel scholars are to be found in each of these issues. From the plethora of articles and books relating to Heschel, the following works are of particular note; while they differ greatly in scope and focus, each of them adds an important dimension to an understanding of Heschel's work: Alan Brill, "Aggadic Man: The Poetry and Rabbinic Thought of Abraham Joshua Heschel," *Meorot* 6, no. 1 (2007) http://www.yctorah.org/content/view/211/10/; Dror Bondi, *Ayyekah? She'elato shel Elohim ve-Tirgum haMasoret be-Haguto shel Avraham Yehoshua Heschel* (Jerusalem: Shalem, 2008); Joseph Harp Britton, *Abraham Heschel and the Phenomenon of Piety* (London: T. and T. Clark, 2013); Samuel H. Dresner, *Heschel, Hasidism and Halakha* (New York: Fordham University Press, 2002); Robert Erlewine, "The Legacy of Abraham Joshua Heschel," *Tikkun* 26, no. 4 (2011): 11–14, 36–9; Alexander Even-Chen and Ephraim Meir, *Between Heschel and Buber: A Comparative Study* (Brighton, MA: Academic Studies Press, 2012); Arthur Green, "Three Warsaw Mystics," in

Rachel Elior and Joseph Dan, eds., *Kolot Rabim: Sefer ha-Zikaron le-Rivka Shatz-Uffenheimer* (Jerusalem: Hebrew University, 1996), Part 2: 1*–58*; Shai Held, *Abraham Joshua Heschel: The Call of Transcendence* (Bloomington: Indiana University Press, 2013); Reuven Kimelman, "Abraham Joshua Heschel's Theory of Judaism and the Rewriting of Jewish Intellectual History," *Journal of Jewish Thought and Philosophy* 17, no. 2 (2009): 207–38; David Novak, "Heschel's Phenomenology of Revelation," in Stanisław Krajewski and Adam Lipszyc, eds., *Abraham Joshua Heschel: Philosophy, Theology and Interreligious Dialogue* (Wiesbaden, Germany: Harrassowitz, 2009), 36–46; Lawrence Perlman, *Abraham Joshua Heschel's Idea of Revelation* (Atlanta, GA: Scholars Press, 1989).

2 Eugene B. Borowitz, "After Kaplan's 'Heschel,' What Is There Left to Be Said?" *Conservative Judaism* 60, no. 4 (2008): 89–96 (hereafter "What Is There Left to Be Said?").

3 Abraham Joshua Heschel, *God in Search of Man: A Philosophy of Judaism* (New York: Farrar, Straus and Cudahy, 1955), 212 (hereafter *Search*). Unless otherwise noted, italics in quotations are Heschel's.

4 It is curious to note in this context that a letter dated 11 May 1953 from Reinhold Niebuhr's secretary, Nola Meade, to Heschel notes that as an editor at Faber and Faber, Eliot had written to Niebuhr concerning one of Heschel's manuscripts. I have not been able to locate the letter itself.

5 T.S. Eliot, "Tradition and the Individual Talent," in T.S. Eliot, *Selected Prose* (London: Penguin, 1953), 212.

6 I am most grateful to Shai Held for coining this felicitous phrase in a private conversation.

7 Eliot, "Tradition and the Individual Talent," 24.

8 Ralph Waldo Emerson, "Quotation and Originality," in *The Collected Works of Ralph Waldo Emerson*, vol. 8: *Letters and Social Aims* (Cambridge, MA: Harvard University Press, 210), 107.

9 Particular attention will be paid in some chapters to *God in Search of Man.*

10 These categories are discussed in Marmur, "In Search of Heschel."

11 For an emphasis on phenomenology, see Novak, "Heschel's Phenomenology of Revelation," and Perlman, *Heschel's Idea of Revelation.*

12 On the centrality of pathos, see Fritz A. Rothschild, introduction in Fritz A. Rothschild, ed., *Between God and Man: An Interpretation of Judaism* (New York: Free Press, 1959), 7–32. For an attempt to offer a systematic reading of Heschel's theology in the spirit of Rothschild's introduction, see John C. Merkle, *The Genesis of Faith: The Depth Theology of Abraham Joshua Heschel* (New York: Macmillan, 1985). See also Michael A. Chester, *Divine Pathos and Human Being: The Theology of Abraham Joshua Heschel* (London:

Vallentine Mitchell, 2005). For a critical reading that places pathos at the heart of Heschel's thought, see Eliezer Berkovits, "Dr. A. J. Heschel's Theology of Pathos," *Tradition* 6, no. 2 (1964): 67–104.

13 Joseph Harp Britton, *Abraham Heschel and the Phenomenon of Piety* (London: Bloomsbury, 2013).

14 See Bondi, *Ayyekah?* esp. 6–54.

15 See Einat Ramon, "Avodah Zarah ve-Sanvarei ha-Neorut be-Hagut Avraham Yehoshua Heschel," *Daat* 71 (2011): 105–31; Byron Sherwin, "The Assimilation of Judaism: Heschel and the 'Category Mistake,'" *Judaism* 55, no. 3–4 (2006): 40–50.

16 For a description of Heschel as a non-traditional traditionalist, see Shaul Magid, "Abraham Joshua Heschel and Thomas Merton: Heretics of Modernity," *Modern Judaism* 50, no. 2–3 (1998): 112–25. Magid promotes a reading of the liberal Heschel, but is well aware of the complexity of this exercise. See Shaul Magid, "The Role of the Secular in Abraham Joshua Heschel's Theology: (Re)Reading Heschel After 9/11," *Modern Judaism* 29, no. 1 (2009): 138–60. See also Michael Lerner, "Heschel's Legacy for the Politics of the Twenty-First Century," *Modern Judaism* 29, no. 1 (2009): 34–43.

17 Held, *The Call of Transcendence*.

18 Abraham Joshua Heschel, *The Earth Is the Lord's: The Inner Life of the Jew in Eastern Europe* (New York: Henry Schuman, 1950), 30–1.

19 Two exceptions, *The Earth Is the Lord's* and *Who Is Man?* were both originally lectures.

20 Abraham Joshua Heschel, *Don Jizchak Abravanel* (Berlin: E. Reiss, 1937), 6.

21 Kaplan and Dresner, *Prophetic Witness*, 145.

22 Abraham Joshua Heschel, *Moral Grandeur and Spiritual Audacity*, ed. Susannah Heschel (New York: Farrar, Straus and Giroux, 1996), 384 (hereafter *Moral Grandeur*).

23 Perlman, *Heschel's Idea of Revelation*, 165.

24 Edward K. Kaplan, *Holiness in Words: Abraham Joshua Heschel's Politics of Piety* (Albany: SUNY Press, 1996), 149.

25 Abraham Joshua Heschel, *Heavenly Torah as Refracted through the Generations*, trans. Gordon Tucker (New York: Continuum, 2005) (hereafter *Heavenly Torah*). Throughout this work, unless otherwise stated, references will be from Heschel's original work, *Torah min Hashamayim be-Aspaklaria shel ha-Dorot*, vol. 1 (London: Soncino, 1962), vol. 2 (London: Soncino, 1965), and vol. 3 (New York: Jewish Theological Seminary of America, 1995) (hereafter *Torah min Hashamayim*).

26 See Jeffrey Shandler, "Heschel and Yiddish: A Struggle with Signification," *Journal of Jewish Thought and Philosophy* 8, no. 2 (1993): 245–99; Annette

Aronowicz, "Heschel's Yiddish *Kotsk*: Some Reflections on Inwardness," in Krajewski and Lipszyc, eds., *Abraham Joshua Heschel: Philosophy, Theology and Interreligious Dialogue*, 112–21.

27 "I am the most maladjusted person in society," from " A Conversation with Rabbi Abraham J. Heschel," an interview with Frank Reynolds, aired on ABC, 21 November 1971.

28 The relationship between Heschel and his readers is discussed in Jon D. Levenson, "Religious Affirmation and Historical Criticism in Heschel's Biblical Interpretation," *AJS Review* 25, no. 1 (2000–2001): esp. 37–9.

29 See Antoine Compagnon, *La seconde main, ou, le travail de la citation*, (Paris: Seuil, 1979).

30 Hillel Goldberg, *Between Berlin and Solobodka: Jewish Transition Figures from Eastern Europe* (Hoboken, NJ: Ktav, 1989), 130.

31 See Arnold Eisen, "Re-Reading Heschel on the Commandments," *Modern Judaism* 9, no. 1 (1989): 1–2. On 28 n6, Eisen lists Eugene Borowitz and Marvin Fox among those who have attributed undue centrality to *Search*.

32 See Arnold Eisen, *Taking Hold of Torah: Jewish Commitment and Community in America* (Bloomington: Indiana University Press, 1997), 17–18.

33 Gerard Genette, *Palimpsests: Literature in the Second Degree*, trans. Channa Newman (Paris: Seuil, 1982); Gerard Genette, *Paratexts: Thresholds of Interpretation*, trans. Jane E. Newman (Paris: Seuil, 1987). Genette listed five forms of transtextual relationship, and he risked confusion by calling the first of these forms by Julia Kristeva's term *intertextuality*. Quotation is adduced as the most direct version of this first type. See also Heinrich F. Plett, "Intertextualities," in Heinrich F. Platt, ed., *Intertextuality* (Berlin: Walter de Gruyter, 1991) esp. 8–17; Graham Allen, *Intertextuality* (London: Routledge, 2000).

34 Some scholars have reacted against the tendency to collapse all distinctions regarding the act of quotation. For a creditable example of such an attempt, see James H. Charlesworth's "Intertextuality: Isaiah 40:3 and the Serek Ha-Yahad," in Craig E. Evans and Shemaryahu Talmon, eds., *The Quest for Context and Meaning; Studies in Biblical Intertextuality in Honor of James A. Sanders* (Leiden, NL: Brill, 1997). I agree with Beal's assertion that "for the practice of intertextual reading … as opposed to theories of intertextuality, one must have … lines of delineation, no matter how arbitrarily they may be set, and no matter how quickly they may be transgressed." Timothy K. Beal, "Ideology and Intertextuality: Surplus of Meaning and Controlling the Means of Production," in Danna Nolan Fewell, ed., *Reading Between Texts; Intertextuality and the Hebrew Bible* (Louisville, KY: Westminster John Knox Press, 1992), 28.

35 Moshe Idel, *Absorbing Perfections: Kabbalah and Interpretation* (New Haven: Yale University Press, 2002), 5.

36 See Michael Marmur, "Why Jews Quote," *Oral Tradition* 29, no. 1 (2014): 5–46. In that article, the six dimensions noted here are discussed at length. There are major and significant distinctions in the style and indeed the intensity of quotation in premodern Jewish literature. Sarah Stroumza notes, for example, that when compared with Abraham Ibn Ezra, Rav Saadia Gaon is rarely quoted. See Sara Stroumza, "Masoret Tzitut," in *Masoret Ve'Shinui beTarbut Yehudit-Aravit bi Yemei Habeinayim* (Ramat Gan: Bar Ilan University, 1999), 168–9.

37 See Tanchuma Buber, Numbers 27. See also Midrash Proverbs 6.16, where misattribution of sources is listed as one of seven deadly sins. The verse from Proverbs is not used here, only the verse from Esther. See also the introduction to *Siftei Cohen* (Hamburg: 1690), 1b–2b. The author, Mordechai Hacohen of Safed, offers an important reading of the term *three degrees of separation*. His claim is that his only sources are Rabbenu Bahya, Rashi, R. Menahem Recanati, and the Zohar.

38 Two highly significant works in this context are the introduction to Reuven Margaliot, *Shem Olam* (Jerusalem: Mossad HaRav Kook, 1989), 7–37, and Abraham Shechter, *Dovev Siftei Yeshenim* (Jerusalem: Tiferet Publications,, 1957). They both provide highly valuable compendia of rabbinic sources on citation. For a recent discussion of the role of source quotation in twentieth-century Jewish thought, see Michael Marmur, "Are You My Witnesses? The Use of Sources in Modern Jewish Thought," *Modern Judaism*, 32, no. 2 (2012): 155–73.

39 See S. Morawski, "The Basic Function of Quotation," in C.H. van Schooneveld, ed., *Sign, Language, Culture* (The Hague: Mouton, 1970), 690–705. In Morawski's model, the stimulatory-amplificatory and the ornamental are distinct functions. I have elided the two for my purposes.

40 "The Eastern European Era in Jewish History," *YIVO Annual of Jewish Social Science* 1 (1946): 101. See "Existence and Celebration" in *Moral Grandeur*, 27, and "A Time for Renewal" in ibid., 47, where Rabbi Akiva is invoked.

41 Abraham Joshua Heschel, *Man's Quest for God: Studies in Prayer and Symbolism* (New York: Charles Scribner's Sons, 1954), 112. These words found their way into a later speech. See *Moral Grandeur*, 9.

42 A recording is in the American Jewish Archives.

43 "Existence and Celebration," in *Moral Grandeur*, 27 and 32. See also the 1972 essay "A Time for Renewal," in *Moral Grandeur*, 47.

44 "Existence and Celebration," in *Moral Grandeur*, 29.

45 From the Abraham Joshua Heschel Papers, Rubinstein Library, Duke
    University.
46 Idel used the term in relation to the study of Hasidism, but it can be more
    broadly applied. See Moshe Idel, "Martin Buber and Gershom Scholem on
    Hasidism: A Critical Approach," in Ada Rapoport-Albert, ed., *Hasidism
    Reappraised* (London: Littman Library of Jewish Civilization, 1996), 397.
47 See for example *Search*, 341, and *A Passion for Truth* (New York: Farrar,
    Straus and Giroux, 1973), xiii–xv.
48 *Search*, 23n2.
49 Ibid., 12. See also 205.
50 Ibid., 206. For an extended discussion of this contrast, see *The Sabbath: Its
    Meaning for Modern Man* (New York: Farrar, Straus and Young, 1951), 109–
    11. This appendix to the original work was written in response to criticism
    from various quarters that Heschel's concentration on the dimension of
    time was one-sided. See also *Search*, 88–90.
51 Ibid., 143n6. The reference is to Plato, *Epistles*, VII, 341. See also 124n9. This
    particular epistle was first quoted by Heschel in *Die Prophetie* (Cracow:
    Polish Academy of Sciences, 1936), 11n5, and it also makes an earlier
    appearance in *Search*, 103n1.
52 Abraham Joshua Heschel, *The Prophets* (Philadelphia: Jewish Publication
    Society of America, 1962), 169n81. The context of these remarks is different
    in *The Prophets* and *Die Prophetie*, although the footnote in the later English
    work is translated from the German original, including references to sec-
    ondary literature by Stenzel and Plaut.
53 Indeed, the Epistle in question hardly serves as a prooftext for the concept
    of spontaneous artistic inspiration. Instead, Plato was interested in distin-
    guishing between the common people and those rare individuals who, by
    dint of their wisdom and application, may have the fire of understanding
    kindled, There are differences in the imagery of Plato on the one hand,
    and Maimonides and the Zohar on the other. For the two Jewish sources,
    the exposure to the flash of insight remains sporadic, even if the elect few
    can be privileged to experience revelation more regularly. For Plato, one
    spark may ignite a flame which is then self-sustaining. Despite this signifi-
    cant difference, it seems to me that Heschel cited Plato because of the es-
    sential similarity of his message: a privileged elite may pass beyond the
    occasional flash of insight to a more sustained understanding. By citing
    the Platonic source alongside the Jewish ones, Heschel is implying a fun-
    damental commonality of purpose, while acknowledging a plurality of
    cultural expression.

54 *Search*, 134–5n6. This is an important discussion which provides the underpinning for a key Heschelian concept. The Bible and both the Babylonian
and Palestinian Talmuds are also cited in the note.
55 Ibid., 78n4.
56 Ibid., 133n5, 150n1.
57 Ibid., 248n1. These sources include ancient works such as Ben Sira, various
midrashic works, and the Talmuds, alongside medieval and modern authors. See, for example, *Search*, 32n9, 70n4, 71n16, 100n13, 134n6, 333n12,
334n32. In 277n14, Maimonides appears alongside the Zohar, Azulai's
Hesed le-Avraham, Leviticus Rabbah, and commentaries by Abravanel and
Sforno.
58 Ibid. See 71n16, 14 n5, 256n8.
59 Ibid. See 78n6, 79n8.
60 Ibid. See 32n5, 408n2.
61 Ibid. See 306n1, 308n4, 337n3, 408n2.
62 Ibid. See 358n12, 359n13.
63 Ibid. On 295 Heschel asserted that "The good deeds of any man, to whatever nation or religion he may belong ... will be rewarded." The reference
in the earlier part of this sentence is listed on 304 n5 as *Kuzari*, 1, iii. This is
an error; in fact, the reference is to i, iii.
64 Ibid., 418. It seems clear that Heschel is alluding here to Kaplan's famous
1934 work, *Judaism as a Civilization*.
65 Note Idel's important discussion of the development of a "mosaic" style of
composition in Moshe Idel, *Rabbi Menachem Recanati ha-Mekubal* (Jerusalem:
Schocken, 1998). See also Haim Shirman, *Toldot ha-Shira ha- Ivrit be-Sefarad
ha-Muslemit* (Jerusalem: Magnes and Ben Zvi Institute, 1996), esp. 47–51.
See Julia Kristeva, *The Kristeva Reader*, ed. Toril Moi (New York: Columbia
University Press, 1986), 37, in which Kristeva represents Bakhtin as suggesting that "any text is constructed as a mosaic of quotations." See also
Robert Alter, *Necessary Angels: Tradition and Modernity in Kafka, Benjamin
and Scholem* (Cambridge, MA: Harvard University Press in association
with HUC Press, Cincinnati, OH, 1991), 11.
66 *Passion for Truth*, 64. The reference, not cited, is to PT Shabbat 1.1, 3a. The
source also appears in PT Kiddushin 1.7, 61a. These and other references
are cited in the Yiddish parallel to this work, *Kotzk: Ein Gerangl far
Emesdikeyt*, vol. 1 (Tel-Aviv: Hamenorah, 1973), 58–60, and the notes on 331.
67 Ibid., 64.
68 See PT Shekalim 2.7 47a. This is an extraordinarily rich source for understanding rabbinic attitudes to citation, and it deserves close attention.

Immediately preceding this saying, for example, is a reflection on King David finding eternal comfort in the fact that his words are quoted in synagogues and houses of study. For parallels to these traditions, see Yevamot 96b; Midrash Shmuel (Buber), 19. In Tanhuma Ki Tissa 3, the tradition takes another turn, as the Sages left in this world refuse to give the departed Master any peace in the grave!

69 *Passion for Truth*, 63.

70 Arnold Jacob Wolf, "Abraham Joshua Heschel after Twenty-Five Years," *Judaism*, 47, no. 1 (1998), 112.

71 Hannah Arendt, "Introduction: Walter Benjamin: 1892–1940," in Walter Benjamin, *Illuminations* (New York: Schocken, 1968), 4. See Alter, *Necessary Angels*, 72–82.

72 Arendt, *Illuminations*, 38.

73 That Heschel maintained both of these views is stated by Maurice Friedman in *You Are My Witnesses: Abraham Joshua Heschel and Elie Wiesel* (New York: Farrar, Straus and Giroux, 1987), xviii. On 9, Friedman recalled asking Heschel, who had expressed envy that Friedman had spent a Sabbath in the ultra-Orthodox community of Williamsburg, why he himself would not go to live in such a community. Heschel replied, "I cannot. When I left my home in Poland, I became a modern Western man. I cannot reverse this."

74 Abraham Joshua Heschel, *Man Is Not Alone: A Philosophy of Religion* (Philadelphia: Jewish Publication Society of America, 1951), 164 (hereafter *Man Is Not Alone*). In a footnote, Heschel quotes *Panim Me'iroth* (an eighteenth-century response by Meir Eisenstadt) on the first words of the *Amidah* prayer.

75 Abraham Joshua Heschel, *Who Is Man?* (Stanford, CA: Stanford University Press, 1965), 99.

76 See Harold Bloom, *The Anxiety of Influence: A Theory of Poetry*, 2nd ed. (New York: Oxford University Press, 1997). Bloom described misprision as "a complex act of strong misreading." See also Harold Bloom, *A Map of Misreading*, 2nd ed. (New York: Oxford University Press, 2003).

77 Milner and Brady on East Asian culture, quoted in Mary Orr, *Intertextuality: Debates and Contexts* (Cambridge, MA: Polity 2003), 88.

78 *Torah min Hashamayim*, vol. 2, 242–4.

79 Abraham Joshua Heschel Papers, Box 34, Folder 1, Rubinstein Library, Duke University. The source of the quotation is Nachman of Bratslav, *Likkutei MoHaRan*, Mahadura Kamma, 12.

80 Moshe Idel, "Abraham J. Heschel on Mysticism and Hasidism," *Modern Judaism* 29, no. 1 (2009), 86.

81 Abraham Joshua Heschel, "Jewish Education," in *The Insecurity of Freedom: Essays in Applied Religion* (New York: Farrar, Straus and Giroux, 1966), 237 (hereafter *Insecurity of Freedom*).

82 On 70n5, he cites Rabbi Eliezer of Mayence rather than Rabbi Eliezer ben Samuel of Metz. Another kind of error relating to a name can be found in one of the three places where Azulai's *Or ha-Hammah* is quoted: on 144n13, the work is attributed to Rabbi Mordecai Azulai. Given the fact that on the two other occasions it is Abraham Azulai who is correctly cited, this could be seen to be little more than an error of proofreading. On imprecise quotation, see Devorah Dimant, "Use and Interpretation of Mikra in the Apocrypha and Pseudepigrapha," in Martin Jan Mulder, ed., *Mikra – Text, Translation, Reading and Interpretation of the Bible in Ancient Judaism and Early Christianity* (Philadelphia: Fortress Press, 1988), esp., for example, 391; Gershon Brin, *Sugiot beMikra vebeMegilot* (Tel Aviv: University of Tel Aviv and Kibbutz Meuchad, 1994), 144; Mendel Piekarz, "Hasidism as a Socio-Religious Movement on the Evidence of *Devekut*," in Ada Rapoport-Albert, ed., *Hasidism Reappraised* (London: Littman Library of Jewish Civilization,1996), 229.

83 Compare *Search*, 23n2 with *Who Is Man?* 19. Earlier, in *Man Is Not Alone*, he or his editors had perpetrated another error, confusing these two similarly named philosophers and creating the name Xenophones. See *Man Is Not Alone*, 113, and again on 143. In those cases it is in fact Xenophanes, not Xenophon, he had in mind.

84 I am very grateful to Professor Neusner for agreeing to share some recollections of his time with Heschel at the Seminary in a private telephone conversation.

85 On p. 155 Heschel quoted Judges 6:13 but called it Nehemiah 6:13; on 256n8, the reference should be to Psalms 51:13, not Isaiah. On 366n3, the reference to *Sanhedrin* 17a should in fact be to *Berakhot* 17a, where the term "well-laden with mitzvot" can be found. Note also that on 32n9, the reference should be to *II Barukh*.

86 *Search*, 289.

87 See Bloom, *Anxiety of Influence* and also his *A Map of Misreading*.

88 See *Torah min Hashamayim*, vol. 3, 88–9. In *Heavenly Torah*, 88, Tucker and Levin add an extensive note to explain the wordplay.

89 "Symbolism and Jewish Faith," in Ernest F. Johnson, ed., *Religious Symbolism* (New York: The Institute for Religious and Social Studies, 1954), 90.

90 Abraham Joshua Heschel, "Al Yichudo shel ha-Kiyum ha-Yehudi," *Molad* 15, no. 107–8 (1958): 237. In the English translation of this paper, Heschel paraphrased the remark. See "The Individual Jew and His Obligations,"

in *Insecurity of Freedom*, 188: "To interpret our history in the light of mere facts is to distort it. To be literal is to be ludicrous."

91 See *Torah min Hashamayim*, vol. 1, 3–23, esp. 13–15.

92 He gave eloquent expression to this idea in *Torah min Hashamayim*, vol. 3, 88, translated by Tucker in *Heavenly Torah*, 708, as: "Observe [guard] the plain meaning, but remember the esoteric meaning." In a highly significant Hebrew essay, Heschel suggested a hierarchy of significance between the two realms. See "Pikuach Neshama: To Save a Soul," in *Moral Grandeur*, 56. There he states that "the hidden is greater than the obvious," which is a view he was later to associate with Rabbi Akiva.

93 Ephraim E. Urbach, *ChaZaL: Pirkei Emunot ve-Deot* (Jerusalem: Magnes, 1975): 14n26. The comment is not to be found in the English translation of the work. According to the late Shmuel Avidor Hacohen (in conversation), Urbach apologized to Heschel for the comment – but he did not take it out of the Hebrew edition.

94 Anecdotal evidence for the disregard in which Heschel was held by these scholars is to be found in the Heschel Archive at the Jewish Theological Seminary Library in New York. More tangible evidence can be adduced from excerpts from the correspondence between Lieberman and Scholem. See Aviad Hacohen, "Shlumiel, Shlemazel ve-Nebich," *Haaretz*, 25 April 2000, Arts and Literature Supplement: 1. In the Heschel papers at Duke University two letters (one incomplete) from Lieberman to Heschel concerning his view of *Torah min Hashamayim* have come to light, and they suggest that Lieberman had a number of methodological reservations about Heschel's approach to rabbinic literature.

95 Seymour Siegel, "Abraham Joshua Heschel's Contributions to Jewish Scholarship," *Proceedings of the Rabbinical Assembly of America*, vol. 32 (1968), 72–85.

96 Gerson D. Cohen, "Abraham Joshua Heschel: The Interpreter of Classical Jewish Thought, *Proceedings of the Rabbinical Assembly*, vol. 45 (1983), 110. In a conversation with the late Louis Jacobs it emerged that in Jacobs's view Heschel had an extremely solid grounding in classical Jewish sources of all eras.

97 Jacob Neusner, review of *Theology of Ancient Judaism, Conservative Judaism* 20, no. 3 (1965): 66–73 and also "The Intellectual Achievement of Abraham Joshua Heschel," in J. Neusner and N. Neusner, eds., *To Grow In Wisdom: An Anthology of Abraham Joshua Heschel* (Lanham, NY: Madison Books, 1990), 13–22 (hereafter *To Grow in Wisdom*).

98 Steven T. Katz, "Abraham Joshua Heschel and Hasidism," *Journal of Jewish Studies* 31 (1980): 89. For examples of a positive if nuanced reception of

Heschel's studies of Hasidism, see Ada Rapoport-Albert, "Hasidism After 1772: Structural Continuity and Change," in Ada Rapoport-Albert and Joseph George Weiss, eds., *Hasidism Reappraised* (London: Littman Library of Jewish Civilization, 1996), 90; Rivka Schatz-Uffenheimer, *Hasidism as Mysticism: Quietistic Elements in Eighteenth Century Hasidic Thought* (Princeton NJ: Princeton University Press/Jerusalem: Magnes, 1993), 51. See, however, 231 and esp. 235n52. For a critique of his work on Nachman of Kosov, see Mendel Piekarz, *Biymei Tzemichat he-Chasidut* (Jerusalem: Bialik Institute, 1978): 26–31.See also Marc B. Shapiro, "Scholars and Friends: Rabbi Jehiel Jacob Weinberg and Professor Samuel Atlas," *Torah u-Madda Journal* 7 (1997): 109–10.

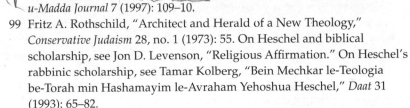

99 Fritz A. Rothschild, "Architect and Herald of a New Theology," *Conservative Judaism* 28, no. 1 (1973): 55. On Heschel and biblical scholarship, see Jon D. Levenson, "Religious Affirmation." On Heschel's rabbinic scholarship, see Tamar Kolberg, "Bein Mechkar le-Teologia be-Torah min Hashamayim le-Avraham Yehoshua Heschel," *Daat* 31 (1993): 65–82.

100 *Insecurity of Freedom*, 203.

101 To judge from Heschel's 1958 letter to Ben Gurion in response to the political crisis over the Law of Return, Heschel did not bemoan the passing of this kind of religious authority. He asserted in that letter, "We cannot force people to believe. Faith brought about by coercion is worse than heresy. But we can plant respect in the hearts of our generation." "We Cannot Force People to Believe," in *Moral Grandeur*, 45.

102 Abraham Joshua Heschel, "The Quest for Certainty in Saadia's Philosophy," *Jewish Quarterly Review*, n.s., 33, no. 3 (1943): 287n118.

103 Ibid., 286.

104 *The Prophets*, vol. 1, 15. See also *Die Prophetie*, 175.

105 All of these quotations appear in "Reason and Revelation in Saadia's Philosophy," *Jewish Quarterly Review*, n.s., 34, no. 4 (1944): 402.

106 Ibid., 403.

107 *Man's Quest for God*, 79.

108 Marc Saperstein, *Jewish Preaching 1200–1800* (New Haven: Yale University Press, 1989), 60.

109 It also appears in a footnote to the chapter, where the verse is altered in order to make a point. See *Search*, 89 n4: "It would, of course, be meaningless to assume that in the most sublime prophetic vision the seraphim would proclaim, 'Holy, holy, holy is the Lord of hosts. The whole earth is full of His fame.'"

110 Isaiah 40:26 appears in *Search,* 98, 99, and 100n12. See also 31, 124n9, and
     417. On the repetitive approach to the theme-verse in a sermon, see
     Saperstein, *Jewish Preaching,* 70–1. On the refrain and its relationship to
     citation, see Compagnon, *La seconde main,* 50–5. On the use of set phrases
     in various literary contexts, see Charlotte Schapira, *La Maxime et le dis-
     cours d'autorité* (Liege: SEDES, 1997). The *locus classicus* for an analysis of
     repetition as a rhetorical technique is to be found in Book IX of
     Quintilian's *Institutes of Oratory.*
111 For some exceptions to the observation that Heschel did not offer close
     readings or literary analyses, see 23n13, 71n16, 99, 311, 370, and 390.
     However, these counter-examples do not constitute a significant excep-
     tion to the rule.
112 See Anthony Grafton, *The Footnote: A Curious History* (Cambridge, MA:
     Harvard University Press, 1977). A recent article ascribed to Noel Coward
     the saying that "having to read a footnote resembles having to go down-
     stairs to answer the door while in the midst of making love." See Alexandra
     Horowitz, "Will the E-book Kill the Footnote?" *The New York Times,* 7
     October 2011. http://www.nytimes.com/2011/10/09/books/review/
     willthe-e-book-kill-the-footnote.html
113 *Search,* 48.
114 Ibid., 53n12.
115 Ibid. See 72n19, 87n7, 124n9, 133n1, 135n7, 183n1, 217n5, 256n6, and
     313n9, and elsewhere.
116 Aristotle saw quotations of ancient maxims and sources as akin to the
     calling of witnesses, adding that "ancient witnesses are the most trust-
     worthy of all, for they cannot be corrupted." *Rhetoric* I, XV.17.
117 Shaul Magid, "Associative Midrash: Reflections on a Hermeneutical Theory
     in Likkutei MoHaRan," in Shaul Magid, ed., *God's Voice from the Void: Old
     and New Studies in Bratslav Hasidism* (Albany: SUNY Press, 2002), 39.
118 Abraham Joshua Heschel, *Israel: An Echo of Eternity* (New York: Farrar,
     Straus and Giroux, 1968), 109–10 (hereafter *Echo of Eternity*). See also 27
     and 38 for examples of sections ending with biblical verses in this apposi-
     tional style.
119 *Passion for Truth,* 15.
120 See S. H. Blumberg, "Educating for Religious Experience: An Analysis of
     the Definitions of Four Major American Theologians and the Implications
     of Their Thought for Jewish Educational Curriculum and Practice" (PhD
     diss., Hebrew Union College – Jewish Institute of Religion, 1991); Paul F.
     Peri, "Education for Piety: An Investigation of the Works of Abraham
     Joshua Heschel" (EdD diss., Columbia University Teachers College, 1980).

121 *Moral Grandeur*, 412.
122 See Yehudah Mirsky, "The Rhapsodist," *The New Republic*, 19 April 1999.
123 "Death as Homecoming," in *Moral Grandeur*, 378.

2 Heschel's Bible and the Hermeneutic of Surprise

 1 "Die Bibel ist sich selbst der einzig angemessene Kommentar," in a
    review of a Bible concordance, *Gemeindeblatt der Jüdischen Gemeinde zu
    Berlin*, 27 June 1937, 3.
 2 *Search*, 247.
 3 *Search*, 253.
 4 "Interview at Notre Dame," in *Moral Grandeur*, 389.
 5 "Choose Life!" in *Moral Grandeur*, 251–2.
 6 "Sacred Image of Man," in *Insecurity of Freedom*, 163.
 7 *Who Is Man?* 97.
 8 Ibid., 107.
 9 "Religion in a Free Society," in *Insecurity of Freedom*, 4.
10 Abraham Joshua Heschel, "Teaching Jewish Theology in the Solomon
    Schechter School," *The Synagogue School* 28, no. 1 (1969): 19.
11 "A Time for Renewal," in *Moral Grandeur*, 53.
12 *Echo of Eternity*, 47.
13 "Carl Stern's Interview with Dr. Heschel," in *Moral Grandeur*, 399, 400.
    For an example of Heschel's application of the Bible to the question of
    Race in America, see "The White Man on Trial," in *Insecurity of Freedom*,
    102–3.
14 Abraham Joshua Heschel, "The Concept of Man in Jewish Thought," in
    Neusner and Neusner, eds., *To Grow In Wisdom*, 102. See also "Carl Stern's
    Interview" in *Moral Grandeur*, 408. The claim that Heschel took this idea
    unattributed from S.R. Hirsch can be found in Mordechai Breuer, "Shitat
    Torah im Derech Eretz be-Mishnato shel Rabbi Shimshon Raphael
    Hirsch," *HaMa'yan* 9 (1969): 12n49.
15 "Teaching Religion to American Jews," in *Moral Grandeur*, 151.
16 "Jewish Education," in *Insecurity of Freedom*, 235.
17 *Torah min Hashamayim*, vol. 2, 189.
18 *Heavenly Torah*, 458.
19 Daniel S. Breslauer, "Abraham Joshua Heschel's 'Biblical Man' in
    Contextual Perspective," *Judaism* 25, no. 3 (1976): 344.
20 For important insights into the privileged role of the Bible in American
    history and society, see Nathan A. Hatch and Mark A. Noll, eds., *The Bible
    in America: Essays in Cultural History* (Oxford: Oxford University Press,

1982). See also Abraham I. Katsh, *The Biblical Heritage of American Democracy* (New York: Ktav, 1977).

21 "Idols in the Temples," in *Insecurity of Freedom*, 52. It is significant that this paper was delivered both to the Rabbinical Assembly and to the multi-denominational Religious Education Association. His remarks were aimed simultaneously at a Jewish and non-Jewish audience, presumably because the biblical deracination he witnessed was occurring in both communities.

22 Jon D. Levenson, "Religious Affirmation and Historical Criticism in Heschel's Biblical Interpretation," 25–44. This paper is based on a paper delivered at the Heschel 25th Yahrzeit Conference at the Jewish Theological Seminary, December 1997. The argumentation of the second part of *Search* is also criticized in Arnold Eisen, "Re-Reading Heschel on the Commandments."

23 Arthur A. Cohen, *The Natural and Supernatural Jew* (New York: Pantheon, 1962), 244. The essay on Heschel is one of the most trenchant and substantial critiques of Heschel's approach. Levenson consciously invoked Cohen in his attempt to restore a modicum of criticism into discussion of Heschel's significance as a modern Jewish thinker. Levenson rightly pointed out that Cohen was not unmitigatingly negative about Heschel's "rhetoric of faith."

24 *Search*, 243.

25 "Carl Stern's Interview," in *Moral Grandeur*, 397.

26 "Reason and Revelation in Saadia's Philosophy," 394.

27 Ibid., 399–400.

28 Ibid., 403.

29 *Search*, 266.

30 Ibid., 268.

31 The example he brought—namely of a teaching by Moses in the name of God that is regarded by the rabbis as the result of Moses's own imagination—carries a dual message. On the one hand, it relates to the readiness of the prophet to challenge the Divine. On the other hand, it carries the implication that a morally reprehensible section of the Bible may in fact be of human rather than divine provenance. Heschel devoted a section of *Torah min Hashamayim* to this question. See vol. 2, 166–80.

32 *Search*, 270.

33 *Search*, 271.

34 On approaches to the Bible worthy of comparison with Heschel's approach, see Michael Fishbane, *The Garments of Torah: Essays in Biblical Hermeneutics* (Bloomington: Indiana University Press, 1989), esp. 93–8; Roy A. Harrisville and Walter Sundberg, *The Bible in Modern Culture: Theology*

and Historical-Critical Method From Spinoza to Kasemann (Grand Rapids,
Michigan: Eerdmans,1995); Eliezer Schweid, "Hermann Cohen's Biblical
Exegesis," in Helmut Holzhey, Gabriel Motzkin, and Hartwig Wiedebach,
eds., *Religion of Reason: Out of the Sources of Judaism – Tradition and the
Concept of Origin in Hermann Cohen's Later Work* (Hildesheim: Georg Olms,
2000): 353–79; Benyamin Uffenheimer, "Buber and Modern Biblical Scholar-
ship," in H. Gordon and J. Bloch, eds., *Martin Buber: A Centenary Volume*
(New York: Ktav, 1984), 163–211. Heschel's approach to ethical interpretation of the Bible is contrasted with that of Buber in Even-Chen and Meir,
Between Heschel and Buber, esp. 146–7.

35 *Search*, 272.
36 See *Torah min Hashamayim*, vol. 3, 30.
37 See Dror Bondi, *Gishato Haparshanit shel Avraham Yehoshua Heschel*
(PhD diss., Bar Ilan University, 2011), 155. Bondi believes that there
is a significant shift which can be discerned in Heschel's work from
philosophy to interpretation. He reads *The Prophets*, published in 1962,
as being replete with extended and close readings of Amos, Hosea,
Habakkuk, and other prophetic works. In my view, however, there is
hardly anything in that voluminous work that can be described as close
textual interpretation.
38 Indeed, Bondi's *Ayekka?* is a thorough explication of this approach.
39 *Search*, 183.
40 Even-Chen and Meir, *Between Heschel and Buber*, 142–5.
41 *Search*, 239.
42 See, for example, *Moral Grandeur*, 406.
43 *Echo of Eternity*, 142.
44 "Protestant Renewal: A Jewish View," in *Insecurity of Freedom*, 171–2. I am
grateful to Susannah Heschel for recounting that as a student in Berlin one
of Heschel's professors ascribed the repetition of the phrase "Comfort you,
comfort you, my people" (Isaiah 40:1) to scribal error. In such ways the
grandeur of the biblical text may be overlooked by those engaged in its
scientific dissection.
45 *Search*, 260.
46 Ibid., 264.
47 See *Torah min Hashamayim*, vol. 2, esp. chap. 16, 381–416.
48 *Search*, 273.
49 Ibid., 258.
50 "Depth Theology," in *Insecurity of Freedom*, 118.
51 In a talk to HUC students in the early 1950s, a recording of which can be
found in the American Jewish Archives in Cincinnati, he remarked with a

good deal of sarcasm that while everyone claimed to know everything about the Bible, he was lucky to know a few verses.

52 See *Die Prophetie*, 151–2, where Heschel decried the tendency of nineteenth century to explain away what it saw as the primitive irrational layer of biblical thinking. See also the remarkable statement in the 1953 essay "The Spirit of Prayer,"*in Moral Grandeur*, 114, on the distinction between Torah and *Wissenschaft des Judentums*.

53 This platform is quoted in a variety of sources. See, for example, Richard N. Levy, *A Vision of Holiness: The Future of Reform Judaism* (New York: URJ Press, 2005), 264.

54 *Moral Grandeur*, 13.

55 *Search*, 273. See also Jacob M. Chinitz, "The Elusive Revelation," *Judaism* 14, no. 2 (1965): 198–200.

56 See William E. Kaufman, "A. J. Heschel, Hasidic Prayer and Process Philosophy," *Proceedings of the Rabbinical Assembly of America*, vol. 45 (1983), 163–8; Sol Tanenzapf, "A Process Theory of Torah and Mitzvot," in Sandra B. Lubarsky and David Ray Griffin, eds., *Jewish Theology and Process Thought* (Albany: SUNY Press, 1996), 35–58.

57 It is particularly interesting in the light of this to note the recollection of J. A. Sanders in a commemorative tribute. He told of how from the mid-1960s Heschel would engage with members of the faculty of the Union Theological Seminary in Bible study, "poring over Biblical texts as though we had just discovered them in a Qumran cave ... as he peeled off layer after layer of meaning from the text." "An Apostle to the Gentiles," *Conservative Judaism* 28, no. 1 (1973): 62.

58 *Search*, 191.

59 In *Torah min Hashamayim*, vol. 2, 435, he discussed the status of the Book of Job, and in n2 he quoted at length the opinion of R. Zerahiah ben Isaac ben Shealtiel of Barcelona concerning the Mosaic authorship of Job. On Heschel and Job, see Michael S. Siegel, "Searching the Whirlwind for Heschel's God of Pathos," in Karp, Jacobs, and Dimitrovsky, eds., *Threescore and Ten: Essays in Honor of Rabbi Seymour J. Cohen on the Occasion of His Seventieth Birthday* (Hoboken, NJ: Ktav, 1991), 219–34.

60 Many of the references to Second Temple literature are relevant in this regard. See Sirach 1:4 on 276n7; 3:21f. on 62n4; 25:12–13 on 78 n1; and 40:1 on 100 n11. Wisdom of Solomon 6:10 on 78n12; 7:25 and 7:27 on 150n1; 9:9 on 276n7; 13:1f. on 32n9; and 17:12 on 77n7.

61 The endnotes of chapters 2, 4, 6, 7, 8, 9, 12, and 24 account for 143 of the 185 biblical references to be found in the notes altogether. In other words, one does not find many biblical verses and passages dispersed among the footnotes.

62 A rare example of unattributed biblical allusion can be found on 62:
    "The hidden things belong to the Lord," and from Him alone must come
    the knowledge and the answer." The reference to Deuteronomy 29:28 is
    not made explicit.

63 *Search*, 93. Isaiah 47:10 is then quoted without comment.

64 See *Search*, 288, where a number of verses are employed to further the view
    that the Torah is "primarily *divine ways* rather than *divine laws*." See 243n3
    for an extraordinary list of verses in a footnote.

65 *Search*, 19.

66 For a similar example in a later section of the book, see Psalms 100:2 on
    406.

67 *Search*, 92–3.

68 Note Siker's observation that "Niebuhr's appeal to Scripture often comes
    at the end of a discussion or section." Jeffrey S. Siker, *Scripture and Ethics:
    Twentieth-Century Portraits* (New York: Oxford University Press, 1997), 15.

69 The only case of a section beginning with a verse in *Man Is Not Alone* is on
    47. The reference is to Exodus 3:14. For sections ending with Biblical vers-
    es, see 117, 118, 122, 155–7 (where an entire psalm is quoted), 174, 247, 259,
    and 264.

70 Ibid., 155–7. It is Psalm 44 which is appended. For an analysis of the ways
    in which this psalm articulates a theological protest following destruction
    and exile, see Dalit Rom-Shiloni: "Psalm 44: The powers of protest,"
    Catholic Biblical Quarterly 70, no. 4 (2008): 683–98.

71 The dedication to *The Prophets* is "To the martyrs of 1940–5" followed by
    some verses from Psalm 44, ending with "Why dost Thou hide Thy face?"

72 *Search*, 272 and 278n33, 302, and 304n10. See also 356, where the reference
    to Leviticus 16:16 seems to be taken from the first chapter of Sifrei to the
    Book of Numbers.

73 For the first of these readings, see Shabbat 99a. See also Zohar I, 48b; for
    the second interpretation, see Shabbat 11a. For the third, see Zohar III, 109b.

74 *Search*, 65.

75 Ibid., 11. See the interpretation in Genesis Rabbah 10:8.

76 Abraham, Joshua Heschel, "The Mystical Element in Judaism," in Louis
    Finkelstein, ed., *The Jews: Their History, Culture and Religion* (Philadelphia:
    Jewish Publication Society of America, 1949), 619. The quotation is from
    Psalm 119.

77 It is instructive to review the alterations Heschel made in the first para-
    graph of this section. In the original essay the text reads: "The yearning for
    mystic living, the awareness of the ubiquitous mystery, the nameless nos-
    talgia for the noble nucleus, have rarely subsided in the Jewish soul. This
    longing for the mystical has found many and varied expressions …" (*Moral*

Grandeur, 181) Three years later, Heschel altered the text in order to suit it to his current purposes and also edited out an overly alliterative phrase "The yearning for spiritual living, the awareness of the ubiquitous mystery, the noble nostalgia for God, have rarely subsided in the Jewish soul. It has found many and varied expressions ..." (*Man Is Not Alone*, 254).

78 "The Spirit of Jewish Prayer," in *Moral Grandeur*, 109–10. The quotation is attributed to E.S. Ames's 1929 work, *Religion*. This passage is reproduced in *Man's Quest for God*, 61, as part of the critique of religious behaviourism and solipsism. Susannah Heschel has pointed out in conversation that Ames was an outstanding representative of American pragmatism, a position to which Heschel was implacably opposed. Indeed, the gulf separating him from Mordecai Kaplan can be understood in these terms. An unpublished and undated note in the Heschel Papers at Duke University is entitled "Errors of Pragmatism."

79 "Confusion of Good and Evil," in *Insecurity*, 133. This passage is reproduced in a 1960 essay, "The Concept of Man in Jewish Thought," in Neusner and Neusner, eds., *To Grow in Wisdom*, 134.

80 *Passion for Truth*, 201.

81 *Search*, 156–7.

82 Ibid., 256n2.

83 *Degel Mahane Efraim*, Parashat Behar. See also Zohar II, 9a, where the reference to the Shekhinah in exile is explicit.

84 *Midrash on Psalms* (Buber), Psalm 119:10.

85 *Search*, 271–3.

86 *Torah min Hashamayim*, vol. 1, 205.

87 *Torah min Hashamayim*, vol. 3, 53.

88 Avi Sagi, *Etgar Shivah el Hamasoret* (Tel Aviv: Hakibbutz Hameuchad, 1993), 57. In n143 Sagi refers to Soloveitchik's *Five Sermons*. See Harold Kasimow, *Divine-Human Encounter: A Study of Abraham Joshua Heschel* (Washington DC: University Press of America, 1979), 13n65.

89 "Carl Stern's Interview," in *Moral Grandeur*, 398.

90 *Search*, 276.

91 Ibid., 185.

92 *Echo of Eternity*, 46.

93 "The Biblical View of Reality," in *Moral Grandeur*, 355.

94 Susannah Heschel, "Introduction," in *Moral Grandeur*, xiii.

95 Heschel, "No Religion is an Island," in Harold Kasimow and Byron L. Sherwin, eds., *No Religion Is an Island: Abraham Joshua Heschel and Interreligious Dialogue* (Maryknoll, NY: Orbis Books, 1990), 4

96 Ibid.

3 A Living Response: Heschel and the Literature of the Sages

1 According to Prof. Avraham Shapira, this story was told by Heschel himself. See also Jacob Neusner, "Faith in the Crucible of the Mind," *America* (10 March 1973): 208.

2 *Moral Grandeur*, 385. See also Emmanuel Levinas, *Outside The Subject*, transl. Michael B. Smith (Stanford, CA: Stanford University Press, 1994), 13–14; Pinhas Peli, "Datiut Yehudit Nusach Buber," *Kivunim* 10 (1981): 59–72.

3 Neusner and Neusner, eds., *To Grow In Wisdom*, 18.

4 "Teaching Religion to American Jews," in *Moral Grandeur*, 150.

5 Ibid., 151.

6 Kadushin, who died in 1980, is referenced twice in the second volume of *Torah min Hashamayim*, on 26 and 265. Beyond this, I have not been able to find much evidence of a connection between the two men. With Finkelstein, who was chancellor during Heschel's years at the seminary, relations were more complex. Heschel's more extensive quotation of Finkelstein is noted below in chapter 7.

7 *Heavenly Torah*, 7.

8 Ibid., 10.

9 Rebecca Schorsch, "The Hermeneutics of Heschel in Torah Min Hashamayim," *Judaism* 40, no. 3 (1991): 302. Dresner quoted his master as saying: "We are living in one of the periods of Jewish history when aggadah has been devalued." Samuel H. Dresner, "Heschel and Halakhah: The Vital Center," *Conservative Judaism* 43, no. 4 (1991): 25.

10 For Bialik's encouragement of the young Heschel, see Kaplan and Dresner, *Prophetic Witness*, 146.

11 See Alan Brill, "Aggadic Man," 5. Esteban Gottfried has written on this connection in his rabbinic thesis, "Heschel Pinat Bialik," at the Hebrew Union College-Jewish Institute of Religion in Jerusalem, 2012.

12 Some of Heschel's books are particularly reliant on Ginzberg, most particularly *The Sabbath*, where mention can be found of this work on 104n8, 105nn30–1, 112n1, 114n1, and 117n2. See *Search*, 32n9, 60n8, 100n17, and 276n7. An entry by Ginzberg in the *Jewish Encyclopaedia* is mentioned on 394n3. See also *Man Is Not Alone*, 151, and "The Mystical Element in Judaism," 951n11. *Torah min Hashamayim* tends to make use of Ginzberg's other works. *Ginzei Schechter*, for example, is cited in vol. 1, 167n132 and 172n1; and vol. 2, 79n21, 145n21, and 150n24. Other works are cited in vol. 1, xxn35, 54n1, 212n7, 237n39, 265n12, 284n8; vol. 2, 8n7, 13n1, 37n12, 54 n5, and 126 n10. For further examples of Heschel's reliance on Ginzberg,

see vol. 1, 221n4, and vol. 2, 13n1, 43n9, 54n5, 122n12, 126n10, and 236n10. I have not found any references to Ginzberg in vol. 3 of *Torah min Hashamayim*. The one reference to *Legends* made both in *Search* and in *Torah min Hashamayim* can be found in the earlier work on 276n7, and in the later work in vol. 2, 21n16. The subject under discussion is the primordial Torah, and Ginzberg's note can be found in vol. 5, 132f. In *The Sabbath* and *Search*, the reader is referred to *Legends of the Jews* in order to explain motifs from ancient lore. In *Torah min Hashamayim*, on the other hand, Ginzberg's other books and essays are cited frequently. *Legends of the Jews* is cited less intensively than these other works (one such citation appears both in *Search* and in *Torah min Hashamayim*). Ginzberg was instrumental in bringing Heschel to the Seminary. Louis Finkelstein recounted that Ginzberg was "fascinated" by Heschel when they met in 1944. Louis Finkelstein, "Three Meetings with Abraham Joshua Heschel," *Conservative Judaism* 28, no. 1 (1973): 20. Box 20, Folder 9 of the Abraham Joshua Heschel papers at Duke University contain a number of letters from Ginzberg to Heschel, and further research is likely to shed light on this important relationship.

13 Brill, "Aggadic Man," 6–7.

14 Ephraim E. Urbach, *ChaZaL: Pirkei Emunot ve-Deot* (Jerusalem: Magnes, 1975), 14n26. For a more recent scholarly reading of Heschel's approach, see Azzan Yadin, *Scripture as Logos: Rabbi Ishmael and the Origins of Midrash* (Philadelphia: University of Pennsylvania Press, 2004), esp. xxi, 93–4.

15 See Gordon Tucker, "Heschel on the Theology of Rabbis," *Proceedings of the Rabbinical Assembly*, vol. 51 (1990), 211–29.

16 Shabbat 147b.

17 *Search*, 380n3, referring to 369.

18 Avodah Zarah 3b –4a. He also referred his readers to Avot 3.2.

19 Sukkah 52a.

20 "Confusion of Good and Evil," in *Insecurity of Freedom*, 127–49. See Britton, *Heschel and the Phenomenon of Piety*, 214f.

21 *Search*, 50n16, 264n20, 272n33, 276n39, and 329n38.

22 *Search*, 314n1, 58n13, 21n13, and 62n3; 49n13, 46n8, 385n3, and 403n2, respectively.

23 See 281–2. Note 1 on 292 refers the reader to Shabbat 88a. For other examples of the invocation of Jewish tradition in conjunction with a rabbinic text, see 302n10, 377n15, 37n17, and 394n1.

24 A series of notes to a paragraph found on 129 illustrates the way in which Heschel integrated sources from Shabbat 104a and Yoma 39a, creating a hybrid of two ideas while indicating to his reader the sources from which

his insight is taken. See also 403 of *Search*, which uses Hullin 7b (wrongly cited as 7a) and the commentary of Tosafot there.

25 *Search*, 362.

26 *Pikuach Neshama – Mikivshona shel ha-Havaya ha-Yehudit* (New York: Baronial Press, 1949), 10. This is translated in *Moral Grandeur*, 63.

27 Avodah Zarah 2a.

28 Genesis Rabbah 19:6.

29 *Torah min Hashamayim*, vol. 1, 69, quoting PT Sukkah 54c, etc.

30 Ibid., vol. 1, 74, quoting Pesikta Rabbati 31.

31 Ibid., vol. 1, 289.

32 The end of chapter 23, "Israel's Commitment," provides another example of this kind of closing quotation. Note 5 on 17, appended to the last words of the chapter, simply quotes a rabbinic teaching about the Sabbath from the Mechilta.

33 Dow Marmur and Marcel Marcus have translated these pieces for my article, "Traditional Exemplars in a Time of Crisis," in Michael A. Meyer and David N. Myers, *Between Jewish Tradition and Modernity – Rethinking an Old Opposition* (Detroit: Wayne State University Press, 2014), 192–208. Another translation of these articles is scheduled for publication.

34 The articles appearing in the *Gemeindeblatt der Jüdischen Gemeinde zu Berlin* were "Jochanan ben Sakai," 23 February 1936, 14; "Rabbi Gamliel II," 8 March 1936, 15; "Rabbi Akiba," 29 March 1936, 16; "Rabbi Schimon ben Gamliel II," 12 April 1936, 15; "Elischa ben Abuja," 26 April 1936, 16; "Rabbi Meir," 17 May 1936, 16; "Rabbi Jehuda Hanassi," 31 May 1936, 16; and "Rabbi Chija," 16 August 1936, 15. All quotations here are from the translation of these pieces by Marmur and Marcus.

35 See "Traditional Exemplars in a Time of Crisis."

36 "The Individual Jew and his Obligations" (1957), in *Insecurity of Freedom*, 190–1. See also *Who Is Man?* 34, 35, and 59. See also, "The Eastern European Era in Jewish History," 101.

37 The term employed is *eine Lawine der Resignation*.

38 See *Torah min Hashamayim*, vol. 1, 242–56.

39 Ibid., vol. 3, 22.

40 Ibid., vol. 1, 287.

41 See Michael Marmur, "Abraham Joshua Heschel, Teenage Halakhist," in *Abraham Joshua Heschel: Philosophy, Theology and Interreligious Dialogue* (Wiesbaden: Harrassowitz, 2009), 89–101.

42 Baba Kama 62b–64a.

43 In contrast, however, note Heschel's complaint in the essay on Jewish education (*Insecurity of Freedom*, 235) that when he asked adults if they knew

what the thirteen *middoth* were, some may have heard of the Thirteen Principles of Rabbi Ishmael, but none had heard of the Thirteen Divine Attributes.

44 Michael Chernick, *Le-Cheker ha-Middot "Kelal u-Ferat u-Chelal" ve-"ribui u-Miut" be-Midrashim ubeTalmudim* (Lod: Habermann Institute, 1984), 80–2n8, noted that this was not altogether accurate: while it is true that Rabbi Akiva never applies generalization and specification, Rabbi Ishmael does employ amplification and limitation.

45 There is a significant literature devoted to this R. Akiva / R. Ishmael distinction, and Heschel cited some of the classic works dating back to the nineteenth century in the first volume of *Torah min Hashamayim,* 10n1. For an enthusiastic elaboration of the thesis that Nehunyah and Nahum are the source of the distinction, see Louis Finkelstein, *Sifra on Leviticus* (Hebrew), vol. 1 (New York: Jewish Theological Seminary, 1989), 126–43. A later generation of scholars is either more cautious or downright sceptical of the coherence of this distinction. In a private conversation Yehudah Zirkind indicated to me that, around the time of the publication of the first volume of *Torah min Hashamayim,* the Lubavitcher Rebbe offered some reflections on the distinction between Rabbi Ishmael and Rabbi Akiva. I hope that Zirkind will bring this fascinating parallel to light.

46 *Torah min Hashamayim,* 11.

47 Ibid.

48 Vol. 2, 88n3. Tucker translated the body of the text on 379, but the reference to Baba Kama 64b is omitted from the footnote.

49 See Yehudah Mirsky, "Rabbi Akiva: Liberal, Existentialist, Navi – Bein Finkelshtein, Heschel u-Martin Luther King ve-Hagut Chevratit – Teologia Amerikait be-Meah Haesrim," *Daat* 71 (2010–11): esp. 103.

50 Mirsky cited *Torah min Hashamayim,* vol. 1, xliv. See also xlvi, 65, and 83.

51 See, for example, vol. 1, 162 and 174. Even-Chen and Meir take it as a given that Heschel preferred Rabbi Ishmael. See *Between Heschel and Buber,* 128 and 153. For an attempt to systematize Heschel's approach to these two fathers of the universe, see Gedalia Haber, "Ha-Dogmatika shel Avraham Yehoshua Heschel," *Daat* (2010): 323–48.

52 *Search,* 302.

53 Genesis Rabbah 19:3. Rabbi Hiyya was one of the sages profiled in Heschel's 1936 articles.

54 *The Sabbath,* 17n8.

55 *Torah min Hashamayim,* vol. 2, 118n15.

56 Ibid., vol. 3, 105n5.

57 Gedalia Haber, "Ha-Dogmatika shel Avraham Yehoshua Heschel," *Daat* (2010): 323–48.
58 Reuven Kimelman, "Review of *Torah min Hashamayim* and *Heavenly Torah*," *Shofar* 26, no. 1 (2007): 228.
59 Ibid., 229. This claim is contested in Gedalia Haber, "Lost in Translation: Abraham Joshua Heschel's "Heavenly Torah" – A Review Essay," *Modern Judaism* 29, vol. 3 (2009): 405–27.
60 *Heavenly Torah*, xxix.
61 See "Hasidism as a New Approach to Torah," in *Moral Grandeur*, 33–9; *Passion for Truth*, 55–69.
62 *Insecurity of Freedom*, 220.
63 See Dresner, *Heschel, Hasidism, and Halakha*, 84–123; *Search*, 320–35.
64 See, however, Kaplan, *Spiritual Radical*, 323.
65 *Search*, 317n3.
66 See David Ellenson and Michael Marmur, "Heschel and the Roots of *Kavanah*," in Pamela S. Nadell, Jonathan D. Sarna, and Lance J. Sussman, eds., *New Essays in American Jewish History: commemorating the sixtieth anniversary of the founding of the American Jewish Archives* (Jersey City, NJ: American Jewish Archives of Hebrew Union College-Jewish Institute of Religion, 2010), 345–66.
67 *Moral Grandeur*, 104. This section of the lecture is reproduced in *Man's Quest for God*, 53–4.
68 Ibid., 111.
69 Ibid., 120. See *Torah min Hashamayim*, vol. 1, 168–9, where Heschel devoted a short chapter to the concept of *kavanah*. It is interesting to note that there he distinguished between an emphasis on the commandment and a concentration on God Who commands.
70 *Search*, 329–30.
71 The continuation of this discussion includes a rare excursion into close textual reading in which Heschel engaged in a polemic with unnamed "exponents of religious behaviorism." It might be posited that the adversary is Kaplan, but in Mordecai M. Kaplan, *Judaism as a Civilization* (New York: Macmillan, 1935), 375 and 547n35, Kaplan made an almost identical point to that made by Heschel on the interpretation of Jeremiah 16:11 in *Search*, 330n40.
72 *Moral Grandeur*, 138. With a slight alteration, this sentence is reproduced in *Search*, 283. See Jakob J. Petuchowski, "Faith as the Leap of Action: The Theology of Abraham Joshua Heschel," *Commentary* 25, no. 5 (1958): 390–7.
73 *Moral Grandeur*, 143.

74 Ibid., 143.
75 *Man's Quest for God*, 12.
76 *Moral Grandeur*, 136–7.
77 *Search*, 310.
78 Ibid., 298: "The individual's insight alone is unable to cope with all the problems of living. It is the guidance of tradition on which we must reply, and whose norms we must learn to interpret and to apply."
79 Ibid., 295. The appended note on 304 refers the reader to a discussion in *Sifra* concerning unwitting donations.
80 Ibid., 337. The reference in 346 n3 is to Bahya's *Duties of the Heart*, and indeed Heschel was quoting directly without using quotation marks.

4 From Contemplation to Practice: Heschel's Two Maimonides

1 See *Search*, 29n8, 148nn19–23, 151n15, 295n5, and 335n41. See also *Man Is Not Alone*, 231; *Man's Quest for God*, 70n37. See also *Torah min Hashamayim*, vol. 1, xxviin2 and 21n11; vol. 2, 29n9, 30n21, 65n10, 264n3, and 429n46; and vol. 3, 34n11 and 39n3. This last note is a good example of the deployment of teachings of Rabbi Judah Halevi along with those of Maimonides.
2 *Search*, 136.
3 Ibid., 143n2.
4 The attached footnote refers the reader to ed. H. Brody, transl. N. Salamon, *Selected Poems of Jehudah Halevi* (Philadelphia: Jewish Publication Society of America, 1928), 134–5, although Heschel makes a few minor alterations to the translation, as well as skipping a section of the poem after the first verse.
5 Micha Goodman, *Chalomo shel ha-Kuzari* (Or Yehuda: Dvir, 2012), 80. See also 208.
6 See *Search*, 23n2, 32n9, 144n12, 148, 151nn15, 17–18, 306n1, 308n4, 334n31, 337n3, 358n12, 359n13, 365n16, 395nn10–11, and 408n2. There may be some significance to the fact that Heschel often quoted from the introduction to works in this category and others. Apart from the introduction to *Duties of the Heart*, he quoted from the introductions to (or first lines of) Maimonides's *Commentary to the Mishnah* (335n44) and his *Guide* (135n7, 139n6, 143n6); Ibn Saddik's *Haolam Haqaton* (23n2); Edels's Talmud commentary (346n4); Luzatto's *Mesillat Yesharim* (334n31); Heller's *Tosefot Yom Tov* (305n13); and the Hasidic work *Resyse Layla* (395n14).
7 *Search*, 340, which is based on Rashi's commentary to Sanhedrin 98b. Another example of reliance on Rashi in the quotation of a source can be found in the long quotation from *Menahot* on 70. For a reference to Rashi

following rabbinic sources see 59n1.Rashi is often quoted in parentheses to explain a Talmudic source in *Torah min Hashamayim,* e.g. vol. 1, XIII. See Naomi Grunhaus "The Dependence of Rabbi David Kimḥi (Radak) on Rashi in His Quotation of Midrashic Traditions,"*Jewish Quarterly Review* 93, no. 3–4 (2003): 415–30, particularly 423, where Grunhaus notes a case in which "Radak mistakenly includes Rashi's own words in his quotation of a Midrashic passage."

8 For an extensive Albo quotation in and endnote to *Search,* see 134n5. For long references in the body of the text, see 323n5 and 359n14. For other references in that work, see 78n6, 79n8, 277n20, 277n23, 346n15, and 408n2.

9 References to Rashi and commentaries attributed to him cover more than one entire page of the index to *Torah min Hashamayim.*

10 See *The Sabbath,* 105n16, 106n9, 109n2, 111n4, 112n9, and 117n13. *Man's Quest for God,* 12n3, 35n7, 38n14, and 68n31. See Elliot K. Ginsburg, *The Sabbath in the Classical Kabbalah* (New York: State University of New York Press, 1989), 178n244.

11 Micha Goodman, *Sodotav shel Moreh ha-Nevukhim* (Or Yehuda: Dvir, 2010), 366n58.

12 I am grateful to Professors Michael A. Meyer and Barry S. Kogan for their comments and suggestions. On approaches to and influences of Maimonides in modern Jewish thought, see Jacob I. Dienstag, "Maimonides' *Guide* and *Sefer Ha Madda* in Hasidic Literature" (Hebrew), in *Abraham Weiss Jubilee Volume* (New York, 1964), 307–30; Alfred I. Ivry, "Hermann Cohen, Leo Strauss, Alexander Altmann: Maimonides in Germany," in Georges Tamer, ed., *The Trias of Maimonides: Jewish, Arabic and Ancient Culture of Knowledge* (Berlin: Walter de Gruyter, 2005), 175–83; Roland Goetschel, "Le paradigme Maimonidien chez Hermann Cohen," in Ira Robinson, Lawrence Kaplan, and Julien Bauer, eds., *The Thought of Moses Maimonides* (Lewiston, NY: Edwin Mellen, 1990), 384–403; Warren Zev Harvey, "The Return of Maimonideanism," *Jewish Social Studies* 42, no. 3–4 (1980): 249–68; James H. Lehmann, "Maimonides, Mendelssohn and the Me'asfim – Philosophy and the Biographical Imagination in the Early Haskalah," *Leo Baeck Institute Yearbook* 20 (1975): 87–108; Michael A. Meyer, "Maimonides and Some Moderns: European Images of the Rambam from the Eighteenth to the Twentieth Century," *CCAR Journal* (1997): 4–15; Aviezer Ravitzky, "Rabbi J.B. Soloveitchik on Human Knowledge: Between Maimonidean and Neo-Kantian Philosophy," *Modern Judaism* 6, no. 2 (1986): 157–88; Eliezer Schweid, "Hashpa'at Ha'Rambam be-Hagut ha-Yehudit ba-Meah ha-Esrim," in Moshe Idel et al., eds. *Sefer Ha-Yovel le Shlomo Pines* (Jerusalem: Hebrew University, 1990), 293–324.

13 Samuel Atlas, "The Contemporary Relevance of the Philosophy of Maimonides," *CCAR Yearbook* 64 (1954): 187.

14 Atlas, "Contemporary Relevance," 199.

15 Atlas and Heschel both came to the Hebrew Union College as part of the College's Refugee Scholars Project, and the two had a complex relationship. The term "ineffable" had come into theological currency before Heschel's work – Rudolf Otto, Aldous Huxley, and others made use of it earlier – but in the context of Atlas's lecture, it is likely that Heschel was both intended by the lecturer and understood by his audience. For a hint to their relationship, see Marc B. Shapiro, "Scholars and Friends: Jehiel Jacob Weinberg and Professor Samuel Atlas," *Torah u-Madda Journal* 7 (1997): 105–21. For an explicit critique of Heschel's perceived abandonment of the canons of rationality, see Meir Ben-Horin, "The Ineffable: Critical Notes on Neo-Mysticism," *Jewish Quarterly Review* 46, no. 4 (1956): 321–54.

16 Abraham Joshua Heschel, *Maimonides: Eine Biographie* (Berlin: Erich Reiss, 1935); "Ha-he'emin ha-Rambam Shezacha li-Nevua?" *Louis Ginzberg Jubilee Volume*, Hebrew Section (New York: American Academy for Jewish Research, 1945), 159–88. Both are available in English translation: *Maimonides*, trans. J. Neugroschel (New York: Farrar, Straus and Giroux, 1982) and "Did Maimonides Believe That He Had Attained the Rank of Prophet?" in Morris M. Faierstein, ed. and trans., *Prophetic Inspiration After the Prophets* (Hoboken, NJ: Ktav, 1996), 69–126.

17 *Search*, 76n5, 148n15, 187, and 340, respectively.

18 Ibid., 21.

19 Ibid.

20 Ibid., 22.

21 *Maimonides*, 96.

22 Ibid., 92.

23 "Jewish Education" (1953), in *Insecurity of Freedom*, 241.

24 "Teaching Jewish Theology," 13.

25 Heschel, "The Two Great Traditions," *Commentary* 5, no. 5 (1948): 420.

26 *The Prophets*, 252. The Stoics are linked here to the thought of both Maimonides and Spinoza.

27 "Teaching Jewish Theology," 12.

28 Menachem Kellner, *Dogma in Medieval Jewish Thought: From Maimonides to Abravanel* (Oxford: Oxford University Press, 1986). Kellner stated that Maimonides "was the first non-Karaite Jewish author systematically, self-consciously, and explicitly to posit specific beliefs which all Jews *qua* Jews had to accept" (1). Kellner noted dismissively and in passing Neumark's

"tendentious division of all Jewish dogmas into the essential and the historical" (31), which is close to the distinction made by Heschel in *Search*, according to which Principles 6, 8, 12, and 13 relate to the "realm of history" rather than the "realm of ideas" (21).

29 "Teaching Jewish Theology," 16. "For an elaboration of this view, see *Torah min Hashamayim*. Vol. I, II and forthcoming Vol. III."

30 Susannah Heschel, "Social Justice – The Theme of Heschel," in Joshua Stampfer, ed., *Prayer and Politics: The Twin Poles of Abraham Joshua Heschel* (Portland, OR: Institute for Judaic Studies, 1985), 46–7. See also Reuven Kimelman, "The Theology of Abraham Joshua Heschel," *First Things* 198 (2009): 35–9.

31 See Gordon Tucker's comment in the preface to Abraham Joshua Heschel, *Heavenly Torah as Refracted Through the Generations*, ed. and transl. Gordon Tucker (New York: Continuum International Publishing Group, 2005), xxv.

32 Heschel, *Heavenly Torah*, 33.

33 *Maimonides*, 49–50. See also *Torah min Hashamayim*, vol. 1, l.

34 Note, for example, *Torah min Hashamayim*, vol. 3, 98, where Maimonides is used to illustrate the rationalist position, according to which "one measure of precision is to be preferred over nine measures of imagination." (Here and below, references to *Torah min Hashamayim* indicate that the text is not translated in *Heavenly Torah*.)

35 See, for example, *Heavenly Torah*, 74, 75, 249, 252, and 558. See also *Kotzk*, 684 n2, where a debate on human nature between Rabbi Akiva and Rabbi Ishmael is carried on in the Middle Ages by Crescas and Maimonides, respectively.

36 *Heavenly Torah*, 45. In a note to this paragraph Gordon Tucker suggested that Heschel simply trailed off at the end of the chapter, but in my view the clear reference to Maimonides is a deliberately planned climax to the entire introduction of the book.

37 *Heavenly Torah*, 166. See *Maimonides*, 28, 66, 179, and 214.

38 A particularly interesting example is the statement in *Guide* III.9 concerning the weather conditions at Sinai. This appears in *Search*, 258, and in 276 n3 this position is contrasted with the view of Isaac Caro. In a parallel discussion in *Heavenly Torah*, 711, the contrasting position is presented by Rabbenu Hananel. It would appear that in this case it is Maimonides's rigid literalism which incurred Heschel's opposition, although the thrust of the argument of the *Guide* seems quite different. It is not clear if Heschel was simply taking Maimonides out of context in order to illustrate the limitations of literalism, or whether there was a more subtle reading of Maimonides at play here.

39 In a work on the Thirteen Principles, Heschel's presentation of alternative traditional readings of Revelation was used as part of the attempt to loosen the normative hold of the Principles. See Marc B. Shapiro, *The Limits of Orthodox Theology* (Oxford: Littman Library of Jewish Civilization, 2004).

40 *Heavenly Torah*, 202.

41 I am grateful to Dr. Gordon Tucker – the translator and interpreter of this work – for this insight which he expressed in a private conversation.

42 *Heavenly Torah*, 589. In the course of Heschel's Hebrew work, Maimonides is not seen to display exclusively Ishmaelian leanings. To cite another example: while Rabbi Ishmael's principled opposition to supernaturalism led him to suggest that Moses died in a conventional manner, Maimonides took a quite different view in his *Commentary on the Mishnah*. See *Heavenly Torah*, 354. See the sources quoted therein, and also Tucker's comment, n33. For other examples of Maimonides's occasional Akivan leanings, see *Heavenly Torah*, 539–40, although on 541n5 Tucker remarked that both views described there are Akivan "in varying degrees." Confusingly enough, on 628 we find Maimonides agreeing with Rabbi Ishmael that the Torah was given scroll by scroll.

43 *Heavenly* Torah, 558–63. See Gerald J.Blidstein, "Oral Law as Institution in Maimonides," in Robinson et al., eds., *The Thought of Moses Maimonides*, 167–82. On 167 Blidstein noted: "In the course of his investigation of the concept *Torah min Hashamayim*, Abraham Heschel pointed out that Maimonides rejected the notion that the Oral Torah in its entirety was delivered by God to Man at Sinai." In 167n1 Blidstein argued that Heschel "neglects to point out, though, that much Oral Law *is* Sinaitic for Maimonides." See, however, *Heavenly Torah*, 561n30.

44 Abraham Joshua Heschel, "Rabbi Nachman of Kosow: Companion of the Baal Shem," in Samuel H. Dresner, ed., *The Circle of the Baal Shem Tov: Studies in Hasidism* (Chicago: University of Chicago Press, 1985), 142. The implication here is that as Maimonides aged he became increasingly open to this worldly orientation of the Ishmaelian view.

45 *Search*, 22.

46 *Maimonides*, 112.

47 *Torah min Hashamayim*, vol. 3 120–2. See also *Search*, 276.

48 Heschel was commissioned by the publisher Erich Reiss and spent seven months on the commission. See Kaplan and Dresner, *Prophetic Witness*, 202–7. See also Edward K. Kaplan, "Metaphor and Miracle: Abraham Joshua Heschel and the Holy Spirit," *Conservative Judaism* 46, no. 2 (1974): 3–18.

49 Heschel's affinity with Maimonides preceded the biography by far. Indeed, the very first published words of Heschel from 1922 comprise an attempt

to harmonize an opinion from Maimonides's commentary on the Mishnah
in light of a section from the Babylonian Talmud. See Marmur, "Teenage
Halakhist."

50 *Maimonides*, 17.
51 Ibid., 30.
52 Ibid., 32.
53 Ibid., 50.
54 Ibid., 105.
55 Ibid., 96.
56 *Maimonides*, 7–8.
57 In a tribute essay in memory of Zevi Diesendruck, Heschel noted
    Diesendruck's 1935 address in which he "pleaded that the approach
    to Maimonides should not be archeological or sentimental or hero-
    worshipping." "Zevi Diesendruck," *American Jewish Year Book* 43 (1941–2):
    398. It is interesting to consider whether Heschel's treatment of
    Maimonides fell foul of this guideline.
58 *Maimonides*, 135.
59 Rémi Brague, "Leo Strauss and Maimonides," in A. Udoff, ed., *Leo Strauss'
    Thought: Toward a Critical Engagement* (Boulder: Rienner Publications,
    1991), 104.
60 "The Reasons for My Involvement in the Peace Movement" (1973), in
    Moral Grandeur 224–6.
61 *Insecurity of Freedom*, 289–90. There is a curious alteration to the text here,
    since in the original, the perception of abstract concepts constitutes a *geis-
    tigen Akt*, but in this late translation these abstractions are afforded a pure-
    ly intellectual significance. The 1199 letter to Ibn Tibbon may be seen as
    indicative of Maimonides's approach to life in his latter years.
62 *Maimonides*, 210.
63 Ibid., 242.
64 For the term *textpeople*, see *Insecurity of Freedom*, 237.
65 On the provenance of this expression, see Kaplan, *Spiritual Radical*, 415n16.
    See also *Die Prophetie*, 139.
66 "Up and down *Maimonides*, lines, sentences, or paragraphs jump at the
    reader for their obvious dual illumination, their description of author as
    well as subject." Hillel Goldberg, *Between Berlin and Slobodka* (Hoboken,
    NJ: Ktav, 1989), 124.
67 See Barry Kogan, "Review of *Maimonides*," *Journal of Reform Judaism* 30
    (1983): 70–3. Kogan (71) found that Heschel's "persistent attempt to reveal
    the personal dimension of the Rambam's thinking easily slips into eisege-
    sis and even misinterpretation."

68 *Maimonides*, 148. For another reference to Maimonidean pathos, see 86.

69 Barry Kogan, "Review of *Maimonides*," 73.

70 "Did Maimonides Believe …?" 92.

71 See Gershom Scholem, "From Researcher to Kabbalist" (Hebrew), *Tarbiz* 6, no. 3 (1935): 91. Heschel quoted from H. Davidovitz and D. Baneth, eds., *Perakim be-Hatzlachah* (Jerusalem: Mekitze Nirdamim, 1939). Baneth's introduction is particularly emphatic in its refutation of the claim for Maimonidean provenance.

72 Chiara Adorisio, "Philosophy of Religion or Political Philosophy? The Debate Between Leo Strauss and Julius Guttmann," *European Journal of Jewish Studies* 1, no. 1 (2007): 135–55; Jonathan Cohen, "Jew and Philosopher: The Return to Maimonides in Leo Strauss: A Review Essay," *Modern Judaism* 16 (1996): 81–91; James A. Diamond, "Maimonidean Scholarship: Pointing the Way Beyond the Academy," *Jewish History* 18 (2004): 227–41; Kenneth Hart Green, *Jew and Philosopher: The Return to Maimonides in the Jewish Thought of Leo Strauss* (Albany: SUNY Press, 1993); Arthur Hyman, "Interpreting Maimonides," *Gesher* 5 (1976): 46–59; Mari Rethelyi, "Guttmann's Critique of Strauss' Modernist Approach to Medieval Philosophy: Some Arguments Toward a Counter-Critique," *Journal of Textual Reasoning* 3, no. 1 (2004) [e-journal]; Moshe Schwarcz, "The Enlightenment and Its Implications for Jewish Philosophy in the Modern Period" (Hebrew) *Daat* 1, no. 1 (1978): 7–16; Eliezer Schweid, "Religion and Philosophy: the Scholarly-Theological Debate between Julius Guttmann and Leo Strauss," *Maimonidean Studies* 1 (1990): 163–95; Alan Verskin, "Reading Strauss on Maimonides: A New Approach," *Journal of Textual Reasoning* 3, no. 1 (2004) [e-journal].

73 George Y. Kohler, *Reading Maimonides' Philosophy in Ninteenth-Century Germany: The Guide to Religious Reform* (Dordrecht: Springer, 2012), 337–40.

74 Heschel, "Did Maimonides Believe …?" 110n135.

75 See Kaplan and Dresner, *Prophetic Witness*, 114–16; Heschel, *Die Prophetie*, 6.

76 *Search*, 3–23. See Yitzhak Julius Guttmann, *On the Philosophy of Religion*, ed. N. Rotenstreich (Jerusalem: The Magnes Press, 1976), 11–22. See also Eliezer Schweid, *Hayahadut ve-Hatarbut ha-Hilonit* (Tel Aviv, 1981), 203–20; Yehoyada Amir, *Teguvot Eretz-Yisraeliot le-Haguto Shel Franz Rosenzweig* (Jerusalem: Hebrew University, 1993), 362–413. It is interesting to note that an article quotes extensively from the first chapter of *Search* while presenting Heschel as a counter to Leo Strauss. See Sando Frunza, "Jewish Philosophy and the Metaphor of Returning to Jerusalem," *Journal for the Study of Religion and Ideologies* 13 (2006): 128–37.

77 See *Search*, 333n3. Heschel pointed out that Isaac Heinemann held a different view.

78 "Did Maimonides Believe …?" 73–4. On the strategy of "indirection," see, for example, David Blumenthal, "Maimonides: Prayer, Worship and Mysticism," in Roland Goetschel, ed., *Priere, Mystique et Judaisme* (Strasbourg: Presses Universitaires de France, 1987), 89–106.

79 "Did Maimonides Believe …?" 159.

80 *Torah min Hashamayim*, vol. 2, 299. See also vol. 2, 409–12.

81 *Search*, 145.

82 See *Search*, 276n2, 304n6. For evidence of Heschel's awareness of the doctrine of Maimonidean contradiction, see his "Zevi Diesendruck." For a recent reading of this question, see Yair Lorberbaum, "On Contradictions, Rationality, Dialectics and Esotericism in Maimonides's *Guide of the Perplexed*," *Review of Metaphysics* 55, no. 4 (2002): 711–50. See also Julius Guttmann, *Philosophies of Judaism* (Philadelphia: Jewish Publication Society of America, 1964), 432n99.

83 See David Novak, "Responding to Leo Strauss – Four Recent Maimonidean Studies," *Conservative Judaism* 44, no. 3 (1992): 84.

84 While Novak did not note this usage, it supports his thesis. See *Search*, 188, and *Torah min Hashamayim*, vol. 2, 26.

85 Novak, "Heschel's Phenomenology of Revelation," 41.

86 *The Prophets*, 248 and 252.

87 *The Prophets*, 431n2. Heschel quoted from *Guide*, II.32.

88 *The Prophets*, 21. Katz suggested that to compare Heschel in *The Prophets* and Maimonides in the *Guide* would be "a fruitful experience." Steven T. Katz, "Eliezer Berkovits and Modern Jewish Philosophy," in *PostHolocaust Dialogues: Critical Studies in Modern Jewish Thought* (New York: New York University Press, 1983), 129.

89 *Maimonides*, 244. On *imitatio dei* in Maimonides see Howard Kreisel, *Maimonides' Political Thought: Studies in Ethics, Law and the Human Ideal* (Albany: SUNY Press, 1999), 125–58, and for the connection between Maimonides and modern Jewish thought in this regard, see Kenneth Seeskin, *Searching for a Distant God: The Legacy of Maimonides* (New York: Oxford University Press, 2000), 91–123.

90 In the later version of the English translation there is this telling addition: "It took a life-long dedication to intellectual pursuits to be able to attain simultaneity of involvement with people and being absorbed in the contemplation of God." *Insecurity of Freedom*, 290. For an example of the scholarly literature on this passage in *Guide* III.51 and its bearing on Maimonides's thought, see Stephen Harvey, "Maimonides in the Sultan's Palace," in Joel

L. Kraemer, ed., *Perspectives on Maimonides* (New York: Littman Library of Jewish Civilization, 1991) 47–75; Lawrence Kaplan, "I Sleep but My Heart Waketh: Maimonides' Conception of Human Perfection," in Robinson et al., eds., *The Thought of Moses Maimonides*, 131–66; Howard Kreisel, "Maimonides' View of Prophecy as the Overflowing Perfection of Man," *Daat*, 13 (1984): xxi–xxvi.

91 *Maimonides*, 209.

92 "Did Maimonides Believe ...?" 89. It is fascinating to consider Heschel's own works in light of this comment. A number of them, such as *Search* and his earlier essay "The Mystical Element in Judaism," conclude in a remarkable way.

93 A sweeping statement made by Kogan, "review of *Maimonides*," 73, claims that based on evidence which has come to light in recent decades "there is little reason to believe ... that he ever seriously aspired to prophetic inspiration." Gruenwald also asserted that "it appears rather doubtful that Maimonides would actually have claimed prophetic inspiration for himself ...," Ithamar Gruenwald, "Maimonides' Quest Beyond Philosophy and Prophecy," in Joel L. Kraemer, ed., *Perspectives on Maimonides*, 142. See also Jacob S. Levinger, *Moses as Philosopher and Codifier* (Hebrew) (Jerusalem: Bialik Institute, 1989), 83n42. Freudenthal left the question open and cited only Heschel's article as he suggested that "others" will have to decide if Maimonides had indeed attained prophecy. See Gad Freudenthal, "The Biological Limitations of Man's Intellectual Perfection," in G. Tamer, ed., *The Trias of Maimonides*, 149. For an example of citation of the article in contemporary scholarship, see Aviezer Ravitzky, "The Secrets of the 'Guide to the Perplexed': Between the Thirteenth and the Twentieth Centuries," in I. Twersky, ed., *Studies in Maimonides* (Cambridge, MA: Harvard University Centre for Jewish Studies, 1990), 192n124. See also Reuven Shoham, *Poetry and Prophecy: The Image of the Poet as a "Prophet," a Hero and an Artist in Modern Hebrew Poetry* (Leiden: Brill, 2003), 13–20.

94 S. Harvey, "Maimonides in the Sultan's Palace," in Joel L. Kraemer, ed., *Perspectives on Maimonides*, 72. For important discussions of the closing chapters of the *Guide*, see n60 above and also David Shatz, "Worship, Corporeality, and Human Perfection: A Reading of *Guide of the Perplexed* III, 51–4; Robinson et al., eds., *The Thought of Moses Maimonides*, 77–129. Shatz asserted that "III.51 recapitulates the tensions in Maimonides' conception of the person that have run through the *Guide* all along" (105) and suggested that the instruction to ponder God when abed "trains you to occupy yourself with God *while engaged in an activity that to some extent interferes with exclusive occupation with God*" (113). See also Menachem Kellner, *Maimonides on Human Perfection* (Atlanta, GA: Scholars Press, 1990).

95 *Maimonides*, 243–4.

96 Both in the German original and the English translation, Book II is cited, but this would appear to be a typographical error.

97 It is my sense that Heschel was greatly influenced by Diesendruck's discussion of divine and human knowledge. See Zevi Diesendruck, "Hatakhlit veha-to'arim be-torat ha-Rambam," *Tarbits* 2, no. 1 (1931): 35–45.

98 *Search*, 122. In the footnotes on 124 Heschel adduced further sections from the *Guide* to bolster his argument, although his quotations are used in a contentious fashion. With regards to n8, for example, the discussion in the *Guide* II.5 refers not to the relative merits of silence and speech but rather to the nature of the spheres, and neither in that chapter nor elsewhere in the *Guide* can one find the assertion that "silence is preferable to speech." Rather, in I.50 Maimonides argued that one should be like those who have established the truth and represented it to themselves *even if they do not utter it*. This is hardly a prescription for silence, and it is not easy to understand Heschel's insistence that Maimonides prescribed it. Consider, however, the following statement made in reference to the same passage from the *Guide*: "Absolute silence, in the sense of total absence of articulated speech and thought, is essential to the apophatic experience." Jose Faur, *Homo Mysticus: A Guide to Maimonides' Guide for the Perplexed* (Syracuse, NY: Syracuse University Press, 1999), 23. See also *Guide* I.59.

99 "Did Maimonides Believe …?" 94–5.

100 The first sentence in this extended quotation also appears in one of the key paragraphs of the Hebrew essay on Maimonides and prophecy in which a number of sources are marshalled to support the contention that prophecy was superior to philosophical speculation in the Maimonidean worldview. See "Did Maimonides Believe …?" 95. The letter is also quoted in *Search*, 70n4. For a discussion of the authenticity of the letter, see Yitzhak Shilat, *Iggerot Ha-Rambam* (Hebrew) (Jerusalem: Hotzaat Shailat, 1988), 673–7.

101 *Search*, 233.

102 Shlomo Pines, "The Limitations of Human Knowledge According to Al-Farabi, ibn Bajja, and Maimonides," in J.A. Buijs, ed., *Maimonides: A Collection of Critical Essays* (Notre Dame, IN: University of Notre Dame Press, 1988), 111. S. Harvey, "Maimonides in the Sultan's Palace," 51n18 contrasted these two responses to the inadequacy of human reason, but I believe that both interpretations are present in Heschel's approach.

103 *Search*, 283.

104 On the juxtaposition of Maimonides with the Rambam, see for example Jacob I. Dienstag, "Rambam or Maimonides: Unity or Duality? A Bibliographical Survey," in Yaakov Elman and Jeffrey S. Gurock, eds., *Hazon Nahum: Studies in Jewish Law, Thought and History Presented to Dr. Norman*

Lamm on the Occasion of His Seventieth Birthday (New York: Michael Scharf Publication Trust of the Yeshiva University Press,1997), 129–48; Isaac Franck, "Maimonides' Philosophy Today," *Judaism* 4, no. 2 (1955): 99–109.

5 On the Verge of God: Heschel and Kabbalah

1 A transcription of Heschel's talk at Dartmouth can be found in the Duke Archive, Box 82, Folder 6. It is clearly the work of a transcriber unfamiliar with Heschel's work, and therefore the quality of this unedited and unpublished transcript is problematic. It is, nonetheless, a fascinating document.
2 This kabbalistic term has many resonances in Heschel's work. Scholem noted, "In many passages of the Zohar the principle is developed that the Torah is at once hidden and manifest, esoteric and exoteric, *oraitha sethim vegalya*. The author finds this dualism not only in the Torah, but in every conceivable sphere of existence, beginning with God and embracing every realm and aspect of Creation." Gershom G. Scholem, *On the Kabbalah and Its Symbolism* (London: Routledge and Kegan Paul, 1965), 51. See also Elliot R. Wolfson, *Abraham Abulafia – Kabbalist and Prophet: Hermeneutics, Theosophy, and Theurgy* (Los Angeles: Cherub Press, 2000), 30–2.
3 Green, "Three Warsaw Mystics," 48*. See also Reuven Kimelman, "Review of *The Sabbath*," *Shofar* 26, no. 1 (2007): 189.
4 In *Die Prophetie*, Kabbalah and Hasidism are mentioned along with Aggadah in a footnote, 170n2.
5 Green, "Three Warsaw Mystics," 48*.
6 *Ineffable* appears on at least forty pages of *Man Is Not Alone*; *mystery* on twelve pages; and *enigma* on three pages. Other key words in the book are *unity* and *spirit*.
7 *Man's Quest for God*, 62. This section of the work is taken from a paper delivered to the Rabbinical Assembly in 1953.
8 I.75b, II.88b, 128a, III.35b, 136a, 173a, 242b, 257a, 272b as well as *Tikkunei Zohar* 21, 59b and *Zohar Hadash*, Genesis 17b.
9 *Man Is Not Alone*, 6.
10 Ibid., 112. The reference is to *Tikkunei Zohar* 17b. Arthur Green pointed out that this source is recited in the Hasidic rite on the Sabbath eve. It is also cited in ibn Gabbai's *Derekh Emunah*, *Pardes Rimmonim* 4.5, and in chapter 6 of *Sha'ar Hayihud Vehaemunah* of *Sefer Hatanya*.
11 "The Mystical Element in Judaism," in *Moral Grandeur*, 171. The essay was originally published in Louis Finkelstein, ed., *The Jews: Their History, Culture, and Religion*, vol. 2 (Philadelphia: Jewish Publication Society of America, 1949), 602–23.

12 See Yehuda Liebes, *Torat ha-Yetzira shel Sefer ha-Yetzira* (Jerusalem: Schocken, 2000), 31–71. For a discussion of Midrash Temura, see 47–8.

13 *Search*, 63 and 66.

14 Nachmanides to Numbers 4.20. Haviva Pedaya discussed the symbolic dimensions of this interpretation. See Haviva Pedaya, *Ha-Ramban: Hitalut: Zeman Mahzori ve-tekst kadosh* (Tel Aviv: Am Oved, 2003), 352–4. As noted in chapter 1, Heschel was mistaken in attributing the authorship of *Sefer Yere'im* to Rabbi Eliezer of Mayence. He may have simply written this from memory. The book's author is in fact Eliezer ben Samuel of Metz.

15 *Moral Grandeur*, 417.

16 Abraham Joshua Heschel, "Le Toldot Rabbi Pinhas Mekoretz," in *Aley Ayin* (Jerusalem: Schocken, 1952), 215. This translation is from Heschel, "Rabbi Pinhas of Korzec," in Samuel H. Dresner, ed., *The Circle of the Baal Shem Tov: Studies in Hasidism*, 2nd ed. (New York: Jewish Theological Seminary of America, 1985), 5. Arthur Green quoted an expanded version of the latter saying as an epigraph in the prologue to Arthur Green, *Guide to the Zohar* (Stanford, CA: Stanford University Press, 2004), 3.

17 *Search*, 31.

18 Abraham Joshua Heschel, *The Earth Is the Lord's: The Inner Life of the Jew in Eastern Europe* (New York: Henry Schuman, 1950), 29.

19 Scholem uses this phrase to describe how Graetz, Zunz, Geiger, Luzzatto, Steinschneider, and the like related to Jewish mysticism. Gershom G. Scholem, *Major Trends in Jewish Mysticism* (New York: Schocken, 1941), 1.

20 *The Sabbath*, 115. The two sources are quoted differently: the source from *Tikkunei Zohar* is without quotation marks.

21 *Man's Quest for God*, 78. See also the use of *Shenei Luhot ha-Berit* in that work, 101–2.

22 Elchanan Shiloh, *Hakabbalah be-yetzirat Shai Agnon* (Ramat Gan: Bar-Ilan University, 2011), esp. 39–42. See a reference to Rabbi Chaim Vital in *Torah min Hashamayim*, vol. 2, 50n30. See also a direct reference to Luria in *The Sabbath*, 124n11.

23 *Man Is Not Alone*, 149.

24 Two of the most tangible distinctions between the two works are, first, the lack of serious footnotes in *Man Is Not Alone*, and second, the unbridled use of extended and mixed metaphor in that work.

25 However, in *Search* we do read of "the danger of being trapped in lofts without light" (30), that "God is not a pearl at the bottom of the sea" (129), and that accounts of the reasons for faith in God's existence "are like ripe fruit we gather from the trees" (138). Thinking about the ultimate "leads along a path with countless chasms and very few ledges" (152). "What a

sculptor does to a block of marble, the Bible does to our finest intuitions" (164); "Faith is not a silent treasure to be kept in the seclusion of the soul, but a mint in which to strike the coin of common deeds" (295). A musical metaphor is employed in a discussion of the mitzvah (315) and, as shall be discussed at length in a later chapter, many optical terms are employed. Finally, near the book's conclusion the eternal command is compared to a saw, "trying to cut through the callousness of hearts" (406).

26 II.99a. See Daniel Abrams, "Knowing the Maiden Without Eyes: Reading the Sexual Reconstruction of the Jewish Mystic in a Zoharic Parable," *Daat* 50–2 (2003): lix–lxxxiii; Melilah Hellner-Eshed, *VeNahar Yotze Me-Eden* (Tel Aviv: Am Oved, 2005), 251–3; Gershom Scholem, *On the Kabbalah and Its Symbolism*, 56; Frank Talmage, "Apples of Gold: The Inner Meaning of Sacred Texts in Medieval Judaism," in Arthur Green, ed., *Jewish Spirituality from the Bible Through the Middle Ages* (London: Routledge and Kegan Paul, 1986), 316–17; Yehuda Liebes, *Studies in the Zohar* (New York: SUNY Press, 1993), 69; Moshe Idel, *Kabbalah: New Perspectives* (New Haven: Yale University Press, 1988), 227–9; Moshe Idel, *Absorbing Perfections: Kabbala and Interpretation* (New Haven: Yale University Press, 2002), 197–8 and 304–5; Moshe Idel, "Tefisat Hatorah besifrut ha-Hechalot vgilguleha bak-abbalah," *Mekhkarei Yerushalayim be'Makhshevet Yisrael* 1 (1981), 59–60. For a discussion of this text's significance in the thought of Martin Buber, see Israel Koren, *Hamistorin shel Ha'aretz* (Haifa: University of Haifa, 2005), 186 and 278–81.

27 *Search*, 254.

28 Ibid., 266.

29 See Scholem, *Major Trends*, 210; Scholem, *On the Kabbalah and Its Symbolism*, 63–4; Isaiah Tishby, *Wisdom of the Zohar* (Oxford: Oxford University Press, 1989), 126–7; Talmage, "Apples of Gold," 324–5; Liebes, *Studies in the Zohar*, 45–6; Green, *Guide to the Zohar*, 66. The excerpt begins with Rabbi Simeon bar Yohai expressing the view that if the Torah were just an every-day tale, it could have been written better. This ironic suggestion that the text of the Bible could be improved upon stayed in Heschel's consciousness until his last days. In the interview with Carl Stern, speaking about "what is mentioned in the beginning of the Book of Genesis, that God created man in His own image," Heschel said, "Frankly, if Moses had consulted me, I would have told him, 'Don't say it.'" *Moral Grandeur*, 401.

30 *Search*, 341. Idel's comment on this term is enlightening in our present context. Referring to the Hebrew equivalent, he noted that it "is a Kabbalistic coinage which points to the world of the separate Intellects. These entities were defined by the philosophers as separated from matter, whereas the

Kabbalists view them as separated from each other, in opposition to the world of the *sefirot* which is defined as the world of unity." "Differing Concepts of Kabbalah in the Early 17th Century," in Isadore Twersky and Bernard Septimus, eds., *Jewish Thought in the Seventeenth Century* (Cambridge, MA: Harvard University Press, 1987), 186n233.

31 *Search*, 347n10.
32 There are almost no kabbalistic references in the long introduction to the first volume. For a rare exception, see xxin2.
33 *Torah min Hashamayim*, vol. 1, 209–11.
34 *Torah min Hashamayim*, vol. 2, 184–5. For other outstanding examples of the use of kabbalistic sources in vol. 2, see 49–50, and also the extensive discussion of the *aspeklaria*, 277–9. Sources quoted there include the Zohar, and Avraham Azulai's commentary to it; Gikatilla's *Sha'arei Orah*, Cordovero's *Pardes Rimonim*, Rabbi Abraham ben Azriel as quoted in the *Perush HaAggadot*, *Shushan Sodot*, and the commentary of Rabbi Judah Hayyat. Interestingly, a 1930 article by Gershom Scholem is also referenced.
35 *Torah min Hashamayim*, vol. 3, 63–8.
36 Ibid., 70–2. At the end of the section, two later kabbalists are mentioned alongside Rabbi Nachman of Bratslav.
37 Ibid., 73–4.
38 Eliot, "Tradition and the Individual Talent," 23.
39 Abraham Joshua Heschel, "Al Ruach ha-Kodesh bi Yemei ha-Beynayim," in Saul Lieberman, ed., *Alexander Marx Jubilee Volume*, Hebrew Section (New York: Jewish Theological Seminary of America, 1950), 208. This translation from "Prophetic Inspiration in the Middle Ages," in *Prophetic Inspiration*, 67.
40 *Search*, 145.
41 The excerpt is included in the printed edition of the *Siddur Rav Saadia Gaon*, 379, although it was not originally included in the Siddur. There is a clearly elitist context to the *piyyut*: it contends that the select few will be able to find in each generation the dimension of the divine Name to be found at that time. However, in line with the general universalistic thrust of the book, this element of Saadia's approach is left out of the quoted text.
42 The excerpt from the *Wisdom of Solomon* in that note is particularly interesting in view of our discussion of *aspeklaria* in this book. See verses 25–8 of chap. 7.
43 Megillah 12a.
44 Zohar II 148b. The second Zoharic source relates to the Torah, which "is continually being sown in the world and sends forth fresh fruit without ceasing, and the world is nourished by it." That source (II166b–167a) also introduces the factor of Exile, which mitigates against the continued

efficacy of the primordial light. Now, after the Exile, it is the Torah which preserves that light and renders it constantly potent. In a private communication Arthur Green commented that Heschel made no mention here of the context in which the light/seed appears. After all, light is sown for the tzaddik, but the persona of the individual who cultivates the light is not discussed here. See Liebes, *Studies in the Zohar*, 27.

45 "Did Maimonides Believe …?" 162; Heschel, *Prophetic Inspiration*, 175ff.
46 See Alexander Even-Chen, *Kol Min ha-Arafel - Avraham Yehoshua Heschel Bein Phenomenologia le-Mistika* (Tel-Aviv: Am Oved, 1999), 103–4
47 See *Kotzk*, 215.
48 *Torah min Hashamayim*, vol. 3, 36–8. See also 65–6.
49 He quoted this reading in *Search*, 138 and 143n5; and in "Ruach ha-Kodesh," 208n193.
50 *Torah min Hashamayim*, vol. 2, 255–6. See also 259.
51 Arthur Green's "God's Need for Man: A Unitive Approach to the Writings of Abraham Joshua Heschel," *Modern Judaism* 35, no. 3 (2015): 247–61, makes this point brilliantly and persuasively.
52 *Search*, 145. In n3 on 150 he cited a further eight sources from the Zohar.
53 Ibid., 204.
54 *The Sabbath*, 96.
55 *Search*, 145.
56 Ibid., 146.
57 Zohar I.90a.
58 III.69a, and particularly III.179b.
59 *Search*, 151n24 quotes the Zohar and Judah of Barcelona's commentary to *Sefer Yetzirah*. A further comment directs the reader to Rashi's commentary to Sotah 38b, in which possible meanings of the verb *Lesha'er* are discussed.
60 *Search*, 198.
61 Ibid., 225.
62 *Die Prophetie*, esp. 16–17, where Jewish mysticism, including that of the Middle Ages, is mentioned.
63 Ibid., 37. The expression can be translated as "the private experience of ecstasy."
64 *Search*, 198–9. The first and last of these sentences is quoted in Alexander Even-Chen, "Mystika ve-Nevua Al Pi Avraham Yehoshua Heschel," *Kabala* 5 (1999–2000): 366.
65 Ibid., 366n25.
66 "Mystical Element," 619.
67 Ibid., 621.
68 Ibid., 621. Green, "Three Warsaw Mystics," 56* is critical of this final section of the essay.

69 See, for example, *Torah min Hashamayim*, vol. 1, 227, 242, 247–56, 265, and 270; vol. 2, ii, 20–5, 41–5, and 346; and vol. 3, 1. Susannah Heschel has pointed out in conversation that her father's thoughts on the apocalyptic pre-date the emergence of sophisticated scholarship in this field.

70 *Heavenly Torah*, 279. The chapter deals with the four who entered the Pardes, which Heschel saw as a clear reference to the mystical activities of certain Sages, Rabbi Akiva among them.

71 *Torah min Hashamayim*, vol. 2, 255.

72 *Heavenly Torah*, 288.

73 *Torah min Hashamayim*, vol. 2, 314–16. See also vol. 2, 24, and "Ruach ha-Kodesh," 179.

74 "Mystical Element," 621.

75 It is reasonable to assume that Heschel was well acquainted with Hillel Zeitlin's essay in which the esoteric tradition is linked to prophetic origins. See Hillel Zeitlin, "Admut ha-Mistorin be-Yisrael," in Hillel Zeitlin, *Befardes ha-Hasidut veha-Kabbala*, 4th ed. (Tel-Aviv: Yavneh, 1997), esp. 61–3.

76 "Rabbi Akiba," 16.

77 Isaac Hirsch Weiss described Rabbi Ishmael as a nationalist zealot in the second volume of *Dor Dor veDorshav*, vol. 2 (Berlin: Platt and Minkus, 1924), 92. None of this dimension of this persona of Rabbi Ishmael existed for Heschel.

78 *Man Is Not Alone*, 31.

79 See *Search*, 117.

80 See Heschel, "The Biblical View of Reality" (1956), in *Moral Grandeur*, 357.

81 *Who Is Man?* 71 and 76–7.

82 *Search*, 106.

83 Heschel, "Religion in a Free Society," in *Insecurity of Freedom*, 21.

84 "The Holy Dimension," in *Moral Grandeur*, 321. See also "An Analysis of Piety," in *Moral Grandeur*, esp. 308–9.

85 For examples of his anti-esoteric stance in *Search*, see 168 and 198. See also "Al Yichudo Shel ha-Kiyum ha-Yehudi," 240.

86 Abraham Joshua Heschel, "A Preface to an Understanding of Revelation," in *Essays Presented to Leo Baeck on the Occasion of his Eightieth Birthday* (London: East and West Library, 1954), 35. See *Search*, 126–7, 173.

87 "Pikuach Neshama," in *Moral Grandeur*, 56 and 59.

88 *Search*, 65. The note appended to the end of this paragraph is an extraordinary reflection on ineffability, marshalling traditions from Midrash, the Talmud, Rashi, Maimonides, Nachmanides, and the Maharsha. See 71n16.

89 See *Search*, 204–5, 306, 341–2, and 347n10.

90 *Torah min Hashamayim*, vol. 1, 14.

91 "Al Yichudo shel ha-Kiyum ha-Yehudi," 237.

92 *Man's Quest for God*, 133.
93 "Did Maimonides Believe …?" 70.
94 See *Search*, 59 and 60 n16. Heschel refers his reader to Zohar I.159a and I.140a.
95 Ibid., 266.
96 *Torah min Hashamayim*, vol. 3, 90. See also *Search*, 58 and 71n16.
97 *Search*, 58.
98 Note 15 cites Numbers Rabbah 19:6. The reference to 19:5 is an error.
99 *Torah min Hashamayim*, vol. 2, 248n3.
100 *Search*, 262–3.
101 Ibid., 273.
102 Ibid., 264.
103 "The various expressions of Torah mutability in Jewish mysticism fall into four main categories: the astrological, the eschatological, the Neoplatonic, and the combinatory." Moshe Idel, *Absorbing Perfection: Kabbalah and Interpretation* (New Haven: Yale University Press, 2002), 353. This book explores the practice of letter combination from a number of perspectives, and Idel credited Heschel on more than one occasion. See, for example 593n110 and 599n63. See also Moshe Idel, *Language, Torah and Hermeneutics in Abraham Abulafia* (Albany: SUNY Press, 1989).
104 The reference is to Gedaliah of Luninec, *Teshuot Chen* (Berditchev: 1816), 43b. I see no explicit reference to the Ba'al Shem Tov.
105 See *Kotzk*, particularly 60–5; *Passion for Truth*, 75–80.
106 *Search* 264. Note 17 on 277 refers to *Toameha Hayim Zakhu*, a late commentary on *Etz Hayyim* by Aharon Shlomo Maharil. The comment to Vital's work relates to *Shaar* 30, *Derush* 2. See also *Search*, 262, and 276n9.
107 Moshe Halbertal, *Concealment and Revelation: Esotericism in Jewish Thought and Its Philosophical Implications* (Princeton NJ: Princeton University Press, 2009), esp. 172.
108 "Did Maimonides Believe …?" 71.
109 "Perush al ha-Tefillot," in *Kovetz Madai le-Zecher Moshe Schorr* (New York: Vaadat Zikaron, 1945), 113–26.
110 See Leo Strauss, *Liberalism Ancient and Modern* (Chicago: University of Chicago Press, 1995), 8.
111 See Dresner, *Heschel, Hasidism and Halakha*, 120–1.
112 *The Sabbath*, 29.
113 *Search*, 262–3. On Cordovero and Isaiah Horowitz, see 277nn12–13. See Moshe Idel, "Infinities of Torah in Kabbalah," in *Midrash and Literature*, eds. Geoffrey H. Hartman and Sanford Budick (New Haven: Yale University Press, 1986), 141–58.

114 *Torah min Hashamayim*, vol. 3, 88.

115 See *Search*, 118n3, 188n6, and 276n9.

116 Green, "Three Warsaw Mystics," 51*.

117 Some rationalist critics accused him of irrational mystical tendencies. See for example Meir Ben-Horin, "Via Mystica," *Jewish Quarterly Review* 45, no. 3 (1955): 249–58.

118 See Arthur Green, "Hillel Zeitlin and Neo-Hasidic Readings of the 'Zohar,'" *Kabbalah* 22 (2010), 59–78. Einat Ramon once suggested that there is evidence for an unacknowledged debt to A.D. Gordon in Heschel's writing due to the latter's use of the Hebrew term *havayah*, a Gordonian term. However, I believe that it can be shown with some ease that Heschel came to the term through his reading of Zeitlin, and through his reading of William James. For an interesting insight into the Heschelian use of this Hebrew word, see his dictionary of philosophical terms.

119 See *Kotzk*, vol. 1, 334n1; vol. 2, 670n9. Heschel was acquainted with Zeitlin's son Aaron, and wrote an article in Yiddish about his poetry. This 1948 article was translated and appears as an appendix in Morris M. Faierstein, "Abraham Joshua Heschel and the Holocaust," *Modern Judaism* 19, no. 3 (1999): 264–71. There is no reference there to Hillel Zeitlin.

120 See Morris M. Faierstein, "God's Needs for the Commandments" in Medieval Kabbalah," *Conservative Judaism* 36, no. 1 (1982): 45–59. Arthur Green's "God's Need for Man" develops this theme and includes personal testimony to this effect.

121 Heschel, "Reason and Revelation in Saadia's Philosophy," *Jewish Quarterly Review* 34, no. 4 (1944): 408.

122 Attributed to Heschel in Maurice Friedman, "Divine Need and Human Wonder: The Philosophy of Abraham Joshua Heschel," *Judaism* 25 no. 1 (1976): 67.

6 A New Accent: Heschel and Hasidism

1 A photograph of the stone and a translation are found in Kaplan, *Spiritual Radical*, 384–5. The text was composed by Susannah Heschel, and it includes mention of Heschel's mother.

2 *Moral Grandeur*, 33–9.

3 "Le Toldot Rabbi Pinhas Mekoretz," *Aley Ayin* (Jerusalem: Schocken, 1952): 213–44, also published in Yiddish as "Reb Pinkhes Koritzer," *Yivo Bleter* 33 (1949): 9–48; "Rabbi Gershon Kutover – Parashat Chayav ve-Aliyato le-Eretz Yisrael," *Hebrew Union College Annual* 23, Part 2 (1950–1), Hebrew Section, 17–71; "Rabbi Yitzhak mi-Drohobycz," *Hadoar Jubilee*

Volume (New York: Hadoar, 1957): 86–94; "Rabbi Nachman mi- Kosow, Havero Shel ha-Besht," in Saul Lieberman et al., eds., *The Harry A. Wolfson Jubilee Volume*, Hebrew Section (New York: American Academy for Jewish Research,1965): 113–41. These essays were published in an English translation of Samuel H. Dresner, ed., *The Circle of the Baal Shem Tov* (Chicago: University of Chicago Press, 1985). A further essay is "Umbekante Dokumenten Zu Der Geschichte Fon Hasidus," *Yivo Bleter* 36 (1952): 113–35.

4　For an appraisal of the value of these works, see Ada Rapoport-Albert, "Hasidism after 1772: Structural Continuity and Change," in Ada Rapoport-Albert, ed., *Hasidism Reappraised* (London: Littman Library of Jewish Civilization, 1996), 90–3.

5　"Rabbi Pinhas of Korzec," in *The Circle of the Baal Shem Tov*, 23.

6　"Rabbi Nachman of Kosow," in *The Circle of the Baal Shem Tov*. For more on Rabbi Nachman of Kosov, his emphasis on cleaving to the divine Name and his relationship with the Besht, see Joseph Weiss,"Reshit Tzmichatah Shel ha-Derekh ha-Chasidit," *Zion* 16 (1951): esp. 60; Immanuel Etkes, *Ba'al Hashem* (Jerusalem: Zalman Shazar Center, 2000), 185–9.

7　*Search*, 78n4.

8　*Kotzk*, 18–22, and esp. *Passion for Truth*, 9–12.

9　See Jeffrey Shandler, "Heschel and Yiddish: A Struggle with Signification," *Journal of Jewish Thought and Philosophy* 2, no. 2 (1993): 245–99; Faierstein, "Heschel and the Holocaust," 255–75.

10　Annette Aronowicz, "Heschel's Yiddish *Kotsk*: Some Reflections on Inwardness," 113. In light of this comment it is fascinating to note that thanks to the indefatigable Dror Bondi, a Hebrew version of the Yiddish *Kotzk* has been published. A non-Yiddish–speaking Israeli public will have an opportunity to encounter the Yiddish Heschel.

11　See Byron L. Sherwin, review of *The Earth Is the Lord's* and *Passion for Truth*, *Shofar* 26, no. 1 (2007), 183–4.

12　*Passion for Truth*, xiv.

13　*Man Is Not Alone*, 87.

14　See for example "Faith" (1944), in *Moral Grandeur*, 388. See also "Reason and Revelation in Saadia's Philosophy," 404–8.

15　*Kotzk*, 175.

16　*Passion for Truth*, 198.

17　*Man Is Not Alone*, 155.

18　"The Individual Jew and His Obligations," in *Insecurity of Freedom*, 201. The Rebbe is referred to as "Rabbi Mandel of Kotzk."

19　*Kotzk*, 170 (the number of the verse is misprinted); *Passion for Truth*, 190, where he linked this teaching to a saying of Kierkegaard.

20 *Search*, 145n6 and 393n14.

21 Ibid., 394.

22 Ibid., 277n19.

23 *Man's Quest for God*, 72, 73, 75; *Insecurity of Freedom*, 132, 148n32.

24 *Search*, 195.

25 Ibid., 388n2; *Insecurity of Freedom*, 139.

26 *Search*, 370; *Insecurity of Freedom*, 135.

27 *Search*, 11.

28 *Man's Quest for God*, 34 n6; *Search*, 99, 361n2; *Insecurity of Freedom*, 127, 139.

29 *The Sabbath*, 20–1.

30 Kaplan, *Spiritual Radical*, 88–9. The reference to the Zohar is somewhat incomplete. It should note that the reference is to volume II, 88b.

31 *The Sabbath*, 31. Note 12 on 106 refers the reader to Yekutiel Arieh Kamelhar's *Dor De'ah* (the reference should read 125f. rather than 127). On 74 of *The Sabbath* two more figures from the early period of Hasidic history, Rabbi Hayim Krasne and Rabbi Shlomo of Karlin, are also referenced, referring to the Sabbath as a foreshadowing of eternity.

32 *The Sabbath*, 75.

33 *Man's Quest for God*, 8; "Existence and Celebration," in *Moral Grandeur*, 18. In the speech Heschel revealed that this is a teaching of Rabbi Moshe Teitelbaum, who he referred to as Rabbi Moshe of Uhely.

34 *The Sabbath*, 88–9. I have not been able to find a Warsaw 1872 edition, but in the Lvov 1864 edition the teaching is to be found on 6b, and not 8c as the notes suggest.

35 *Mei ha-Shiloah*, Vayeshev, 14d–15a.This teaching is discussed in Yehoshua Mondshine, "The Fluidity of Categories in Hasidism: *Averah Lishmah* in the Teachings of R. Zvi Elimelekh of Dynow," in *Hasidism Reappraised*, 311n47. The Izbicer implies the superiority of Judah, pointing out that the Messiah will issue from his loins.

36 *Kotzk*, 643–4 and 688n6. In that footnote Heschel noted that this excerpt is quoted in *Search*.

37 *Passion for Truth*, 59–60.

38 *Moral Grandeur*, 201. This teaching is analysed in Joseph Weiss, "A Late Jewish Utopia of Religious Freedom" (1964), in Joseph Weiss, *Studies in Eastern European Jewish Mysticism* (Oxford: Oxford University Press, 1985), 218–23. I am grateful to Dror Bondi for confirming that the teaching of the Izbicer is indeed in the unpublished chapter of *Torah min Hashamayim*. His work on the missing chapters of this work promises to be of great interest.

39 See 53 n16, where a teaching from *Amarot Tehorot* is paraphrased with reference to Psalm 136. Heschel used this source to introduce the notion that

certain privileged generations are permitted to witness great miracles performed before their eyes. See Eliezer Ish Horowitz of Tarnegrod, *Amaroth
Tehorot* (Warsaw: Sklower, 1838), 39b.

40 *Search*, 154.

41 A casual reader inclined to check the Talmudic source would therefore be
baffled by this reference, since it is not to be found in the classic printed
edition. See *Ein Yaakov* to Berachot, #139. The Aramaic saying is:
"גנבא אפום מחתרתא רחמנא קרי". For a discussion of this source, see Adin Stein-
saltz, "Emunah ve-Yirat Shamayim," in Moshe Halbertal, David Kurzweil,
and Avi Sagi, eds., *Al ha-Emunah – Iyunim be-Musag ha-Emunah uve-Toldotav
ba-Masoret ha-Yehudit* (Jerusalem: Keter, 2005), 483–9.

42 See Aristotle, *Nicomachean Ethics*, 1146a –1147b.

43 *Maamarei Admor ha-Zaken*, vol. 1 (Brooklyn, NY: Otzar ha-Hasidim, 1986),
Lech Lecha 5565, 4. The second of the two sources implies at the beginning
that the faith of the criminal can in some circumstances be as strong as that
of the observant Jew, but then reiterates the point made in the above
source that the praying thief lacks a full internalization of *emunah*. See
Maamarei Admor ha-Zaken, vol. 2, 255–6. See *Search*, 325, for another reference to Shneur Zalman of Lyady.

44 "Hasidism as a New Approach to Torah" (1972), in *Moral Grandeur*, 35.

45 *Moral Grandeur*, 38.

46 Ibid., 33.

47 Ibid., 34. A saying attributed to Rabbi Aaron of Karlin declares that a soul
such as that of the Ba'al Shem Tov comes to the world once in a millenni-
um. The unique status attributed to the Ba'al Shem Tov by Heschel is discussed by Moshe Idel, *Old Worlds, New Mirrors: On Jewish Mysticism and
Twentieth Century Thought* (Philadelphia: University of Pennsylvania Press,
2010), 222f.

48 Faierstein, "Heschel and the Holocaust," 273.

49 Moshe Idel, "Abraham J. Heschel on Mysticism and Hasidism," *Modern
Judaism* 29, vol. 1 (2009), 86.

50 *Moral Grandeur*, 34.

51 *Passion for Truth*, xiii.

52 It is interesting to note that in a late conversation with Pinhas Peli, Heschel
resisted Peli's suggestion that his own resistance to a single-minded emphasis on Halakhic conformity had its roots in Heschel's Hasidic forebears, and preferred to root this sensibility in the biblical Prophets. See
Chamesh Sichot 'im Avraham Yehoshua Heschel (Jerusalem: Merkaz Avraham
Yehoshua Heschel, n.d.), 76.

53 Even-Chen and Meir, *Between Heschel and Buber*, 212.

54 Kaplan and Dresner, *Prophetic Witness*, 45.

55 Dresner, *Heschel. Hasidism and Halakha*, 62–4. Kaplan and Dresner, *Prophetic Witness*, 317 n30. See "An Analysis of Piety" (1942), in *Moral Grandeur*, 310. See *Man Is Not Alone*, 282.

56 *Man's Quest for God*, 98; *Search*, 146n7.

57 For the *Ohev Yisrael*, Rabbi Abraham Joshua Heschel of Apta (1748–1825), see *Moral Grandeur*, 38. For Rabbi Israel of Ruzhin (1796–1850), see *Search*, 311. For a mention of the Maggid of Miedzyrzec, see *Passion for Truth*, 104, and a long section in "Rabbi Pinhas of Korzec,"19–29. This section was published in its Hebrew original as a separate article, "Rabbi Pinhas mi-Koritz veha-Maggid mi-Mezeritch," in Menahem Ribolov, ed., *Hadoar Jubilee Volume* (New York: Hadoar, 1952), 279–85.

58 *Circle of the Baal Shem Tov*, 2.

59 These quotations are taken from "Jewish Theology," in *Moral Grandeur*, 154: "In Search of Exaltation," ibid., 227; and "Carl Stern's Interview," ibid., 395, respectively.

60 See Kaplan and Dresner, *Prophetic Witness*, 38–72; Dresner, *Heschel, Hasidism and Halakhah*, 61–5. A comment reportedly made by Heschel to Maurice Friedman is instructive in this context. Asked by Friedman if he would consider returning to an ultra-Orthodox milieu, Heschel replied, "When I left my home in Poland, I became a modern Western man." Maurice Friedman, *You Are My Witnesses: Abraham Joshua Heschel and Elie Wiesel* (New York: Farrar, Straus and Giroux, 1987), 9. Arthur Green suggested that the "Hasidic world of Warsaw was too narrow for him; he saw the small-mindness that necessarily resulted from the tremendous effort expended to shut out the modern world." Arthur Green, "Recasting Hasidism for Moderns," *Tikkun* 14, no. 1 (1999): 63.

61 According to "an edifying story" recorded by Kaplan and Dresner, *Prophetic Witness*, 71, Heschel's uncle the Novominsker Rebbe agreed to "release" him to Vilna, saying: "You can go, but *only* you."

62 *Kotzk*, 10.

63 "Heschel believed that there was a reliable oral tradition going back to the earliest Hasidic period, if only one knew where to look and how to listen." Dresner, *Heschel, Hasidism and Halakhah*, 70. In parallel, Heschel was keenly involved in the collection and research of literary sources and documents relating to the early years of the Hasidic movement.

64 *The Earth Is the Lord's*, 79n3. For another example of an oral tradition, see *The Circle of the Baal Shem Tov*, 45n5.

65 *Moral Grandeur*, 34.
66 *Kotzk*, 8, translated in Dresner, *Heschel, Hasidism and Halakhah*, 46. See also "Umbekante Dokumenten …," particularly 113–14. In the introduction to *Kotzk*, 7, the fact that the spoken word of the Kotzker has been set down in rather ungainly Hebrew is described as a *tzoreh*, a cause of sadness.
67 Heschel's introduction to Samuel H. Dresner, *The Zaddik* (London: Abelard-Schuman, 1960), 7–8.
68 See Arthur Green, "On Translating Hasidic Homilies," *Prooftexts* 3 (1983): 63–72; Zeev Gries, "The Hasidic Managing Editor as an Agent of Culture," in Ada Rapoport-Albert, *Hasidism Reappraised*, 147–8: "… early Hasidism did not consider the book an important tool for the dissemination of Hasidic ideas or the construction of a distinctive community ethos; both of these functions were performed primarily by the circulation of oral traditions." These ideas are expanded and other related topics area raised in Zeev Gries, *Sefer Sofer ve'Sipur be'Reshit ha-Hasidut: Min ha-Besht ve'ad Menahem Mendel me-Kotzk* (Tel Aviv: Hakibbutz Hemeuhad, 1991). See also Moshe Rosman, *Founder of Hasidism: A Quest for the Historical Ba'al Shem Tov* (Berkeley: University of California Press, 1996), 206, which relates to the political dimensions of the transition from oral tradition to printed text. Moshe Idel noted Heschel's distinction between Hasidic literature and life in *Absorbing Perfections*, 615n45.
69 The search for the sources of these unattributed quotations has been an intricate affair, and I would like to thank of the following for their great help: Prof. David Assaf, the late Rabbi Dr. Louis Jacobs, Rabbi Y.Y Kuzecky, the late Rabbi Yehoshua Mondshine, and Prof. Ada Rapoport-Albert. Only with Hasidic material did Heschel refer to a source in the main body of the text in the name of a sage with no further referential pointer. See references to Rabbi Aaron of Karlin in this way on 143 and 424. See Rabbi Aaron Perlov of Karlin, *Bet Aharon* (Brody: Moses Loeb Hermlin, 1875), 47a. For another example of such citation, see *Search*, 160.
70 *Search*, 271.
71 *Emet ve-Emunah*, #462.
72 *Kotzk*, 72–3.
73 Dresner, *Heschel, Hasidism, and Halakhah*, 59, translating *Kotzk*, 59.
74 *Search*, 160.
75 *Toldot Yaakov Yosef*, Kedoshim, 11.
76 Dresner, *Heschel, Hasidism, and Halakhah*, 70.
77 *Search*, 393–4.
78 Yehezkel Shraga Halberstam, *Divrei Yehezkel*, Ekev. On 394 of *Search*, Heschel collapsed two Besht traditions relating to his final hours into one,

without providing references to their literary parallel. The first of these can be found in Naphtali Zevi Horowitz of Ropczyce's *Zera Kodesh*, Vayera, 15. The second is included in the Mondshine edition of *Shivchei ha-Besht* (Jerusalem: Mondshine, 1982), 274, attributed to the *Hekhal Beracha*.

79 *Prophetic Inspiration after the Prophets.*

80 "Perush Al ha-Tefillot." For the suggestion of Abulafian provenance, see Idel, "Abraham Joshua Heschel on Mysticism and Hasidism," 96.

81 *Circle of the Baal Shem Tov*, 70.

82 "Umbekante Dokumenten," 14. Translated in the preface of the *The Circle of the Baal Shem Tov*, 2nd. ed.

83 See, for example, Mendel Piekarz, *Biymei Tzemichat ha-Chasidut*, 26–7. See also Rivka Schatz-Uffenheimer, *Hasidism as Mysticism: Quietistic Elements in Eighteenth Century Hasidic Thought* (Princeton NJ: Princeton University Press, 1993), 104n30; Shaul Magid, "'A Thread of Blue': Rabbi Gershon Henoch Leiner of Radzyn and his Search for Continuity in Response to Modernity," *Polin* 11 (1998): 39n27 (Magid related to Heschel's work on the Kotzker Rebbe); Rosman, *Founder of Hasidism*, 248n40. Rosman is more appreciative of Heschel's method on 256–7n10.

84 Katz, "Abraham Joshua Heschel and Hasidism," 84. For an example of an appreciative comment regarding his scholarship from a current scholar of the first rank, see David Assaf, "Hebetim Historiim veHevratiim be'Heker ha-Hasidut …," in David Assaf, ed., *Tzaddik ve-Edah: Hebetim Historiim ve-Hevratiim beHeker ha-Hasidut* (Jerusalem: Zalman Shazar Center, 2001), 14n5.

85 For an example of this criticism, in this case advanced in the context of a private correspondence, see Marc B. Shapiro, "Scholars and Friends: Rabbi Jehiel Jacob Weinberg and Professor Samuel Atlas," *The Torah U-Madda Journal* 7 (1997): 109–10, where Weinberg wrote, "I am concerned that Dr. Heschel is wasting his time and strength in 'scientific study,' producing a detailed and boring study of the life of R. Gershon Kotover. People make use of the scholarly approach for insignificant matters." See also Rosman, *Founder of Hasidism*, 248n40; Ron Margolin, *Mikdash Adam* (Jerusalem: Magnes, 2005), 361–2. For an extended critique of Heschel's reading of Nachman of Kosov, see Mendel Piekarz, *Biymei Tzemichat ha-Chasidut*, 25–32.

86 This letter, dated 3 August 1953, can be found in the Heschel archive collected by Kaplan and Dresner and located in the Archives of the Jewish Theological Seminary in the file labelled "Scholem." By all accounts it is in response to a letter sent earlier that year by Scholem to Heschel. This letter is to be found in the Heschel papers at Duke, and it deserves closer attention than I can give it here. In it, Scholem congratulates Heschel on his

contributions to the understanding of Hasidism, but he does raise a num-
ber of methodological concerns. See also the comment made by Joseph
Weiss in his *Studies in Eastern European Jewish Mysticism*, 118n12. See
Gershom Scholem, "Shtei Iggerot Me'Eretz Yisrael ...," in David Assaf
and Esther Liebes, eds., *Hashelav ha-Acharon: Mechkarei ha-Chasidut Shel
Gershom Scholem* (Jerusalem: Am Oved/Magnes, 2008), 150n4.

87 *The Circle of the Baal Shem Tov*, 90.

88 Dresner, *Heschel, Hasidism and Halakhah*, 75.

89 Ibid., 60.

90 See Gloria Wiederkehr-Pollack, *Eliezer Zweifel and the Intellectual Defense of
Hasidism* (Hoboken, NJ: Ktav, 1995).

91 Seymour Siegel, "Abraham Joshua Heschel's Contributions to Jewish
Scholarship," 79.

92 The large and burgeoning literature on this question is beyond the con-
fines of this discussion. For the views of the protagonists themselves, see
"Martin Buber's Interpretation of Hasidism," in Gershom Scholem, *The
Messianic Idea in Judaism* (New York: Schocken, 1971); "Martin Buber's
Conception of Judaism," in Gershom Scholem, *On Jews and Judaism in
Crisis: Selected Essays* (New York: Schocken, 1976); Martin Buber, *Hasidism
and Modern Man*, ed. Maurice Friedman (New York: Horizon Press, 1958);
Martin Buber, "Interpreting Hasidism," *Commentary* 36, no. 3 (1963):
218–25.

93 Friedman, "Interpreting Hasidism: The Buber-Scholem Controversy,"
Yearbook of the Leo Baeck Institute 33 (1988): 450.

94 Even-Chen and Meir, *Between Heschel and Buber*, 205–38.

95 *Passion for Truth*, 292–3.

96 Katz, "Abraham Joshua Heschel and Hasidism," 90–1.

97 Joseph Weiss, "Some Notes on the Social Background of Early Hasidism,"
in *Studies in Eastern European Jewish Mysticism* (Oxford: Oxford University
Press, 1985), 23n5.

98 Gershom Scholem, "Reflections on Jewish Theology," in Werner J.
Dannhauser, ed., *On Jews and Judaism in Crisis: Selected Essays* (New York:
Schocken, 1976), 271.

99 Ibid., 272.

100 Ibid., 274.

101 Moshe Idel, *Hasidism: Between Ecstasy and Magic* (Albany: SUNY Press,
1995), 6.

102 See *The Circle of the Baal Shem Tov*, 44.

103 See Morris M. Faierstein, "On the Origins of Hasidism," *Judaism* 39, no. 2
(1990): 251, where Faierstein argued that in the choice of subjects for

Heschel's portraits of the circle of the Ba'al Shem Tov "Heschel is implicitly arguing against the Scholem-Weiss hypothesis of the origins of Hasidism."

104 It might be instructive to place Heschel in the tradition of Hillel Zeitlin. Such a suggestion is made by, among others, Zanvel Klein in response to Steven Katz. Zanvel E. Klein, "Heschel as a Hasidic Scholar," *Journal of Jewish Studies* 32, no. 2 (1981): 200–2. See Kaplan and Dresner, *Prophetic Witness*, 61–3.

105 See Dresner, *Heschel, Hasidism and Halakhah*, 42. Dresner listed motifs that reveal "clear echoes of Hasidic concepts and concerns," among them the concept of *ruach hakodesh*, the Sabbath as a bride, "divine pathos," the "ineffable," "radical amazement," the "primacy of inwardness," the "endless yearning," and more.

106 Green, "Recasting Hasidism" 65.

107 Ibid., 66.

108 Ibid., 67.

109 Idel, "Abraham J. Heschel on Mysticism and Hasidism," 84.

110 *Passion for Truth*, 37–9.

111 Dror Bondi pointed this out in his recent commentary to a Hebrew translation of the Yiddish work.

112 See Michael Rosen, *The Quest for Authenticity: The Thought of Reb Simhah Bunim* (Jerusalem: Urim, 2008), 135–66; *Kotzk*, esp. 79–80.

113 *Who Is Man?* 42.

114 *Passion for Truth*, 159.

115 *Insecurity of Freedom*, 237.

116 See Yehuda Brandes, *Bemalkhut Hakedushah* (Alon Shevut: Tevunit, 2006), 57 and 71. The connection between these traditions and a number of Heschelian motifs is made by Dror Bondi in *Ayekkah?* (Jerusalem: Shalem Center, 2008), 287 n15. As usual, Bondi shows great sensitivity to these connections.

117 Reuven Kimelman, "Review of *The Sabbath*," *Shofar* 26, no. 1 (2007), 188.

118 Yoram Jacobson, "Kedushat ha-Hullin be-Hasidut Gur – Iyunim be-Tefisat ha-Shabbat be-Drushei Sefat Emet," in Rahel Elior, Israel Bartal, and Hone Shmeruk, eds., *Tzaddikim ve-Anshei Maaseh – Mechkarim be-Hasidut Polin* (Jerusalem: Bialik Institute, 1994): 241–77.

119 *The Sabbath*, 3 n1 refers to *Man Is Not Alone*, 200. *Search*, 200 n1 refers to *The Sabbath*, 7f.

120 *Search*, 200.

121 *Torah min Hashamayim*, vol. 2, 272.

122 See "Space, Time and Reality: The Centrality of Time in the Biblical World View," *Judaism* 1, no. 3 (1952), where references include Genesis Rabbah,

Midrash on Psalms, Pirke de Rabbi Eliezer, as well as Saadia, Maimonides, and Judah Halevi. Significantly perhaps, there are more non-Jewish sources quoted in that essay.

123 *The Sabbath,* 98.

124 See, for example, *Sefat Emet. Hayei Sarah,* 5658.

125 *Sefat Emet, Pikkudei,* 5655.

126 "Evenings – palaces in time …"

127 Tzadok Hacohen of Lublin, *Peri Tzadik* (Lublin: Schneidmesser and Hirschenhorn, 1907), 231.

128 Abraham Joshua Heschel, "Architecture of Time," *Judaism* 1, no. 1 (1952): 49.

129 *Moral Grandeur,* 227.

130 "The Eastern European Era in Jewish History," *YIVO Annual of Jewish Social Science* 1 (1946), 102.

131 *Search,* 211–12.

132 Ibid., 37. See Abraham Joshua Heschel, *Ohev Yisrael* (Zhitomir: Schapira, 1863), 86b, at the beginning of Ki Tetze.

133 "The Individual Jew and his Obligations," in *Insecurity of Freedom,* 190–1. See also *Who Is Man?* 34, 35, and 59; "Israel and Diaspora" (1958), in *Insecurity of Freedom,* 213–14.

134 *Passion for Truth,* 143. Compare with *Kotzk,* vol. 1, 154–9.

135 I am very grateful to Shai Held for sharing with me the manuscript of his *The Call of Transcendence.*

136 See 11, in which he quotes Bunam's definition of a Hasid: "A Hasid goes beyond the law; he will not even deceive his own self." Although no attribution is made here, this source can be identified. See *Sefer Kol Mevasser,* a collection of traditions attributed to Reb Simcha Bunam, vol. 1, Behar, quoting from *Ma'ayanah shel Torah.*

137 *Search,* 388. On 394n2 Heschel simply wrote "Raphael of Bersht," with no further attribution. In fact, the teaching is to be found in *Midrash Pinhas,* 137, section 56.

138 *Search,* 394. Note 17 on the following page ascribes this teaching to Epstein's *Maor Vashamesh,* 29b. In fact, this teaching appears on 209b. On Buber's use of this teaching, see Barry J. Hammer, "Resolving the Buber-Scholem Controversy in Hasidim," *Journal of Jewish Studies* 47, no. 1 (1996): 107.

139 "The Values of Jewish Education," *Proceedings of the Rabbinical Assembly,* vol. 26 (1962), 94.

140 *Moral Grandeur,* 105. See Louis Jacobs, *Religion and the Individual: a Jewish Perspective* (Cambridge, UK: Cambridge University Press, 1992), 38–40.

141 See Yehuda Brandes, *Bemalkhut Hakedushah,* 42.

7 An Affinity of Strangers

1 *Passion for Truth*, 85f.
2 Ibid., 86.
3 For this Heschelian expression, see *Man Is Not Alone*, 165.
4 *Passion for Truth*, 239.
5 *Search*, 12
6 "Faith" (1944), in *Moral Grandeur*, 335.
7 "No Religion Is an Island" (1966), in *Moral Grandeur*, 237.
8 "Confusion of Good and Evil" (1956), in *Insecurity of Freedom*, 127–49. This essay, originally published in a volume devoted to the thought of Niebuhr, was intended "to examine some of Niebuhr's views in the light of Jewish thinking" (128). On the close relationship between these two men, see Kaplan, *Spiritual Radical*, for example 181.
9 See 124 and 543n9. On 321n2 Heschel indicated to his Yiddish readers that a longer discussion of the affinity between the two men can be found in the English version of that work. Heschel had first suggested a link between the two thinkers in a short 1959 Hebrew essay. See "Rabbi Mendel mi-Kotzk," *Hadoar* 38, 28 Iyyar 5719 (1959): 519–21.
10 See *Torah min Hashamayim*, vol. 1, 55 and 177, with reference to Islam.
11 The Gospel According to Matthew, for example, is cited in *Torah min Hashamayim*, vol. 1, 165n10 and 231n33; vol. 2, 43n16, 80n7, 116n16, and 117n18; and vol. 3, 67n37.
12 See for example references to the work of R.H. Charles in *Torah min Hashamayim*, vol. 2, 36nn10–11; J.G. Davies and others with reference to the Ascent of Enoch in vol. 2, 43, and a fascinating short chapter on the motif of sacred writings in the heavens in Islam and other religions in vol. 2, 24–6.
13 The same can be said of his Yiddish work. For a rare counter-example, see Kotzk, 652n6, where one of Jean de La Fontaine's seventeenth-century fables is cited as a source.
14 See Michael Marmur, "Are You My Witnesses? The Use of Sources in Modern Jewish Thought," *Modern Judaism* 32 (2012): esp. 156.
15 "Faith," in *Moral Grandeur*, 334. For echoes of this notion, see Ha'amek Davar to Deuteronomy 16:3 and Kedushat Levi, Terumah. This statement appears in his Hebrew essay from the late 1940s, "Pikuach Neshama," in *Moral Grandeur*, 64.
16 *Man is Not Alone*, 161. The quotations are from *Two Essays on Analytical Psychology* and *Psychological Types*.
17 *Search*, 39–40. The poems quoted are "Song at the Feast of Brougham Castle" and "The Old Cumberland Beggar."

18 Ibid., 373.

19 Henri Bergson, *The Two Sources of Morality and Religion* (Garden City, NY: Doubleday Anchor, 1954), 76–7.

20 *Torah min Hashamayim*, vol. 1, xxxiin21.

21 *The Prophets*, 299–306.

22 *Search*, 293–5.

23 It is interesting to note that in *Man Is Not Alone* Heschel quoted excerpts from *Measure for Measure* (182) and *Much Ado about Nothing* (185) in a non-polemical way. Indeed, in both of these cases the verses are applied much like biblical verses.

24 Martin Jay, "Name-Dropping or Dropping Names?" in *Force Fields: Between Intellectual History and Cultural Critique* (New York: Routledge, Chapman and Hall, 1993), 169.

25 *Man's Quest for God*, 113.

26 *Search*, 209–10.

27 *Search*, 222–3.

28 In "The Vocation of the Cantor," in *Insecurity of Freedom*, 246, Heschel wrote, "I am neither a musician nor an expert on music. But the shattering experience of music has been a challenge to my thinking on ultimate issues." See also Avraham Holtz, "Religion and the Arts in the Theology of Abraham Joshua Heschel," *Conservative Judaism* 28, no. 1 (1973): esp. 34–6. Musical metaphors have also been used to describe his work. Lou H. Silberman, "The Philosophy of Abraham Heschel," *Jewish Heritage* 2, no. 1 (1959): 24. In a real sense, Heschel's writings must be looked at from the point of view of a symphony, which is above and beyond its parts. His literary style is theme and variations, in which, to use the musical figure, each note must be listened to not by itself but together with that which has gone before and that which is yet to come. The broad sweep of his works is necessary for complete understandings. It is also worth noting that Heschel's wife, Sylvia, was a pianist by profession.

29 Heschel, *Search*, 380n2.

30 Ibid., 52n6. It may not be coincidental that in that Supplement Schopenhauer mounted stiff resistance to Spinoza, claiming that "Spinoza's doctrine that the world is the only possible and absolutely necessary substance is incompatible with our wonder and astonishment at its existence and essential nature." Heschel's disapproval of Schopenhauer was to a certain extent mitigated by his emphasis on wonder, and perhaps also by his rejection of Spinoza.

31 *Search*, 143n6.

32 Epistles 341c, quoted in the body of the text in *Search*, 103. For another example of this interpolation of non-Jewish with Jewish sources, see ibid.,

151n15, Heschel once again juxtaposed Jewish and non-Jewish teaching: Maimonides, Bahya, ibn Ezra, and Ben Yehuda are linked to al-Ghazali and Aristotle. See also ibid., 23n2. The issue of self-knowledge is mentioned first in relation to "philosophy" with citations of Plato, Aristotle, Xenophanes, Plotinus, and others, followed by references to cognate sources in Jewish literature.

33 *Search*, 15.

34 *Who Is Man?* 21. Some thirteen references from the topics of politics, ethics and poetics are cited on that page.

35 Abraham Joshua Heschel, *Between God and Man: An Interpretation of Judaism* (New York: Free Press, 1959), 25. The term "the most moved mover" is often attributed to Heschel himself, and it is possible that Rothschild was quoting Heschel's teaching here. However, I have not been able to find the phrase in any of Heschel's published works. The reference to Aristotle's concept appears in *Die Prophetie*, 139. See also *The Prophets*, 234, and his 1964 piece "The White Man on Trial," in *Insecurity of Freedom*, 102. See *The Prophets*, 259.

36 See Heschel's summary of Kierkegaard's either/or in *Passion for Truth*, 112, where Plato stands against Protagoras in asserting that God is the measure of all things.

37 *Search*, 57 and 59n5.

38 Ibid., 98.

39 Ibid. See 377, where the Platonic phrase is employed to illustrate an opinion with which Jewish thought disagrees. See also 400 n1.

40 Ibid. See 12, 14, 15, 18, 24, 25, and 184.

41 See Julius Guttmann, "Kant ve'Yahadut," in *Dat u-Mada* (Jerusalem: The Magnes Press, 1957): 218–29.

42 *Search*, 285–6.

43 Ibid., 38–9, and 42n7.

44 Ibid., 378–9.

45 Ibid., 294–5. For other examples of a less than enthusiastic treatment of Kantian views in *Search*, see 88 and 108–9. For an important discussion of this question, see Lawrence Perlman, "Heschel's Critique of Kant," in Jacob Neusner, Ernest S. Frerichs, and Nahum M. Sarna, eds., *From Ancient Israel to Modern Judaism: Intellect in Quest of Understanding*, vol. 3 (Atlanta: Scholars Press, 1989), 213–26. See also J. Hyman, "Abraham Heschel: Alienation and the Trope of Meaning" (PhD diss., Stanford University, 1996), 84–94.

46 *Search*, 39.

47 *Search*, 21. The paragraph in which this sentence appears is in fact a quotation from *Man Is Not Alone*, 84–5. The idea of the hundred dollars appears

in the fourth section of the *Critique of Pure Reason*. For a discussion of the context, see Oded Balaban, "The Belief in Reality and the Reality of Belief," *Giornale de Metafisica* 17, 1–2 (1995): 71–85. This mention of Kant does not suggest any identification on Heschel's part with typically Kantian philosophic positions but rather an employment of well-known Kantian rhetoric.

48 *Search*, 10.
49 Ibid., 51 and 53n18.
50 *Passion for Truth*, 106.
51 *Search*, 18.
52 *Man's Quest for God*, 60.
53 Ibid., 88. I believe that the mention of Dewey in both this litany and the previous note reflects Heschel's silent polemic against Mordecai Kaplan. For another list, in this case invoking the names of Kepler and Newton, see *Man Is Not Alone*, 30. As we will see below, any reference to Spinoza in Heschel's work is far from impartial. The God of Spinoza is not a God to whom one can turn in prayer. The Alexander mentioned here is most likely Samuel Alexander, an Australian-born ethicist and metaphysician of Jewish extraction whose Gifford Lectures were published in 1920 as *Space, Time, and Deity*.
54 Heschel held up Plato, Schelling, William James, and Bergson as examples of thinkers who would not be termed philosophers if philosophy is to be understood as synonymous with rationalism. Here is a good example of the technique of mention: these four thinkers evoke a certain philosophical sensibility. For a contrasting list, see 24, where Hegel, Hobbes, Locke, and Schopenhauer are mentioned in a satirical and unflattering light.
55 "Israel and Diaspora," in *Insecurity of Freedom*, 218. For more on Heschel's approach to Freud, see *Man's Quest for God*, 60. Freud was something of a bugbear for Heschel. See, for example, his critique of pan-psychology in *Man Is Not Alone*, 221–7. See David Barnard, "Abraham Heschel's Attitude toward Religion and Psychology," *Journal of Religion* 63, no. 1 (1983): 26–43. See also *Search*, 54.
56 Kaplan, *Spiritual Radical*, 17. See Heschel's response to Einstein's "Science and Religion," abridged and published in German, "Antwort an Einstein," *Aufbau* 6, no. 38 (20 September 1940): 3.
57 Abraham Joshua Heschel, "Space, Time and Reality: The Centrality of Time in the Biblical World View," *Judaism* 1, no. 3 (1952): 264–5.
58 Faierstein, "Heschel and the Holocaust," 273.
59 *Search*, 24.
60 Ibid., 322.

61 Ibid., 333n3.
62 *Die Prophetie*, 139. The way in which Spinoza's approach to the affects is
    dealt with here is reminiscent of Hermann Cohen. See *Religion of Reason*,
    18 and 140–1. Cohen describes Spinoza's position with reference to Stoic
    philosophy, and this may have been influenced Heschel's discussion. For
    other references to Spinoza in *Die Prophetie*, see 125, 130, 157, and 162.
63 *Search*, 322. See Julius Guttmann, "Yerushalayim" le-Mendelssohn ve- "ha-
    Masekhet ha-Teyologit-ha Medinit" le-Spinoza," in *Dat u-Mada*, 192–217;
    Julius Gutmann, *Philosophies of Judaism: The History of Jewish Philosophy
    from Biblical Times to Franz Rosenzweig* (Philadelphia: Jewish Publication
    Society of America, 1964), 299–300; Yitzhak Heinemann, "Ha-Achdut
    be'Philosofia ha-Datit shel Moshe Mendelssohn," *Metzuda* 7 (1953–4): 197–
    219. See also Michael L Morgan, "History and Modern Jewish Thought:
    Spinoza and Mendelssohn on the Ritual Law," *Judaism* 30, no. 4 (1981):
    467–89. Heschel is in good company in his reliance on Guttmann's thesis
    about the role of Mendelssohn as a mediating force between Spinoza and
    Kant, and indeed in his entire presentation of the relationship between
    Mendelssohn and Spinoza. In his great biography, *Moses Mendelssohn:
    A Biographical Study* (London: Routledge and Kegan Paul, 1973), 842n39,
    Alexander Altmann stated that in his analysis of the second part of
    Jerusalem, "we follow, in the main, Julius Guttmann's essay." In *Spinoza and
    Other Heretics*, vol. 2 (Princeton NJ: Princeton University Press, 1989), 9,
    Yirmiyahu Yovel stated that Kant probably did not read the *Tractatus* at
    first hand, and that "in all probability, as Julius Guttmann has shown, he
    was indirectly influenced by Spinoza's ideas – the mediating link being
    Moses Mendelssohn…"
64 In *Search*, 322, Heschel quoted from *Jerusalem*, and referred the reader
    in 333n4 simply to Part II, with no more specific reference. The first of
    the two sentences is a loose translation of the text – see *Jerusalem* in the
    Gesammelte Schriften (Leipzig: Brodhaus, 1843), vol. 3, 311. The second sen-
    tence does not appear in *Jerusalem*, although a similar statement can be
    found in a letter from Mendelssohn to Wolf Dessau dated 11 July 1782.
    Heschel's text reads, "The spirit of Judaism is freedom in doctrine and
    conformity in action," and the text of the letter reads, "The spirit of
    Judaism demands conformity in action and freedom in respect of doc-
    trine." In the *Jewish Encyclopedia*'s entry on Moses Mendelssohn, written
    by Meyer Kayserling, the text of both the quotations brought by Heschel
    appears word for word.
65 See, for example Nathan Rotenstreich, *Jewish Philosophy in Modern Times:
    From Mendelssohn to Rosenzweig* (New York: Holt, Rhinehart and Winston,

1968), esp. 14–15; Steven B. Smith, *Spinoza, Liberalism and the Question of Jewish Identity* (New Haven: Yale University Press, 1997), esp. 170; Zeev Levy, *Spinoza ve-Musag ha-Yehadut* (Tel Aviv: Sifriat Poalim, 1974), 84–95.

66 Franz Nauen argued that over time Hermann Cohen's "dislike of Spinoza ripened into hate." Fritz Nauen, "Hermann Cohen's Perception of Spinoza: A Reappraisal," *AJS Review* 4 (1979): 123. Nauen discussed the various explanations of this apparent change suggested by Rosenzweig, Simon, and Strauss.

67 "The Two Great Traditions," 420.

68 *The Sabbath*, 4.

69 "Space, Time and Reality: The Centrality of Time in the Biblical World View," *Judaism* 1, no. 3 (1952): 268.

70 "Yisrael: Am, Eretz, Medinah: Ideological Evaluation of Israel and the Diaspora," *Proceedings of the Rabbinical Assembly of* America, vol. 22 (1958), 127.

71 "Teaching Jewish Theology," 6. See also "The People of the Covenant" (interview), *Ararat* 30 (1967): 75: "Judaism is not religious behaviorism as Spinoza and Moses Mendelssohn thought. These men were under the erroneous impression that the only authentic expression of Judaism is the science of law."

72 See *The Prophets*, 190–1.

73 For more damning critique, see *Torah min Hashamayim*, vol. 3, 162. See Daniel S. Breslauer, "Spinoza's Théologico-Political Treatise and A.J. Heschel's Theology of Biblical Language," *CCAR Journal* 24, no. 1 (1977): 19–26.

74 *Man's Quest for God*, 53.

75 *Torah min Hashamayim*, iv.

76 *Search*, 325.

77 See, for example, "Sacred Image of Man," in *Insecurity of Freedom*, 166, where he suggests that in the future, the nations listed by Isaiah in 19:25 – Egypt, Assyria, and Israel – "will be equally God's chosen people." I have recently completed a more comprehensive study of Heschel's ambivalent approach to the concept of the Chosen People, which I hope to publish in the future.

78 *Man Is Not Alone*, 169.

8 Heschel's *Aspaklaria*

1 Kaplan, *Spiritual Radical*, 163.

2 Chapter 16 contains one reference to the Palestinian Talmud, one paraphrase of a teaching from the Ba'al Shem Tov, and two references to *Man Is*

Not Alone; chapter 17 has no footnotes, but one verse from Deuteronomy is quoted in the body of the chapter; chapter 22 quotes two contemporary non-Jewish sources; chapter 39 quotes Plato and Heschel.

3 There is a passing reference to Hegel in the chapter, and the only notes refer the reader to William James, Nicolai Hartmann, and Heschel's own *Man Is Not Alone*. Heschel's interest in William James goes back well before his arrival in the United States. Dresner and Kaplan recorded Heschel's discussions of James in Berlin in 1930 (*Prophetic Witness*, 132–3; Edward Kaplan, "Jewish Renewal in Pre-Nazi Berlin – Abraham Heschel Interprets William James," *CrossCurrents* 53, no. 3 (2003): 436–44). See *Die Prophetie*, 46 and 118; see also Abraham Joshua Heschel, "The Religious Message," in John Cogley, ed., *Religion In America: Original Essays on Religion in a Free Society* (New York: Meridian Books, 1958), 246; "Idols in the Temples" (1962), in *Insecurity of Freedom*, 65; and *Passion for Truth*, 118, where the Jamesian expression "the will to believe" is mentioned; and 179. It may be argued that the distinction between ends and needs in *Man Is Not Alone* is adopted from James. See also Hal Bridges, *American Mysticism from William James to Zen* (New York: Harper and Row, 1970), 63. For an important comment on the nature of freedom, see *The Earth Is the Lord's*, 63. I am grateful to my colleague Yehoyada Amir for first pointing out to me the importance of the chapter on freedom in *Search*.

4 See *Search*, 100n13, 332n2, and 333n4.

5 In the first of these references, *Search*, 100 n7, the reference is to statements by Herberg, which are meant to provide a contrast with the views of Francis Thompson on nature. It is most likely that the particular sentence to which Heschel was referring his readers on 34 of Will Herberg, *Judaism and Modern Man – An Interpretation of Jewish Religion* (Philadelphia: Jewish Publication Society of America, 1951) is this: "We must break through the natural limitations of life and establish vital contact with what is beyond."

6 *Search*, 360n4.

7 Ibid., 313n7.

8 In *Die Prophetie* he cited thinkers such as Leo Baeck (62) and Martin Buber (34, 40, 125, and 179), but none of them is discussed at length. Scholars such as Saul Lieberman, Louis Finkelstein, and Gershom Scholem are mentioned in *Torah min Hashamayim*. For Lieberman see vol. 1, 160, 214, 237, and 284; and vol. 2, 40. For references to Finkelstein, see vol. 1, xxxvii, xxxviii, 10, 13, 37, 105, 120, and 137; and vol. 2, 71, 79, 96, 120, 135, 147, 152, 169, 194, 213, and 234. Scholem is mentioned in vol. 1, 13, 64, 209, 244, and 279; and in vol. 2, 40. There is work to be done appraising Heschel's professional appreciation of these and other scholars whom he knew and with whom he often had complex relationships. In view of what is known

about his relations with Scholem, for example, it is interesting to note the glowing review Heschel gave *Major Trends in Jewish Mysticism*. See *Journal of Religion* 24, no. 2 (1944): 140–1.

9 His short appreciation of Diesendruck does not rise to this level. See "Zevi Diesendruck," *American Jewish Year Book* 43 (1941–2): 391–8.

·10 This comment is made in his Hebrew work on Crescas. See Warren Zev Harvey, *Great Spirit and Creativity within the Jewish Nation: Rabbi Hasdai Crescas* (Jerusalem: Zalman Shazar Center, 2010), 63. This whole question needs to be explored further as part of a study of Jewish quotational practices.

11 See *Search*, 112n9 and 121n4; the reference is to *Man Is Not Alone* 135n8, 153n2, 205n3, 233n5, and 312n10.

12 See ibid., 7n3, 39n8, 74n3, 85n6, 138n4, 200n1, 244n3, and 344n13.

13 There are examples of this kind of citation, when the fact that the book referred to is by the author seems incidental. See ibid., 124n1, 150n1, 234n1, 335n41, 347n8, and 419n2.

14 *Man's Quest for God*, 104.

15 *Search*, 20.

16 Examples of paraphrase close to the original source can be found in *Search*, 23 n8 and 160 n1, although this latter source is wrongly cited: rather than referring to 74 of *Man Is Not Alone*, the intention appears to be to 128 of that work.

17 *Search*, 100n13; *Don Jizchak Abravanel* (1937), chap. 3n3.

18 *Search*, 205.

19 *Torah min Hashamayim*, vol. 3, 133. The term is to be found in Mishnah Tamid, 1.2.

20 "Did Maimonides Believe …?" 166. See also *Kotzk*, 328n5, where a similar phrase is used in relation to the experience of prayer: he cites Rabbi Nachman of Bratslav to the effect that it is not possible to maintain a constant level of intensity throughout prayer.

21 See "Ruach ha-Kodesh …," 175, and "Did Maimonides Believe …?" 175–6.

22 *The Sabbath*, 8.

23 For a further complex example of self-quotation see "The Concept of Man in Jewish Thought," which appeared as a chapter in S. Radhakrisnan and P.T. Raju, *The Concept of Man* (London: Allen and Unwin, 1960), 108–57. The first two sections are mainly comprised of *Man Is Not Alone*, 191–9, 207, and 209–15, although this borrowing is unattributed. In his later *Who Is Man?* however, Heschel noted that some paragraphs in chapter 4 were taken from the two earlier works. See *Who Is Man?* 50. "Sacred Image of Man," in *Insecurity of Freedom*: 150–67 is in fact a patchwork of these three earlier writings.

24 Abraham Joshua Heschel, *The Ineffable Name of God: Man*, transl. Morton Leifman (New York: Continuum, 2005), 69. See Green, "Recasting Hasidism," 66, and Even-Chen and Meir, *Between Heschel and Buber*, 78.

25 For explicit references to optics in his philosophical lexicon, see Abraham Joshua Heschel, "A Concise Dictionary of Hebrew Philosophical Terms" (unpublished manuscript, Cincinnati, 1941), 40 and 51.

26 For the term *aspaklaria* and its development in Jewish and Christian literature, see David H. Gill, "Through a Glass Darkly: A Note on 1 Corinthians 13:12," *Catholic Biblical Quarterly* 25 (1963): 427–9; Anne Chantal, "Kierkegard lecteur de Spinoza et la Question de l'Éternite," *Studia Spinoziana* 10 (1994): 135–53; Emmanuel Lev, "Aspaklaria," in I. Low, *Fauna und Minerallen der Juden* (Hildesheim: Georg Olms, 1969), 175–81; Yehoshua Brand, "Aspakalaria," in *Sefer Zikaron le'Binyamin De-Vries* (Tel Aviv: University of Tel Aviv, 1968–9), 110–18.

27 See Sifrei to Numbers, 103; Tanchuma, Tzav 13; Rashi to Numbers 12:8. See W.Z. Harvey, "Torat haNevua ha-Sinestetit shel RiHaL ve-Heara al Sefer ha-Zohar," *Kolot Rabim* 1 (1996): 141–55.

28 Leviticus Rabbah 1:14; Yevamot 49b; Pesikta Zutarta (Lekach tov) Beha'lotecha 104a. This latter source refers to perception according to one's ability, a theme developed in Exodus Rabbah 5:9; Midrash Shemuel 4; and elsewhere.

29 See I Corinthians 13:12.

30 Elliot R. Wolfson, *Through a Speculum That Shines: Vision and Imagination in Medieval Jewish Mysticism* (Princeton, NJ: Princeton University 1994). See also Rachel Neis, *The Sense of Sight in Rabbinic Culture: Jewish Ways of Seeing in Late Antiquity* (Cambridge: Cambridge University Press, 2013).

31 See Ovadiah of Bertinoro to Mishnah Kelim, chap. 30 Mishnah 2. See Abravanel to Numbers 12:8.

32 *The Earth Is the Lord's*, 32–3, 35.

33 Ibid., 84. See also *Man Is Not Alone*, 60, for a reference to "mere reflection."

34 *Who Is Man?* 34.

35 *Passion for Truth*, 86.

36 *The Ineffable Name of God: Man*, 30–1.

37 *Man's Quest for God*, 126. This section also appears in "The Concept of Man in Jewish Thought" (1960), in Neusner and Neusner, eds., *To Grow in Wisdom*, 126.

38 *The Prophets*, vol. 1, 15. See also *Die Prophetie*, 175.

39 "The Meaning of This War" (1944), in *Moral Grandeur*, 211.

40 Sefat Emet to Va'era 1896. For more on the mirror as a motif, see Sabine Melchior-Bonnet, *The Mirror: A History* (London: Routledge, 2002). For a parallel in English literature, see W. David Shaw, "The Optical Metaphor;

Victorian Poetics and the Theory of Knowledge," *Victorian Studies* 23, no. 3 (1980): 305: "a Baconian model of the poem as self-reflecting mirror and a Hobbesian model of the poem as transparent glass or window." For a parallel in modern Jewish thought, A.D. Gordon's use of mirror imagery is informative. See Avraham Shapira, *Or Hayyim be Yom Ktanot* (Tel-Aviv: Am Oved, 1996), 113–14. For an example of Gordon's use of *aspaklaria*, see A.D. Gordon, *Mivchar Ketavim* (Jerusalem: ha-Sifriya ha-Tziyonit, 1983), 60–1. I am indebted to Yehoyada Amir for drawing my attention to the Gordonian mirror.

41 *Torah min Hashamayim*, vol. 1, 276.
42 *The Earth Is the Lord's*, 54; *Man's Quest for God*, 105; *Search*, 351. For another image, see *Moral Grandeur*, 77.
43 "Al Yichudo shel ha-Kiyum ha-Yehudi," 238.
44 *Torah min Hashamayim*, vol. 1, 83. The same sentence appears ibid., xlvi.
45 Ibid., xlv.
46 *Torah min Hashamayim*, vol. 2, 403. Heschel also repeated this in vol. 3, 16.
47 *The Earth Is the Lord's*, 54.
48 See Harold Kasimow, "Heschel's View of Religious Diversity," *Studies in Christian-Jewish Relations* 2, no. 2 (2007): 19–25, http://ejournals.bc.edu/ojs/index.php/scjr/article/view/1419; Arnold Eisen, "Abraham Joshua Heschel and the Challenge of Religious Pluralism," *Modern Judaism* 29, no. 1 (2009): 4–15.
49 For an example of use of the term *aspaklaria* in this sense, see *Chamesh Sichot 'im Abraham Joshua Heschel* (Jerusalem: Mossad Abraham Joshua Heschel, Hebrew Publication Committee, 1975), 41.
50 Ibid., 70.
51 "On Prayer," in *Moral Grandeur*, 259.
52 He also translated the word in a different way. The phrase ישראל בימינו נסתכל באספקלריה של תולדות appears in "Al Yichudo shel ha-Kiyum ha-Yehudi," 238. In the English version, "The Individual Jew and His Obligations," in *Insecurity of Freedom*, 190, the phrase is translated thus: "Let us look at our recent history."
53 *Echo of Eternity*, 155. In this version of the dichotomy, prophecy and apocalypse are on the same side of the equation. In *Torah min Hashamayim*, vol. 1, 247–70, they are presented as essentially different phenomena.
54 See *Torah min Hashamayim*, vol. 1, lv–lvi.
55 "Interview at Notre Dame," in *Moral Grandeur*, 389.
56 He stated in a 1969 essay that "this has been my personal challenge, ever since I began working on my dissertation; that is: How to maintain a Jewish way of thinking?" "Jewish Theology," in *Moral Grandeur*, 156.

57 "Choose Life!" in *Moral Grandeur*, 256.

58 "Existence and Celebration," in *Moral Grandeur*, 20.

59 See for example Zohar I.122a; Zohar Hadash, 27b, 28b,

60 *Torah min Hashamayim*, vol. 1, lv; see also ibid., 220.

61 *Torah min Hashamayim*, vol. 3, 89. See also *Chamesh Sichot*, 59.

62 "Toward an Understanding of Halacha,"in *Moral Grandeur*, 388–9. See also *Insecurity of Freedom*, 33 and 130.

63 *The Prophets*, vol. 1, xiv.

64 Ibid., x.

65 Ibid., 138. See the section entitled "From the Point of View of God," in *Man's Quest for God*, 94–6.

66 Ibid., 15; *Die Prophetie*, 175. See also *The Prophets*, vol. 2, 93. Heschel used Spinoza's term in *Search*, 15 and in this telling comment on 418: "In the language of the Jew, living *sub specie aeternitatis* means living *sub specie Sabbatis*."

67 For a parallel in the thought of Soloveitchik, see Joseph B. Soloveitchik, *The Halakhic Mind: An Essay on Jewish Tradition and Modern Thought* (1944; reprint, New York: Free Press, 1986), 45. See also Steven Nadler, *Spinoza's Heresy: Immortality and the Jewish Mind* (Oxford: Clarendon, 2001), 121; Piero di Vona, *La conoscenza "sub specie aeternitatis" nell'opera di Spinoza* (Naples: Loffredo, 1995), esp. 79; Chantal, "Kierkegard lecteur de Spinoza," 135–53. Descartes's expression "au regard de l'Éternité" is mentioned in Charles Taylor, *A Secular Age* (Cambridge, MA: Harvard University Press, 2009), 132.

68 There are several references to *aspaklaria* in *Torah min Hashamayim*. See, for example, vol. 1, 227–31.

69 Ibid., vol. 2, 299.

70 *Echo of Eternity*, 155.

71 Ibid., 159.

72 *Who Is Man?* 35.

73 See, for example, Rashi to Sukkah 45b. Heschel made reference to the Maimonidean concept in "Did Maimonides Believe…?" 102–3. Halbertal suggested that "the esoteric … is reflected … through piercing the fearsome veils in order to arrive at the experience of the vision of the hidden God." Halbertal, *Concealment and Revelation*, 19.

74 Leviticus Rabbah 1:14.

75 *Search*, 277n23. On 85 a number of works are adduced to enhance the idea that one may have eyes and yet not see.

76 Heschel related to Maimonides's notion of moral perfection as a ladder to prophecy in "Did Maimonides Believe …?"105–6.

77 See Maimonides's Commentary to Tractate Kelim 30.2 and the beginning of the seventh of his Eight Chapters on Tractate Avot.

78 *The Prophets*, 193.

79 "Did Maimonides Believe …?" 103n105, which refers the reader to Yesodei Hatorah, 4.7, and also mentions the concept of the eye of the heart, discussed below. See also 110–11, where Heschel quoted the Guide II.36 regarding the process of self-perfection.

80 See both Heschel, "The Holy Dimension," in *Moral Grandeur*, 318 and "Faith," in ibid., 330.

81 Ramon, "Avodah Zarah ve-Sanvarei ha-Neorut," 105.

82 *The Earth Is the Lord's*, 105.

83 *Echo of Eternity*, 7.

84 "Religion and Race," in *Insecurity of Freedom*, 87.

85 *Heavenly Torah*, 710.

86 *Search*, 87n12.

87 "The God of Israel and Christian Renewal," in *Moral Grandeur*, 275.

88 Ken Koltun-Fromm, "Vision and Authenticity in Heschel's The Sabbath," *Modern Judaism* 31, no. 2 (2011): 143.

89 Ibid., 143.

90 Ibid., 162.

91 "The Holy Dimension," in *Moral Grandeur*, 319. The motif of facing up can be found in many of his works. It is particularly prominent in *Who Is Man?* where references to the face and face-to-face encounter are to be found on 1, 34, 38, 76, 84, 88, 90, and 113.

92 *Search*, 148.

93 See, for example, ibid., 87n12, 151n24, 188n5, and 276n1. For metaphors of hearing, see for example 144n13, 145n3, and 188n6.

94 Ibid., 148.

95 Ibid., 151n15, with reference to the inner eye of the "chosen ones," in *The Kuzari*, iv, 3. The references to Halevi at the end of this section are somewhat confused: n22 refers the reader to *Selected Poems* and n23 to a German edition of the *Diwan*, but in fact the attribution is the other way round. The long excerpt of poetry can be found in Heinrich Brody, ed., *Selected Poems of Jehudah Halevi* (Philadelphia: Jewish Publication Society of America, 1924), 94, and here Heschel was faithful to the printed translation.

96 Wolfson, *Through a Speculum that Shines*, esp. 294–5. See also 163–87.

97 The link between issues of perception and Judah Halevi was also made in *Search*, 29, where Heschel quotes the poet expressing to see the face of God within his heart.

98 "A Concise Dictionary of Hebrew Philosophical Terms."

99 *Search*, 148.

100 Ibid., 151n16.

101 See Megillah 24b. See Tosafot to Avodah Zarah, 28b. See also the quotation from Philo's "De Opificio Mundi" in *The Prophets*, vol. 2, 112.

102 *The Prophets*, vol. 2, 11.

103 Abraham Joshua Heschel, "Ilya Schor," *Conservative Judaism* 16, no. 1 (1961): 20: "Authenticity of insight is being corroded." An additional example can be found in "On Prayer,"in *Moral Grandeur*, 267: "We of this generation are afflicted with a severe case of dulling or loss of vision."

104 "Ilya Schor," 21.

9 Heschel and the Call to Action

1 "The Reasons for My Involvement," in *Moral Grandeur*, 224.

2 *The Ineffable Name of God: Man*, 175.

3 Faierstein, "Heschel and the Holocaust," 272.

4 At a discussion involving a number of students and faculty members from the Jewish Theological Seminary during the period of mourning for Sylvia Ettenberg in 2012, it was suggested that Heschel had been almost alone among his faculty contemporaries in not condemning the 1968 student protests at neighbouring Columbia University. Most faculty members viewed the prospect of protesting hordes of students as the prelude to a pogrom. Heschel saw it as evidence that this time the young people were not prepared to let injustice pass with equanimity.

5 "Religion in a Free Society," in *Insecurity of Freedom*, 4.

6 "Religion and Race," in *Insecurity of Freedom*, 85.

7 *The Prophets*, 16. In a 1971 essay, we find Heschel again reprising this aphorism, in opposition to American involvement in Vietnam. See "Required: A Moral Ombudsman" (1971), in *Moral Grandeur*, 220. For another example of Heschel's frequent use of this phrase, see Kaplan, *Spiritual Radical*, 305. See also "Religion and Race," in *Insecurity of Freedom*, 93.

8 "The Reasons for My Involvement," in *Moral Grandeur*, 225.

9 Two significant discussions of the prophetic dimension in Heschel's thinking are to be found in Hebrew: Eliezer Schweid, "Ha-Filosof ke-Nevi ha-Nevuah: ha-Yahas bein Filosofia le-Dat be-Mishnato shel Avraham Joshua Heschel," in *Neviim le-Amam ve-le-Enoshut: Nevuah ve-Neviim be-Hagut ha-Yehudit shel ha-Meah ha-Esrim* (Jerusalem: Magnes Press, 1999), 234–54; Arnold Eisen, "Nevuah ke- 'Vokatsia': Perspectivot Chadashot al

Machshavato ve-Peiluto shel HaRav Abraham Joshua Heschel," in
Yehoyada Amir, ed., *Derech HaRuach: Sefer ha-Yovel le-Eliezer Schweid*
(Jerusalem: Hebrew University of Jerusalem and Van Leer Institute,
2005), 835–50. Another highly significant study relating specifically
to Heschel's treatment of the theme in his dissertation is Nathan
Rotenstreich, "On Prophetic Consciousness," *Journal of Religion* 54
(1974): 185–98.

10 *The Prophets*, 19.

11 "Carl Stern's Interview with Dr. Heschel," in *Moral Grandeur*, 400.

12 See Martin Kavka, "The Meaning of That Hour: Prophecy, Phenomenology, and the Public Sphere in the Early Writings of Abraham Joshua
Heschel," in Clayton Crockett, ed., *Religion and Violence in a Secular World*
(Charlottesville: University of Virginia Press, 2006), 108–36; Shaul Magid,
"A Monk, A Rabbi and 'The Meaning of the Hour': War and Non-violence
in Abraham Joshua Heschel and Thomas Merton," *Cross Currents* 55,
no. 2 (2005): 184–213; Yoel Finkelman, "Dat u-Hayim Tsiboriyim: Galut
u-Medina be-Hegutam shel Y.D. Soloveitchik, A.J. Heschel ve-Mordechai
Kaplan," in Aviezar Ravitsky, ed., *Dat u-Medina be-Hagut Hayehudit be-
Meah Haesrim* (Jerusalem: Israeli Democracy Institute, 2005), esp. 379–90.

13 "Religion and Race," in *Insecurity of Freedom*, 93.

14 Abraham Joshua Heschel, "The Moral Outrage of Vietnam," in Robert
McAfee Brown, Abraham Joshua Heschel, and Michael Novak, *Vietnam:
Crisis of Conscience* (New York: Herder and Herder, 1968), 56.

15 Ibid., 273.

16 *The Prophets*, vol. 1, 189.

17 *Search*, 282–3.

18 Ibid., 291. Elsewhere we see "the deed" referring explicitly to social action.
See *Moral Grandeur*, 239.

19 *Insecurity of Freedom*, 267.

20 See Michael Marmur, "Heschel's Rhetoric of Citation: The Use of Sources
in *God in Search of Man*" (PhD diss., the Hebrew University of Jerusalem,
2005), 68–74.

21 *Heavenly Torah*, 736. See also 594.

22 Ibid., 738. In a footnote Heschel pointed out that according to one commentary this was not a one-time ruling.

23 Ibid., 191, quoting Sotah 14a.

24 *Torah min Hashamayim*, vol. 1, 105.

25 Ibid., 157.

26 *Torah min Hashamayim*, vol. 1, 66.

27 See ibid., 65–92.

28 "Teaching Jewish Theology," 26.

29 "Did Maimonides Believe…?" For some thoughts on the distinction between the concept of *nevuah* and that of *ruach hakodesh*, see Yoel Ben-Nun,
"Me'et Hashem Mitoch ha-Neshama – Hashra'at Ruach ha-Kodesh Al-Pi
ha-Ra'ya Kook," in Benjamin Ish-Shalom, ed., *BeDarkei Shalom: Iyunim be-
Hagut Yehudit Mugashim le-Shalom Rozenberg* (Jerusalem: Bet Morasha,
2006), 353–76; Eliezer Schweid, "Nevua Mitchdeshet Le'et Reshit haGeula –
ha-Nevua ba-Mishnat ha-Ra'ya Kook," in Eliezer Schweid, *Nevi'im le-
Amam vela-Enoshut* (Jerusalem: Magnes, 1999), 190–214. These articles
provide a fascinating corollary to the ideas discussed here and invite a
systematic comparison of Kook and Heschel on the contemporary possibility of prophecy.

30 Note Heschel's comment in *Prophetic Inspiration*, 2n3, and in *Torah min
Hashamayim*, vol. 2, 247n17. This work was never published, and to the
best of my knowledge no manuscript has yet been found.

31 See *National Jewish Monthly* 69, no. 10 (1955): 7, 27–8.

32 "The Last Days of Maimonides," in *Insecurity of Freedom*, 289–90. There is
a curious alteration to the text here, since in the original, the perception
of abstract concepts constitutes a *geistigen Akt*, but in this late translation
these abstractions are afforded a purely intellectual significance.

33 *Insecurity of Freedom*, 290.

34 *Torah min Hashamayim*, vol. 3, 122.

35 "Mystical Element," 604.

36 *Search*, 145.

37 Ibid., 146. The reference is to Zohar, III, 95a.

38 The Ba'al Shem Tov discusses the dilemma of a person hesitating before
performing a deed that seems to have a hint of transgression. The Kotzker
casts doubt on the rabbinic tradition that application of Psalm 119:126 provided the legal basis for committing the Oral Law to writing. Albeit with
no explicit quotation of our verse, this tradition is brought by Heschel at
the end of the second part of one of his most important works, *Search*, 276.
See also *Kotzk*, 125.

39 "God, Torah and Israel," in *Moral Grandeur*, 197.

40 See Annette Aronowicz,"Heschel's Yiddish *Kotzk*: Some Reflections on
Inwardness," 112–21.

41 See Kaplan, *Spiritual Radical*, 323–4. See Ellenson and Marmur,"Heschel
and the Roots of Kavanah."

42 *Kotzk*, vol. 1, 51. Note 9 on 329 quotes from *Mei Shiloach*, vol. 1, *Likkutei
Hashas*, #160, according to which a Jew of unblemished pedigree may be
entitled to rely on the desire of his heart to decide how he should behave.

43 *Kotzk*, 645.
44 *Search*, 342. See *Kotzk*, 688–9n6. See also "God, Torah and Israel," in *Moral Grandeur*, 201, where the source is brought as an example of the tension between Halakhah and Aggadah. This teaching is discussed in Weiss, "A Late Jewish Utopia…" 218–20; Yehoshua Mondshine, "The Fluidity of Categories in Hasidism: *Averah Lishmah* in the Teachings of R. Zvi Elimelekh of Dynow," in *Hasidism Reappraised*, 311n47. The Izbicer implies the superiority of Judah, pointing out that the Messiah will issue from his loins.
45 *Kotzk*, 646. This is a translation of Heschel's rendering of *Mei Shiloach* to Balak, quoted in 689n11. I am grateful to my father, Dow Marmur, for his assistance with the Yiddish texts.
46 Arnold Eisen, "Nevuah ke-Vokatsia," 836.
47 "Teaching Jewish Theology" 27.
48 *Search*, 313n9.
49 The source is wrongly listed as being on 11a, In fact, it is to be found earlier in the work. Moses Almosnino, *Sefer Tefillah le-Moshe* (Cracow, 1900), 3a.
50 *Search*, 371; *Insecurity of Freedom*, 135.
51 Zohar III.80b. Heschel quoted this section in a later essay; see Neusner and Neusner, eds., *To Grow In Wisdom*, 135.
52 Exodus Rabbah 5:9.
53 *Search*, 255.
54 Seder Eliahu Rabbah 10, "Devorah Isha Neviah." This expression, calling heaven and earth as witnesses, appears on two further occasions in Seder Eliahu Rabbah.
55 See, for example, *Search*, 257–78.
56 *Search*, 161.
57 "Sacred Image of Man," in *Insecurity of Freedom*, 166. It is interesting to note that Heschel quoted the verses and offered an explanation in *The Prophets*, vol. 1, 186 and in *Echo of Eternity*, 128. In both cases he omitted the bold statement about three chosen peoples.
58 "Jewish Theology," in *Moral Grandeur*, 156
59 Borowitz, "What Is There Left to Be Said?" 95.
60 Ibid.
61 Susannah Heschel, "Theological Affinities in the Writings of Abraham Joshua Heschel and Martin Luther King, Jr.," *Conservative Judaism* 50, no. 2–3 (1998): 126–43. See also Mirsky, "Rabbi Akiva: Liberal, Existentialist, Prophet": 93–104. For an example of King's invoking of the Hebrew prophets as a basis for his activism, see Martin Luther King, Jr., "Letter from Birmingham Jail" (16 April 1963), http://www.africa.upenn.edu/Articles_Gen/Letter_Birmingham.html.

62 See Kaplan, *Spiritual Radical*, 325–6.

63 Kaplan, *Spiritual Radical*, 23–4 and elsewhere. See Abraham Cronbach, "The Prophets: Our Concurrence and Our Dissent," in Harry M. Orlinsky, ed., *Interpreting the Prophetic Tradition: The Goldenson Lectures 1955–1956* (Cincinnati, OH: Hebrew Union College Press, 1969); *Prophetic Tradition*, 23–42. See also Shlomo Shafir, "The View of a Maverick Pacifist and Universalist: Rabbi Abraham Cronbach's Plea for Clemency for Nazi War Criminals in 1945," *American Jewish Archives* 42, no. 2 (1990): 147–54.

64 *Prophetic Tradition*, 24.

65 Here the Reform Jew rejects the over-strident antiritualism of some of the classical prophets.

66 *Prophetic Tradition*, 41.

67 It is interesting to note that Cronbach wrote an article aiming to illustrate that an aspect of religion "is that of extolling certain texts as sacred and then using those texts to convey meanings far different from anything that their authors had in mind." See Abraham Cronbach, "Unmeant Meanings of Scripture," *Hebrew Union College Annual* 36 (1965): 99–123. His analysis ignores rabbinic and medieval literature.

68 *Heavenly Torah*, 738.

69 "No Religion Is an Island," in *Moral Grandeur*, 244.

70 *Search*, 262, quoting Moses Cordovero.

71 *Search*, 210.

72 For references to the verse in Deuteronomy and related teachings in *Avot*, the Zohar, and elsewhere, see *Search*, 138 and 143 n5; and in his essay "Ruach ha-Kodesh," 208n193. See also *Kotzk*, vol. 1, 215. See also *Torah min Hashamayim*, vol. 2, 255–6 and 259; and vol. 3, 36–8 and 65–6.

73 *Search*, 426.

74 *Search*, 147. The quotation is from Zohar I 77b. Heschel changed the Soncino translation, which reads "Ye that are the Lord's remembrancers, keep not silence," to "Ye that stir the Lord to remember, take no rest."

75 *Echo of Eternity*, before 1. See Bondi, *Ayyekah?* 235and 249.

76 *The Sabbath*, 101.

77 *Don Jizchak Abravanel*, 6.

78 Jacob Neusner, "Abraham Joshua Heschel: The Man," in Neusner and Neusner, eds., *To Grow In Wisdom*, 8.

79 Pinhas Peli, "Heschel and the Hasidic Tradition," in Neusner and Neusner, eds., *To Grow In Wisdom*, 84.

80 "Jewish Education," in *Insecurity of Freedom*, 237.

81 *Passion for Truth*, 107.

82 *The Sabbath*, 16.

83 Ibid., 100.
84 Dresner, *Heschel, Hasidism, and Halakha*, 92.
85 Quoted in Faierstein, "Heschel and the Holocaust," 269.
86 "Teaching Religion to American Jews," in *Moral Grandeur*, 149.
87 Berkovits, "Heschel's Theology of Pathos," 98.
88 *Who Is Man?* 99.
89 Emerson, "Quotation and Originality," 107.
90 I am grateful to Rachel Sabath Beit-Halachmi for this rapture/rupture distinction.

Sources Index

Subject Index

Moses Judah, 115

Moses, among the prophets, 156; as foil for divine mystery, 96–7; compared with other prophets, 149; Deuteronomy and, 87; ontology of, 100

Moshe ben Nahman. *See* Nachmanides

Moshe Chaim Ephraim of Sudilkov, 200n83

Moshe of Uhely. *See* Teitelbaum, Moshe

mystery, in Heschel's thought, 17

mysticism, 40, 54–5, 87, 100; antiquity of, 101; appeal of, 84; as problematic, 81; criticized, 65; definition of, 100; distinguished from prophecy, 92; Heschel and, 81–101; in modern Judaism, 98; inner eye and, 159–60; Maimonides and, 72, 77–8; prophecy and, 84; revelation and, 118; visions, 108. *See also* apocalyptic; apocalypticism; esotericism; inspiration; Kabbalah; *Ma'arekhet ha-Elohut*; mekhilta; mystery; prophecy; revelation; Sephirot; vision; Zohar

Nachman of Bratslav, 20, 106, 135, 190n79, 219n36, 240n20

Nachman of Kosov, 71, 104, 193n98, 224n6

Nachmanides, 17, 83, 217n14

Nadler, Steven, 243n67

Nagasaki, 178

Nahum of Chernobyl, 106

Nahum of Gimzo, hermeneutics of, 57, 204n45

National Conference on Religion and Race (Chicago, IL), 164

National Socialism (Nazism), 6, 44–5, 151; impact on Heschel, 54–5, 72, 113

nationalism, Heschel and, 123

Nauen, Franz, 238n66

Nazism. *See* National Socialism

Nehunyah ben ha-Kanah, 204n45; hermeneutics of, 57

Neis, Rachel, 241n30

Neumark, David, 208n28

Neusner, Jacob, 8, 180, 191n84, 192n97, 201n1, 201n3, 249n78; criticism of Heschel, 22, 47; on Heschel's use of sources, 20

Neusner, N., 201n3

New Testament, 149; as source, 128

New, as theological term, 123–4

Newton, Isaac, 236n53

Niebuhr, Reinhold, 41, 128, 142, 145, 174, 176, 178, 233n8; Heschel's reading of, 51

No'am Elimelech (Elimelech of Lyzhansk), 107

Noll, Mark A., 195n20

Novak, David, 76, 184n1, 184n11, 213n83–5

Novominsker Rebbe or Warsaw, 111–12, 227n61

Numbers Rabbah, 97

Nuremberg laws, 53

Ohev Yisrael. *See* Heschel, Abraham Joshua, of Apta

Oifn Weg (Hager), 113

HaOlam HaQaton (ibn Saddik), 15

Olympic Games of Berlin, 53

Onkelos, 89

oral law, 87, 115, 168; writing of, 247n38

orality, importance of, 113–15

Orr, Mary, 190n77
Orthodox Judaism, 118
Otto, Rudolf, 208n15
Ovadiah of Bertinoro, 241n31
Ovanta deliba, meaning, 160

pacifism, 54. *See also* activism;
  Civil Rights movement; Peace
  movement
Panim Me'iroth (Eisenstadt), 190n74
parable, in the Zohar, 82
Pardes Rimmonim, 97, 216n10
particularism, Hasidism and, 126;
  Heschel and, 173; in Jewish learning, 128–9. *See also* universalism
A Passion for Truth (Heschel), 10, 17,
  105, 109; on radicalism, 171–2;
  philosophy in, 134
pathos, divine, and Akiva, 58; as
  informing a vision of God, 67; as
  root of human agency, 168–9; contrast with Aristotelian theology,
  133; in *God in Search of Man*, 12; in
  Heschel's thought, 52; in Judaism
  and Christianity, 181; Maimonides
  and, 76, 79; mysticism and, 92;
  Spinoza and, 136; *tzorech gavoah*
  and, 101
Peace movement, 162
Pedaya, Haviva, 217n14
Peli, Pinhas, 8, 180, 201n2, 226n52,
  249n79
Peri Etz Hayyim (Vital), 97–8
Peri, Paul F., 194–5n120
Perlman, Lawrence, 184n1, 184n11,
  185n23, 235n45; on Heschel's use
  of sources, 8–9
Perlow family, 112
perspective, Heschel on, 153
perspectivism, 153

Peshat. See Bible—interpretation of,
  plain meaning
Petuchowski, Jakob J., 205n72
phenomenology, 91, 93, 119, 155
Philo of Alexandria, 76
Philo, 135, 245n101
philosophy, contrasted with science, 136; diversity of, 16; Hebrew
  and Greek, 132–3; prophecy
  and, 79, 215n100; vocabulary of,
  160; wonder and, 132. *See also*
  Aristotelianism; binaries; epis-
  temology; ethics; existentialism;
  functionalism; individualism;
  pacifism; particularism; perspectivism; phenomenology; pluralism; radicalism; rationalism;
  reason; reductionism; secularism;
  thought; time; universalism
Piekarz, Mendel, 191n82, 193n98,
  229n83, 229n85
Pikuach Neshama (Heschel), 52, 95
Pines, Shlomo, 79, 215n102
Pinhas of Korzec, 103, 112; on the
  Zohar, 84
piyyut, 64–5
Plato, 15, 188n51, 236n54; anthropology of, 29; epistle of, 16; in Heschel's
  work, 132; as source, 129
Plett, Heinrich F., 186n33
Pluralism, in Heschel's thought, 59,
  152–3. *See also* universalism
Plutarch, 129
poetic inspiration, 16
polarity, in Heschel's thought, 95
politics, Heschel and, 94
Post, Emily, 131–2
pragmatism, 200n78
prayer, Heschel on, 33, 85, 134–5;
  in Judaism, 60–1; in synagogue

The Kenneth Michael Tanenbaum Series in Jewish Studies